AAT

INTERACTIVE TEXT

Intermediate Unit 6

Cost Information

In this May 2000 edition

- Layout designed to be easier on the eye - and easier to use

- Icons to guide you through a 'fast track' approach if you wish

- Thorough reliable updating of material to 1 May 2000

- **FOR 2000 AND 2001 ASSESSMENTS**

BPP Publishing
May 2000

First edition 1998
Third edition May 2000

ISBN 0 7517 6213 X (Previous edition 0 7517 6155 9)

British Library Cataloguing-in-Publication Data
A catalogue record for this book
is available from the British Library

Published by

BPP Publishing Limited
Aldine House, Aldine Place
London W12 8AW

www.bpp.com

Printed in Great Britain by Ashford Colour Press, Gosport, Hants

We are grateful to the Lead Body for Accounting for permission to reproduce
extracts from the Standards of Competence for Accounting, and to the AAT for
permission to reproduce extracts from the mapping and Guidance Notes.

Page

BPP PUBLISHING

HOW TO USE THIS INTERACTIVE TEXT

Aims of this Interactive Text

To provide the knowledge and practice to help you succeed in the devolved and central assessments for Intermediate Unit 6 *Recording Cost Information*.

To pass the central and devolved assessments you need a thorough understanding in all areas covered by the standards of competence.

To tie in with the other components of the BPP Effective Study Package to ensure you have the best possible chance of success.

Interactive Text

This covers all you need to know for central and devolved assessment for Unit 6 *Recording Cost Information*. Icons clearly mark key areas of the text. Numerous activities throughout the text help you practise what you have just learnt.

Devolved Assessment Kit

When you have understood and practised the material in the Interactive Text, you will have the knowledge and experience to tackle the Devolved Assessment Kit for Unit 6 *Cost Information*. This aims to get you through the devolved assessment, whether in the form of the AAT simulation or in the workplace. It contains the AAT's sample simulation for Unit 6 plus other simulations.

Central Assessment Kit

As well as tackling the devolved assessments, you need to get to grips with the types of question that come up in central assessments. The Central Assessment Kit for Unit 6 contains the AAT's sample Central Assessment for Unit 6 plus relevant questions from the AAT's central assessments set under the previous version of the standards.

Recommended approach to this Interactive Text

(a) To achieve competence in Unit 6 (and all the other units), you need to be able to do **everything** specified by the standards. Study the text very carefully and do not skip any of it.

(b) Learning is an **active** process. Do **all** the activities as you work through the text so you can be sure you really understand what you have read.

(c) After you have covered the material in the Interactive Text, work through the **Devolved** and **Central Assessment Kits**.

(d) Before you take the central and devolved assessments, check that you still remember the material using the following quick revision plan for each chapter.

    (i) Read through the **chapter learning objectives**. Are there any gaps in your knowledge? If so, study the section again.

    (ii) Read and learn the **key terms**.

    (iii) Look at the **assessment alerts.** These show the sort of things that are likely to come up.

    (iv) Read and learn the **key learning points**, which are a summary of the chapter.

    (v) Do the **quick quiz** again. If you know what you're doing, it shouldn't take long.

This approach is only a suggestion. Your college may well adapt it to suit your needs.

Remember this is a **practical** course.

(a)   Try to relate the material to your experience in the workplace or any other work experience you may have had.

(b)   Try to make as many links as you can to your study of the other Units at Intermediate level.

(c)   Keep this Text - you will need it as you move on to Technician, and (hopefully) you will find it invaluable in your everyday work too!

INTERMEDIATE QUALIFICATION STRUCTURE

The competence-based Education and Training Scheme of the Association of Accounting Technicians is based on an analysis of the work of accounting staff in a wide range of industries and types of organisation. The Standards of Competence for Accounting which students are expected to meet are based on this analysis.

The Standards identify the **key purpose** of the accounting occupation, which is **to operate, maintain and improve systems to record, plan, monitor and report on the financial activities of an organisation,** and a number of **key roles** of the occupation. Each key role is subdivided into **units of competence**, which are further divided into **elements of competences**. By successfully completing assessments in specified units of competence, students can gain qualifications at NVQ/SVQ levels 2, 3 and 4, which correspond to the AAT Foundation, Intermediate and Technician stages of competence respectively.

Whether you are competent in a Unit is demonstrated by means of:

- *either* a Central Assessment (se t and marked by AAT assessors)

- *or* a Devolved Assessment (where competence is judged by an Approved Assessment Centre to whom responsibility for this is devolved)

- or *both* Central *and* Devolved Assessment.

Below we set out the overall structure of the Intermediate (NVQ/SVQ Level 3) stage, indicating how competence in each Unit is assessed. In the next section there is more detail about the Devolved Assessments for Unit 6.

Intermediate Qualification Structure

NVQ/SVQ **Level 3 - Intermediate**

All units are mandatory

Unit of competence

Elements of competence

Unit 5 Maintaining financial records and preparing accounts **Central *and* Devolved Assessment**	**5.1** Maintain records relating to capital acquisition and disposal
	5.2 Record income and expenditure
	5.3 Collect and collate information for the preparation of financial accounts
	5.4 Prepare the extended trial balance account

Unit 6 Recording cost information **Central *and* Devolved Assessment**	**6.1** Record and analyse information relating to direct costs
	6.2 Record and analyse information relating to the allocation, apportionment and absorption of overhead costs
	6.3 Prepare and present standard cost reports

Unit 7 Preparing reports and returns **Devolved Assessment *only***	**7.1** Prepare and present periodic performance reports
	7.2 Prepare reports and returns for outside agencies
	7.3 Prepare VAT returns

Unit 21 Using information technology **Devolved Assessment *only***	**21.1** Obtain information from a computerised Management Information System
	21.2 Produce spreadsheets for the analysis of numerical information
	21.3 Contribute to the quality of the Management Information System

Unit 22 Monitor and maintain a healthy, safe and secure workplace (ASC) **Devolved Assessment *only***	**22.1** Monitor and maintain health and safety within the workplace
	22.2 Monitor and maintain the security of the workplace

UNIT 6 STANDARDS OF COMPETENCE

The structure of the Standards for Unit 6

The Unit commences with a statement of the **knowledge and understanding** which underpin competence in the Unit's elements.

The unit of Competence is then divided into **elements of competence** describing activities which the individual should be able to perform.

Each element includes:

(a) A set of **performance criteria** which define what constitutes competent performance

(b) A **range statement** which defines the situations, contexts, methods etc in which competence should be displayed

(c) **Evidence requirements**, which state that competence must be demonstrated consistently, over an appropriate time scale with evidence of performance being provided from the appropriate sources

(d) **Sources of evidence**, being suggestions of ways in which you can find evidence to demonstrate that competence. These fall under the headings: 'observed performance; work produced by the candidate; authenticated testimonies from relevant witnesses; personal account of competence; other sources of evidence.' They are reproduced in full in our Devolved Assessment Kit for Unit 6.

The elements of competence for Unit 6: *Recording Cost Information* are set out below. Knowledge and understanding required for the unit as a whole are listed first, followed by the performance criteria, and range statements for each element. Performance criteria are cross-referenced below to chapters in this Unit 6 *Cost Information* Interactive Text.

Unit 6:   Recording Cost Information

What is the unit about?

This unit is concerned with recording, analysing and reporting information relating to both direct and indirect costs. It involves the identification, coding and analysis of all costs, the apportionment and absorption of indirect costs and the presentation of all the information in standard cost reports. The candidate is required to carry out variance analyses, different methods of allocation, apportionment and absorption and adjustments for under/over recovered indirect costs. There is also a requirement for information to be systematically checked and any unusual or unexpected results to be communicated to management.

Knowledge and understanding

The business environment

- Main types of materials: raw materials; part finished goods; materials issued from stores within the organisation; deliveries (Elements 6.1 & 6.2)

- Methods of payment for labour: salaried labour; performance related pay; profit related pay (Elements 6.1 6.2)

- Main types of expenses: expenses directly charged to cost units; indirect expenses; depreciation charges (Elements 6.1 & 6.2)

Accounting techniques

- Basic analysis of variances: usage; price; rate; efficiency; expenditure; volume; capacity (Elements 6.1, 6.2 & 6.3)

- Procedures for establishing standard materials costs, use of technical and purchasing information (Element 6.1)

- Methods of analysing materials usage: reasons for wastage (Element 6.1)

- Procedures for establishing standard labour costs: use of information about labour rates (Element 6.1)

- Analysis of labour rate and efficiency: idle time; overtime levels; absenteeism; sickness rates (Element 6.1)

- Methods of stock control (Element 6.1)

- Methods of setting standards for expenses (Elements 6.1 & 6.2)

- Procedures and documentation relating to expenses (Elements 6.1 & 6.2)

- Allocation of expenses to cost centres (Elements 6.1 & 6.2)

- Analysis of the effect of changing activity levels on unit costs (Elements 6.1 & 6.2)

- Procedures for establishing standard absorption rates (Element 6.2)

- Bases of allocating and apportioning indirect costs to responsibility centres: direct; reciprocal allocation; step down method (Element 6.2)

- Activity based systems of allocating costs: cost drivers; cost pools (Element 6.2)

- Bases of absorption (Element 6.2)

- Methods of presenting information orally and in written reports (Element 6.3)

- Control ratios of efficiency, capacity and activity (Element 6.3)

Accounting principles and theory

- Relationship between technical systems and costing systems - job, batch, unit, systems (Elements 6.1 & 6.2)

- Principles and objectives of standard costing systems: variance reports (Elements 6.1, 6.2 & 6.3)

- Relationships between the materials costing system and the stock control system (Element 6.1)

- Relationships between the labour costing system and the payroll accounting system (Element 6.1)

- Relationships between the expenses costing system and the accounting system (Elements 6.1 & 6.2)

- Objectives of depreciation accounting (Elements 6.1 & 6.2)

- The distinction between fixed, semi-fixed and variable costs (Elements 6.1 & 6.2)

- Effect of changes in capacity levels (Element 6.2)

- Arbitrary nature of overhead apportionments (Element 6.2)

- The significance of and possible reasons for variances (Elements 6.1, 6.2 & 6.3)

The organisation

- Understanding of the ways the accounting systems of an organisation are affected by its organisational structure, its administrative systems and procedures and the nature of its business transactions (Elements 6.1, 6.2 & 6.3)

- The reporting cycle of the organisation (Element 6.3)

Element 6.1 Record and analyse information relating to direct costs

Performance criteria	Chapters in this Text
1 Direct costs are identified in accordance with the organisation's costing procedures	2-4,9
2 Information relating to direct costs is clearly and correctly coded, analysed and recorded	2-4, 7-9
3 Direct costs are calculated in accordance with the organisation's policies and procedures	2-4, 9
4 Standard costs are compared against actual costs and any variances are analysed	10, 11
5 Information is systematically checked against the overall usage and stock control practices	10, 11
6 Queries are either resolved or referred to the appropriate person	2-4, 7

Range statement

1 Direct costs: standard and actual material costs; standard and actual labour costs; standard and actual expenses

- Materials: raw materials; part finished goods; materials issued from stores within the organisation; deliveries

- Labour: employees of the organisation on the payroll; sub-contractors; agency staff

- Expenses: direct revenue expenditure

2 Variance analysis: Materials variances: usage, price; Labour variances: rate, efficiency

Element 6.2 Record and analyse information relating to the allocation, apportionment and absorption of overhead costs

Performance criteria	Chapters in this Text
1 Data are correctly coded, analysed and recorded	2-4, 7
2 Overhead costs are established in accordance with the organisation's procedures	2-4, 9
3 Information relating to overhead costs is accurately and clearly recorded	2-4, 7-9
4 Overhead costs are correctly attributed to producing and service cost centres in accordance with agreed methods of allocation, apportionment and absorption	5
5 Adjustments for under or over recovered overhead costs are made in accordance with established procedures	5
6 Standard costs are compared against actual costs and any variances are analysed	10
7 Methods of allocation, apportionment and absorption are reviewed at regular intervals in discussions with senior staff, and agreed changes to methods are implemented	5
8 Staff working in operational departments are consulted to resolve any queries in the data	2-4, 7

Range statement

1   Overhead costs: standard and actual indirect material costs; standard and actual indirect labour costs; indirect expenses; depreciation charges

2   Methods of allocation and apportionment: direct; reciprocal allocation; step down method

3   Variance analysis: Overhead variances: expenditure, efficiency, volume, capacity; Fixed overhead variances: expenditure, volume, capacity, efficiency

Element 6.3 Prepare and present standard cost reports

Performance criteria	**Chapters in this Text**
1 Standard cost reports with variances clearly identified are presented in an intelligible form	11
2 Unusual or unexpected results are identified and reported to managers	11
3 Any reasons for significant variances from standard are identified and the explanations presented to management	11
4 The results of the analysis and explanations of specific variances are produced for management	11
5 Staff working in operational departments are consulted to resolve any queries in the data	11

Range statement

1   Methods of presentation: written report containing analysis and explanation of specific variances; further explanations to managers

2   Types of variances: Overhead variances: expenditure, efficiency, volume, capacity; Materials variances: usage, price; Labour variances: rate, efficiency

ASSESSMENT STRATEGY

This unit is assessed by both *central* and *devolved* assessment.

Central Assessment

A central assessment is a means of collecting evidence that you have the **essential knowledge and understanding** which underpins competence. It is also a means of collecting evidence across the **range of contexts** for the standards, and of your ability to **transfer skills**, knowledge and understanding to different situations. Thus, although central assessments contain practical tests linked to the performance criteria, they also focus on the underpinning knowledge and understanding. You should in addition expect each central assessment to contain tasks taken from across a broad range of the standards.

*Each Unit 6 central assessment will last for **three hours** plus fifteen minutes' reading time and will be divided into two sections.* The two sections will normally take the same time to complete.

Section 1

This section will assess competence in element 6.1 and will also include standard cost reporting relating to direct costs as detailed in element 6.3 of this unit. Examples of tasks which may be assessed in this section include the following.

(a) Calculation of material price and usage variances.

(b) Calculation of labour rate, efficiency and idle time variances.

(c) Calculation of control ratios such as the labour efficiency ratio.

(d) Consideration of the different types of standard costs and the procedures to be adopted in establishing those standard costs.

(e) Methods of stock control and pricing of materials to include first-in-first-out, last-in-first-out and standard cost.

(f) The use of actual costs for materials and labour and the analysis of those costs.

(g) Application of different cost behaviours to direct costs.

(h) Preparation of cost accounting entries from payroll and stock control systems.

(i) Preparation of standard cost reports for direct materials, which will include an assessment of knowledge and understanding relating to standard cost variances.

Section 2

This section will assess competence in element 6.2 and will also include standard cost reporting relating to indirect costs as detailed in element 6.3 of this unit. Examples of tasks which may be assessed in this section include the following.

(a) The allocation and apportionment of indirect costs to cost centres.

(b) Procedures for the calculation of departmental absorption rates using different absorption bases.

(c) The application of different cost behaviours to indirect costs.

(d) The separation of variable costs from fixed costs and the impact of changing capacity levels.

(e) Comparison of budgeted indirect cost data with actual data and the calculation of indirect cost variances.

(f) The calculation of fixed overhead expenditure and volume variances and the division of the volume variance into efficiency and capacity variances.

(g)   Preparation of cost accounting entries for indirect costs.

(h)   Preparation of standard cost reports for indirect costs, which will include an assessment of knowledge and understanding relating to standard cost variances.

The tasks detailed above are indicative of those which may be assessed but are not exhaustive. It is important to understand that the Central Assessment is based on the Standards of Competence for this unit and that all areas included in the Standards are assessable.

Students will now be required to prepare a report in both sections. Since competence must be demonstrated in both sections, it is important that students practise their report writing.

(a)   Plan the report and check that the plan deals with the tasks set.

(b)   Be aware of the context in which the report is written. (A common scenario will be used for both sections.)

(c)   Use appropriate headings.

(d)   Use clear and concise English.

Devolved Assessment (*more detail can be found in the Devolved Assessment Kit*)

Devolved assessment is a means of collecting evidence of your ability to carry out **practical activities** and to **operate effectively in the conditions of the workplace** to the standards required. Evidence may be collected at your place of work or at an Approved Assessment Centre by means of simulations of workplace activity, or by a combination of these methods.

If the Approved Assessment Centre is a **workplace**, you may be observed carrying out accounting activities as part of your normal work routine. You should collect documentary evidence of the work you have done, or contributed to, in an **accounting portfolio**. Evidence collected in a portfolio can be assessed in addition to observed performance or where it is not possible to assess by observation.

Where the Approved Assessment Centre is a **college or training organisation**, devolved assessment will be by means of a combination of the following.

(a)   Documentary evidence of activities carried out at the workplace, collected by you in an **accounting portfolio**.

(b)   Realistic **simulations** of workplace activities. These simulations may take the form of case studies and in-tray exercises and involve the use of primary documents and reference sources.

(c)   **Projects and assignments** designed to assess the Standards of Competence.

If you are unable to provide workplace evidence you will be able to complete the assessment requirements by the alternative methods listed above.

Part A
Materials, labour and expenses

Chapter 1   Cost information

Chapter topic list

1   Costs in outline

2   Costs in detail

3   Why record cost information?

4   Product costing

5   Functional costs

6   Standard costs and variances

7   Cost accounting and financial accounting

Learning objectives

On completion of this chapter you will be able to:

	Performance criteria	Range statement
• recognise cost elements	n/a	n/a
• distinguish between different types of cost	n/a	n/a
• appreciate the reasons for recording cost information	n/a	n/a
• decide on appropriate costing methods	n/a	n/a
• use costing terms	n/a	n/a

BPP PUBLISHING

1 COSTS IN OUTLINE

1.1 Before proceeding, a brief note on how to go about your studies. Unit 6 *Recording Cost Information* is a very practical subject: at its heart it is about manipulating numbers. This Interactive Text tells you how to manipulate the numbers and it also tells you why you might want to do so in different circumstances. Unless you actually practise and see the results for yourself, however, you will not fully appreciate what you are learning.

1.2 Let us suppose that in your hand you have a red biro which you bought in the newsagent's down the road for 50p. Why does the newsagent charge 50p for it? In other words what does that 50p represent?

1.3 From the newsagent's point of view the cost can be split into two.

Price paid by newsagent to wholesaler	Z
Newsagent's 'mark-up'	Y
	50 p

1.4 If the newsagent did not charge more for the biro than he paid for it (Y) there would be no point in him selling it. The mark-up itself can be split into further categories.

Pure profit	X
Amount paid to shop assistants	X
Expenses of owning and operating a shop (rent, electricity, cleaning and so on)	X
	Y

1.5 The newsagent's **profit** is the amount he personally needs to live: it is like your salary. Different newsagents have different ideas about this: this is why you might pay 60p for an identical biro if you went into another newsagent's. The shop expenses are amounts that have to be paid, whether or not the newsagent sells you a biro, simply to keep the shop going. Again, if other newsagents have to pay higher rent than our newsagent, this might be reflected in the price of biros.

1.6 The amount paid to the wholesaler can be split in a similar way: there will be a profit element and amounts to cover the costs of running a wholesaling business. There might also be a cost for getting the biro from the wholesaler's premises to the shop and, of course, there will be the amount paid to the manufacturer.

1.7 The majority of the remainder of this Interactive Text takes the point of view of the manufacturer of products since his costs are the most diverse. If you understand the costing that a manufacturer has to do, you will understand the costing performed by any other sort of business.

1.8 This chapter provides a brief introduction to recording cost information.

2 COSTS IN DETAIL

Production costs

2.1 Look at your biro and consider what it consists of. There is probably a red plastic cap and a little red thing that fits into the end, and perhaps a yellow plastic sheath. There is an opaque plastic ink holder with red ink inside it. At the tip there is a gold plastic part holding a metal nib with a roller ball.

2.2 Let us suppose that the manufacturer sells biros to wholesalers for 20p each. How much does the little ball cost? What share of the 20p is taken up by the little red thing in the end of the biro? How much did somebody earn for putting it there?

2.3 To elaborate still further, the manufacturer probably has machines to mould the plastic and do some of the assembly. How much does it cost, per biro, to run the machines: to set them up so that they produce the right shape of moulded plastic? How much are the production line workers' wages per biro?

2.4 Any of these separate production costs are known as **direct costs** because they can be traced directly to specific units of production. These direct costs could be calculated and recorded on a unit cost card which records how the total cost of a unit (in this instance, a biro) is arrived at.

BIRO - UNIT COST CARD	£	£
Direct materials		
Yellow plastic	X	
Red plastic	X	
Opaque plastic	X	
Gold plastic	X	
Ink	X	
Metal	X̲	
		X
Direct labour		
Machine operators' wages	X	
Manual assembly staff wages	X̲	
		X̲
		X
Direct expenses		
Moulding machinery - operating costs	X	
Assembly machinery - operating costs	X̲	
		X̲
Total direct cost (or prime cost)		X
Overheads (production)		X̲
Manufacturing cost (or factory cost)		X
Overheads (administration, distribution and selling)		X̲
Total cost		X̲

Don't worry if you are a bit unsure of the meaning of some of the terms in the unit cost card above as we will be looking at them in detail as we work through this Interactive Text.

Cost units

> **KEY TERM**
>
> A **cost unit** is a unit of product which has costs attached to it. The cost unit is the basic control for costing purposes.

2.5 A cost unit is not always a single item. It might be a batch of 1,000 if that is how the individual items are made. For example, a cost per 1,000 (or whatever) is often more meaningful information, especially if calculating a cost for a single item gives an amount that you cannot hold in your hand, like 0.003p. Examples of cost units are as follows.

- A batch of 1,000 pairs of shoes
- A passenger mile (for a bus company)
- A patient night (for a hospital)

Cost centres

> **KEY TERM**
>
> **Cost centres** are the essential 'building blocks' of a costing system. They act as a collecting place for certain costs before they are analysed further.

2.6 A **cost centre** might be a **place**, and this is probably what you think of first because the word 'centre' is often used to mean a place. On the other hand it might be a **person**. For example, the company solicitor would incur costs on books and stationery that were unique to his or her function. It might be a **group of people**, all contributing to the same function, the accounting staff, say, or the laboratory staff. Or it might be an **item of equipment** such as a machine which incurs costs because it needs to be oiled and maintained.

2.7 Cost centres may vary in nature, but what they have in common is that they **incur costs**. It is therefore logical to **collect costs** initially under the headings of the various different cost centres that there may be in an organisation. Then, when we want to know how much our products cost, we simply find out how many cost units have been produced and share out the costs incurred by that cost centre amongst the cost units.

Profit centres

> **KEY TERM**
>
> A **profit centre** is similar to a cost centre but is accountable for both costs *and* revenues.

2.8 We have seen that a cost centre is where costs are collected. Some organisations, however, work on a **profit centre basis**. Cost centres only have costs attributed to them. Profit centres, on the other hand, also receive **revenues** associated with those costs. For example, an organisation with two departments each making a different product will allocate the revenues from each product to the department where each product is made. This ensures that the organisation has some idea as to the relative **profitability** of each product.

2.9 Profit centre managers should normally have control over how revenue is raised and how costs are incurred. Not infrequently, several cost centres will comprise one profit centre.

Direct and indirect costs

2.10 To summarise so far, the cost of an item can be divided into the following cost elements.

(a) Materials
(b) Labour
(c) Expenses

Each element can be split into two, as follows.

Materials	=	Direct materials	+	Indirect materials
+		+		+
Labour	=	Direct labour	+	Indirect labour
+		+		+
Expenses	=	Direct expenses	+	Indirect expenses
Total cost	=	Direct cost		Overhead

2.11 As you study this introductory chapter, you must make sure that you have a clear understanding of what makes a cost **direct** or **indirect** since this is the main focus of elements 5.1 and 5.2 in Unit 6: *Recording Cost Information*. We shall look at direct costs in more detail when we look at materials, labour and expenses, later on in this Interactive Text.

Overheads

2.12 **Overheads** (or indirect costs) include costs that go into the making of the biro that you do not see when you dismantle it. You can touch the materials and you can appreciate that a combination of man and machine put them together. It is not so obvious that the manufacturer has had to lubricate machines and employ foremen to supervise the assembly staff. He also has to pay rent for his factory and for somewhere to house his stock of materials, and he has to pay someone to buy materials, recruit labour and run the payroll. Other people are paid to deliver the finished biros to the wholesalers; still others are out and about persuading wholesalers to buy biros, and they are supported at head office by staff taking orders and collecting payments.

2.13 In addition certain costs that could be identified with a specific product are classified as **overheads** and not direct costs. Nails used in the production of a cupboard can be identified specifically with the cupboard. However, because the cost is likely to be relatively insignificant, the expense of tracing such costs does not justify the possible benefits from calculating more accurate direct costs. Instead of keeping complex and time consuming records which might enable us to trace such costs directly to specific units of production, we try to apportion them and other overheads (indirect costs) to each cost unit in as fair a way as possible.

2.14 Overheads are the biggest problem for cost accountants because it is not easy to tell by either looking at or measuring the product, what overheads went into getting it into the hands of the buyer. Overheads, or indirect costs, unlike direct costs, will not be identified with any one product because they are incurred for the benefit of all products rather than for any one specific product.

Activity 1.1

List all of the different types of cost that a large supermarket might incur. Arrange them under headings of materials, labour used and other expenses.

Fixed costs and variable costs

2.15 There is one other important distinction and that is between fixed costs and variable costs.

(a) If you produce two identical biros you will use twice as many direct materials as you would if you only produced one biro. Direct materials are in this case a **variable cost**. They vary according to the volume of production.

(b) If you oil your machines after every 1,000 biros have been produced, the cost of oil is also a variable cost. It is an indirect material cost that varies according to the volume of production.

(c) If you rent the factory that houses your biro-making machines you will pay the same amount of rent per annum whether you produce one biro or 10,000 biros. Factory rental is an indirect expense and it is **fixed** no matter what the volume of activity is.

2.16 The examples in (b) and (c) are both indirect costs, or overheads, but (b) is a variable overhead and (c) is a fixed overhead. The example in (a) is a variable direct cost. Direct costs usually are variable although they do not have to be.

2.17 We are elaborating this point because it can be a source of great confusion. Variable cost is *not* just another name for a direct cost. The distinctions that can be made are as follows.

(a) **Costs are either direct or indirect, depending upon how easily they can be traced to a specific unit of production.**

(b) **Costs are either variable or fixed, depending upon whether they change when the volume of production changes.**

Activity 1.2

Do you think the following are likely to be fixed or variable costs?

(a) Charges for telephone calls made
(b) Charges for rental of telephone
(c) Annual salary of the chief accountant
(d) Managing director's subscription to the Institute of Directors
(e) Cost of materials used to pack 20 units of product X into a box

---

3 WHY RECORD COST INFORMATION?

3.1 In case you are beginning to think that recording cost information is far more trouble than it is worth we shall now consider why we bother. There are a number of very good reasons.

Determining the selling price

3.2 In the first place, if an item costs 50p and it is sold for 35p then the seller makes a loss on every sale. Before long he will go out of business. It is therefore important to know how much things cost so that a suitable **selling price** can be set.

Decision making

3.3 Before deciding on the selling price, the seller had to decide whether to make the item at all. Suppose he could make one or other of two items, either of which could be sold for £1 each. If one cost 80p to make and the other cost 90p then it would be better to make the one that cost 80p. Costing is therefore essential to **decision making**.

Planning and budgeting

3.4 Having decided to make the item it is then necessary to work out the best way of going about it. Sellers are limited as to the number of items they can sell and as to the amount of money they have available to invest in a project. You might conduct market research that told you you could sell 10,000 items. You would then need cost information so that you could plan what quantity of materials you could afford to buy, how many staff to employ, and how long to keep the machines running each day. Costing is thus an integral part of **planning** for the future.

3.5 Another term for planning of this sort is **budgeting**. You will learn about this later in your studies. For now you can simply think of a budget as a plan that shows how much money you expect to make and how much it will cost to produce the items (or services) that bring this money in.

Control

3.6 There is, of course, no guarantee that everything will go according to plan. You might make and sell your 10,000 items for 50p each, only to discover that the actual cost of each item had gone up to 70p, perhaps because the suppliers of materials had put their prices up, or because workers had demanded higher wages. Costing is not a one-off exercise. Costs can be predicted in advance but they must also be monitored as they are actually incurred. If this is done then an increase in materials costs, say, can be spotted as soon as it arises and the implications for the future assessed. It may be possible to buy cheaper materials and keep costs down to the level planned or it may be necessary to draw up an entirely new plan. The recording of cost information in such a way that it can be monitored is thus vital to maintain **control of the business**.

Reporting

3.7 Finally, **costs have to be recorded so that a business can report its results.** Companies have to prepare accounts to comply with the Companies Acts and all businesses need to have some records so that the **Inland Revenue** knows how much tax is due and **Customs and Excise** know whether VAT is being properly accounted for. Senior managers judge the performance of their subordinates according to whether they have managed to meet targets which include targets for cost control. Cost information is essential for **reporting**.

Activity 1.3

(a) Give five reasons for recording cost information.
(b) How can costs be used to control a business?
(c) Who is interested in cost information?

4 PRODUCT COSTING

Job costing

4.1 There are several different ways of arriving at a value for the different cost elements (material, labour and expenses) which make up a unit cost of production. The most straightforward case is where the thing to be costed is a **one-off item**. For example, a furniture maker may make a table, say, to a customer's specific requirements. From start to finish the costs incurred to make that table are identifiable. It will cost so much for the table top, so much for the legs, and so on. This form of costing is known as **job costing**.

BPP PUBLISHING

Batch costing

4.2 An item like a biro, however, will be produced as one of a **batch** of identical items, because it would clearly be uneconomical to set up the machinery, employ labour and incur overheads to produce each biro individually. There might be a production run of, say, 5,000 biros. The cost of producing 5,000 biros would be calculated and if we wanted to know the cost of one biro we would divide this total by 5,000. The answer would however be a fraction of a penny and this is not very meaningful information.

4.3 This method of costing is called **batch costing** and it applies to many everyday items. So far as costing techniques are concerned, job and batch costing are much the same.

Accounting for overheads

4.4 Whether job costing, or batch costing is used, there is still a problem in attributing to units of product overhead costs like factory rental, canteen costs and head office lighting. The pros and cons of trying to work out an amount per unit for such costs are open to debate. Most businesses actually do try to do this in practice, and one very good reason for doing so is to make sure that all costs are covered when prices are set.

4.5 This practice of working out an amount per unit for overheads is known as **absorption costing**. Absorption costing is a technique that is used in conjunction with the product costing methods described above. We will look at absorption costing in Chapter 5.

5 FUNCTIONAL COSTS

5.1 When we talk about functional costs we are not talking about a different **type** of cost to those we have met already, but about a way of grouping costs together according to what aspects of an organisation's operations (what **function**) causes them to be incurred.

5.2 A convenient set of functions is the following.

(a) **Production costs**. Materials and labour used and expenses incurred to make things and get them ready for sale.

(b) **Distribution and selling costs**. Costs incurred both to get the finished items to the point where people can buy them and to persuade people to buy them.

(c) **Administration costs**. This is a vague term. You might like to think of these costs as the materials and labour used and the expenses incurred in co-ordinating the activities of the production function and the distribution and selling function.

(d) **Financing costs**. The expenses incurred when a business has to borrow to purchase fixed assets, say, or simply to operate on a day to day basis.

5.3 These divisions are not the only ones that could be made, nor are there rigid definitions of what is a production cost, what is an administration cost and so on.

6 STANDARD COSTS AND VARIANCES

6.1 When we were talking about the purposes of costing we hinted that it might involve not only recording what costs were, but also predicting what they ought to be.

6.2 Recognising the usefulness of cost information as a tool for controlling what goes on, many businesses adopt what are known as **standard costs**. They decide what the cost of each element that makes up a product *should* be in advance of the actual cost being incurred. Once the cost has been incurred it is compared with the estimated standard cost and if there is a difference (a **variance**) somebody is asked to explain why.

6.3 To set a standard cost it is necessary not only to know what the level of cost was in the past but also to have an idea of what it is likely to be in the future. In Chapter 9 we shall look at the various problems involved in setting standard costs.

6.4 **Standard costing** is not an alternative to job, batch or unit costing, nor to absorption costing. It is an approach that can be used in addition to those methods.

Activity 1.4

Explain the following terms in your own words.

(a)	Cost unit	(f)	Overhead
(b)	Functional cost	(g)	Cost centre
(c)	Fixed cost	(h)	Variable cost
(d)	Standard cost	(i)	Budget
(e)	Indirect cost	(j)	Direct cost

---

7 COST ACCOUNTING AND FINANCIAL ACCOUNTING

7.1 It is important that cost accounting is clearly distinguished from financial accounting. Cost accounting systems and financial accounting systems in a business both record the same basic data for income and expenditure.

7.2 The main differences between cost accounting and financial accounting are as follows.

Cost accounting	Financial accounting
Cost accounting is used internally, for use within the business only.	Financial accounting information is used to report externally
Cost accounting information is recorded and presented in a manner which is entirely at management discretion.	Financial accounts are required by law, and this is the basis for the manner in which they are presented.
Cost information is an historical record, and used as a tool for future planning.	Financial accounts are an historical record only.

ASSESSMENT ALERT

When completing assessments, always make sure that you present your tasks in a neat and orderly fashion - you are more likely to impress your assessor if you do so.

BPP PUBLISHING

Key learning points

- Costs can be divided into three elements, **materials, labour** and **expenses.**

- A **cost unit** is a unit of product which has costs attached to it.

- A **cost centre** is something that incurs costs. It may be a place, a person, a group of people or an item of equipment.

- A **profit centre** is similar to a cost centre but it is accountable for both costs *and* revenues.

- Costs can be analysed in different ways. For example, direct, indirect, fixed, variable.

- Costs can also be analysed according to their function. For example, production, distribution and selling, administration and financing costs.

- Cost information is recorded to aid price setting, decision making, planning and budgeting, control and reporting.

- Costing using standards is a good way of keeping a business under control.

Quick quiz

1   What is a cost unit?

2   Which cost elements make up overheads?

3   List five reasons for recording cost information.

4   Why is cost information essential for reporting?

5   List four types of functional cost.

6   How is cost accounting distinguished from financial accounting?

Answers to quick quiz

1   A unit of product or service which incurs cost.

2   Indirect materials, indirect labour and indirect expenses.

3   • Determination of selling prices
    • Decision making
    • Planning and budgeting
    • Control
    • Reporting

4   • Companies need to prepare accounts in order to comply with statute
    • In order to keep a record of VAT due to/due from Customs & Excise
    • For senior management to assess whether targets have been met

5   • Production costs
    • Distribution and selling costs
    • Administration costs
    • Financing costs

6   • Cost information is used internally, whereas financial accounts are for external use
    • Cost information is recorded and presented in a manner which is based on what management require
    • Financial accounts are required by law
    • Financial accounts are an historical record, whereas cost information is an historical record *and* also used as a tool for future planning

Answers to activities

Answer 1.1

Materials	*Labour*	*Expenses*
Saleable stocks	Petrol station staff	Heating
Carrier bags	Car park attendant	Lighting
Other packaging	Check-out staff	Telephone
Cleaning materials	Supervisors	Post
Bakery ingredients	Delicatessen staff	Stationery
	Bakery staff	Rent
	Shelf fillers	Business rates
	Warehouse staff	Water rates
	Cleaners	Vehicle running costs
	Security staff	Advertising
	Administrative staff	Discounts
	Managers	Bank charges
	Delivery staff	Waste disposal
	Maintenance staff	

Answer 1.2

(a)   Variable
(b)   Fixed
(c)   Fixed
(d)   Fixed
(e)   Variable

Answer 1.3

(a)   Costs are recorded for the following reasons.

   (i)   To set selling prices
   (ii)   To aid decision making
   (iii)   To help with planning
   (iv)   As a means of control
   (v)   For inclusion in accounts

(b)   If costs are monitored and the results are compared with what was originally planned, a significant difference in a particular area may suggest that area of the business is not being properly managed. The reasons can be investigated and corrective action taken as necessary.

(c)   Parties interested in cost information will include the following.

   (i)   The manager responsible for the costs
   (ii)   The board of directors
   (iii)   Shareholders
   (iv)   Competitors
   (v)   The Inland Revenue and Customs and Excise

Answer 1.4

(a)   A **cost unit** is a unit of product (or service) for which costs are ascertained.

(b)   A **functional cost** is one that relates to a 'function' or area of operations of a business, for example production, administration, research, distribution and so on.

(c)   A **fixed cost** is one that does not increase or decrease when a different number of units are produced.

(d)   A **standard cost** is an estimate of what a cost should be on average in the future.

(e)   An **indirect cost** is one that cannot be identified with one particular product.

(f)   An **overhead** is another name for an indirect cost (as explained in (e)).

(g)   A **cost centre** is a location, a function (a person or a department), an activity or a piece of equipment which incurs costs that can be attributed to cost units.

(h)   A **variable cost** is one that increases when more units are made and decreases when fewer units are made.

(i)   A **budget** is a business's plan for a forthcoming period expressed in money. It shows how many of its products the business expects to sell at what price and how much the costs are expected to be.

(j)   A **direct cost** is one that can be traced directly to a unit of product.

Chapter 2   Materials

Chapter topic list

1   Types of material

2   Buying materials

3   Valuing materials issues and stocks

4   Stock control

5   Computers and stock control

6   Reordering stock

Learning objectives

On completion of this chapter you will be able to:

	Performance criteria	Range statement
• identify and calculate direct material costs in accordance with organisational policies and procedures	6.1.1, 6.1.3	6.1.1
• establish indirect material costs in accordance with organisational procedures	6.2.2	6.2.1
• ensure that information relating to direct material costs is clearly and correctly coded, analysed and recorded	6.1.2	6.1.1
• ensure that data and information relating to indirect material costs is accurately and clearly coded, analysed and recorded	6.2.1, 6.2.3	6.2.1
• ensure that issues are in accordance with overall usage and stock control practices	6.1.5	6.1.1
• deal with queries about direct and indirect materials	6.1.6, 6.2.8	6.1.1, 6.2.1

BPP PUBLISHING

1 TYPES OF MATERIAL

Classifying materials

1.1 There are a number of different ways in which materials can be classified. The three main ways of classifying materials are as follows.

- They can be classified according to the **substances that make them up.**
- They can be classified according to **how they are measured.**
- They can be classified according to their **physical properties.**

1.2 Materials may be made of one or more substances. For example, when classifying materials according to the **substances that make them up**, they may be classified as either **wood, plastic, metal, wool** and so on. Many items may be made up of a **combination of substances.**

1.3 You may also classify materials according to how they are measured. Accounting text books could make it easy for you to believe that all materials come by the **litre, metre** or **kilogram.** In practice however, you will find that materials really come in **bags, packets** or **by the thousand.**

1.4 Materials may also be classified by one or more of their physical properties. The same basic piece of material may be distinguished by one or more of the following features.

- Colour
- Shape
- Fire resistance
- Water resistance
- Abrasiveness
- Flexibility
- Quality

1.5 Finally, material may be classified as either **direct** or **indirect**. This chapter will be focussing on recording and analysing information relating to **direct material costs**.

Raw materials

> **KEY TERM**
>
> **Raw materials** are goods purchased for incorporation into products for sale.

1.6 **Raw materials** is a term which you are likely to come across often, both in your studies and your workplace. But what are raw materials?

1.7 Examples of raw materials are as follows.

- Clay for making terracotta garden pots.
- Timber for making dining room tables.
- Paper for making books.

Activity 2.1

Without getting too technical, what are the main raw materials used in the manufacture of the following items?

(a) A car
(b) A box of breakfast cereal
(c) A house (just the basic structure)
(d) Your own organisation's products

Activity 2.2

How would you distinguish direct materials from indirect materials?

Activity 2.3

Classify the following as either direct or indirect materials.

(a) The foil wrapping around Easter eggs
(b) Paper used for the pages of a book
(c) Lubricant used on sewing machines in a clothing factory
(d) Plastic used to make audio cassette boxes
(e) Shoe boxes
(f) Thread used in the manufacture of hats
(g) Glue used in the manufacture of shoe boxes

Work in progress

> **KEY TERM**
>
> **Work in progress** is a term used to represent an intermediate stage between the manufacturer purchasing the materials that go to make up the finished product and the finished product.

1.8 Work in progress is another term which you are likely to come across often, and valuing work in progress is one of **the most difficult tasks in costing.** Work in progress is another name for **part-finished goods**.

1.9 Work in progress means that some work has been done on the materials purchased as part of the process of producing the finished product, but **the production process is not complete.** Examples of work in progress are as follows.

(a) Terracotta pots which have been shaped, but which have not been fired, and are therefore unfinished.

(b) Dining room tables which have been assembled, but have not been polished, and are therefore not ready for sale.

(c) Paper which has been used to print books, but which has not yet been bound. The books are therefore not yet assembled, and not yet ready for sale.

Finished goods

1.10 Did you notice how all of the examples of work in progress were items which were not ready for sale? It therefore follows that examples of finished goods are as follows.

- Terracotta pots **ready for sale or despatch**
- Dining room tables **ready for sale or despatch**
- Books **ready for sale or despatch**

1.11 The examples in the previous paragraph show terracotta pots which have now been fired, dining room tables which have now been polished, and books which have now been bound. These final processes have transformed our **work in progress** into **finished goods.**

Activity 2.4

Distinguish between raw materials, work in progress and finished goods.

2 BUYING MATERIALS

Purchasing procedures

2.1 All businesses have to buy materials of some sort, and this means that decisions have to be made and somebody has to be responsible for doing the **buying**.

2.2 Large businesses have specialist **buying departments** managed by people who are very skilled at the job. One of the reasons for the success of companies like Tesco's is that they are expert at buying good quality goods at the best prices.

2.3 A buying transaction is not complicated and, in fact, familiar because most people buy things every week and go through the following process.

- You need something.

- You find out where you can buy it.

- If there is a choice you identify which item is most suitable, taking into account the cost and the quality, and from whom you will buy it.

- You order the item, or perhaps several if you will need more in the future.

- You receive the item.

- You pay for the item.

2.4 In a business this process will be more involved, but only because those spending the money are likely to be different from those looking after the goods and those using them, and because none of those people will actually own the money spent. The following diagram illustrates who will be involved.

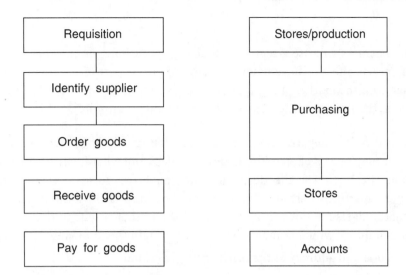

Purchasing documentation

2.5 Clearly there needs to be some means by which different departments can let each other know what they want and what is being done about it, and even the smallest business will need to keep records of some sort. We shall describe a manual system that might be used in a fairly large organisation. In reality it is likely that much of the procedure would be computerised, but this does not alter the basic principles or information flows.

Purchase requisition form

2.6 The first stage will be that the department requiring the goods will complete a **purchase requisition form** asking the **purchasing department** to carry out the necessary transaction. An example is shown below. Note that the purchase requisition will usually need some form of **authorisation**, probably that of a senior person in the department requiring the goods and possibly also that of a senior person in the finance department if substantial expense is involved.

PURCHASE REQUISITION Req. No.			
Department _____ Suggested Supplier:		Date Requested by: Latest date required:	
Quantity	Description	Estimated Cost	
		Unit	£
Authorised signature:			

Order form

2.7   Often the business will use a regular source of supply. The purchasing department may be aware of special offers or have details of new suppliers: part of its job is to keep up to date with what is on the market. Thus once a **purchase requisition** is received in the purchasing department, the first task is to identify the most suitable **supplier**.

2.8   The requisitioning department may specify the goods they require but the buying department may have a choice (for example in deciding what quality paper will be ordered for stationery). Whatever the decision made, an **order form** is then completed by the purchasing department (again, it may have to be authorised by the finance department to ensure that budgets are not being over-stepped) and this is sent to the supplier. The order form, an example of which is shown below, will contain the following details.

(a)   The **name** and **address** of the ordering organisation.

(b)   The **date** of order, and reference numbers for both ordering department and supplier.

(c)   The **address** and **date**(s) for delivery or collection.

(d)   **Details of goods/services**: quantity, code, specification, unit costs and so on.

An order form should be sent even if goods are initially ordered by telephone, to confirm that the order is a legitimate one and to make sure that the supplier does not overlook it.

The **purchase order** is important because it provides a means by which the business can later check that the goods received are the same as those ordered. Copies of the purchase order can be sent to the following people/departments.

- The person who requisitioned the goods
- The stores department
- The accounts department

A purchase order form is shown on the following page.

Purchase Order/Confirmation	Fenchurch Garden Centre Pickle Lane Westbridge Kent			
Our Order Ref: To	Date			
⌐(Address) ⌐	Please deliver to the above address			
	Ordered by:			
	Passed and checked by:			
⌊ ⌋	Total Order Value £			
			Subtotal	
			VAT (@ 17.5%)	
			Total	

Despatch note

2.9 Certain other documents may arise before the goods are actually received. The supplier may acknowledge the order and perhaps indicate how long it is likely to take to be fulfilled. A **despatch note** may be sent to warn that the goods are on their way.

Delivery note

2.10 We now move to the stores department. When the goods are delivered, goods inwards will be presented with a **delivery note** or **advice note** (although bear in mind that smaller suppliers may not go to these lengths). This is the supplier's document (a copy is signed by the person receiving the goods and returned to the supplier) and, as such, there is no guarantee that its details are correct. If the actual goods cannot be inspected immediately, the delivery note should be signed 'subject to inspection'.

Goods received note

2.11 Once the goods have been delivered they should be inspected as soon as possible. A **goods received note (GRN)** will be completed by goods inwards on the basis of a physical check, which involves counting the items received and seeing that they are not damaged. A copy of the GRN would also be sent to the following departments.

(a) The **purchasing department**, so that it can be matched with the **purchase order**. If there are any discrepancies, these would be sorted out with the supplier.

(b) The **accounts department**, so that it can be matched with the **invoice**.

2.12 The transaction ends with payment of the invoice (once any discrepancies have been sorted out). The supplier might issue a credit note if this invoice is wrong or there were problems with delivery.

		ACCOUNTS COPY

GOODS RECEIVED NOTE   WAREHOUSE COPY

DATE: _ _7 March 20X1_ _ _   TIME: _ _ _2.00 pm_ _ _ _ _   NO 5565

ORDER NO: _ _ _ _ _ _ _ _ _ _ _ _ _ _ _ _ _ _ _ .

SUPPLIER'S ADVICE NOTE NO: _ _ _ _ _ _ _ _ _ _ _ _ WAREHOUSE A

QUANTITY	CAT NO	DESCRIPTION
20	TP 400	Terracotta pots, medium

RECEIVED IN GOOD CONDITION: *L. W.*   (INITIALS)

Activity 2.5

Why would you buy roofing slates by the thousand rather than by weight?

Buying and costing

2.13 Clearly the buying department needs to retain cost information for the purpose of identifying suitable suppliers. This is likely to be in the form of **catalogues** and **price lists**. From the point of view of costing products such information will be useful when new products are being assessed and when setting standard costs for materials (see later).

2.14 The costing department is, however, chiefly interested in the actual cost of materials as shown on the **invoice** and included in the accounting records as cash and credit transactions.

2.15 EXAMPLE: BUYING AND COSTING

It is Jo West's first day in the costing department and she has been told to calculate the materials cost of job 3ROC which has just been completed. No invoice has yet been received for the main material used, which is known as LI98. Jo uses her initiative and pops down to the purchasing department to see if they can help. They are rather busy but someone hands her a very well-thumbed catalogue and a thick file of purchase orders, all relating to the supplier of LI98. There are many orders for LI98, one of which has today's date. How should Jo go about costing the LI98 used for job 3ROC?

2.16 SOLUTION

The quickest thing to do would be to phone up the supplier and ask what price will be charged for the order in question, but there might be good reasons for not doing this (for example not wishing to prompt an earlier invoice than usual!) It seems likely that, in the absence of the actual information, the best way of ascertaining a price for LI98 is to consult the catalogue (assuming it is up to date) and to find the most recent purchase order that *has* been invoiced. If there is a discrepancy, previous invoices could be looked at to see if they show a price rise since the date of the catalogue. If the price fluctuates widely it might be better to calculate an average.

2.17 As Jo gets to know her way around the system she will learn which are the most reliable sources of information. Possibly some suppliers make frequent errors on invoices but quote correct unit prices on delivery notes. The moral is: always be on your guard for errors.

Activity 2.6

Draw a flow diagram illustrating the main documents involved in a materials purchase, from its initiation up until the time of delivery.

---

3 VALUING MATERIALS ISSUES AND STOCKS

Just-in-time stock policy

3.1 The implicit assumption in the Jo West example above was that materials were bought specifically for individual jobs and therefore that each order could be identified with a particular job. This is possible in practice. Certainly, keeping large quantities of stock is something to be avoided in the business environment of the new millennium. Holding stock means that you have to have somewhere to put it and so it takes up space that could be used for other purposes. Often it means employing somebody to look after it, perhaps 24 hours a day if it is very valuable.

3.2 Ideally, you should receive an order for so many items of the product in question, buy exactly the right quantity of materials to make that many items and be left with no stocks of finished goods, work in progress or raw materials. This is known as the **just-in-time (JIT) approach,** that is, the just-in-time purchasing of stocks to meet just-in-time production of goods ordered. From the point of view of costing, there is very little difficulty with the JIT approach. The materials costs of each production run are known because the materials used were bought specially for that run. There was no stock to start with and there is none left over.

Buffer stock

3.3 However the approach more common in practice is to keep a certain amount of stock in reserve to cope with fluctuations in demand and with suppliers who cannot be relied upon to deliver the right quality and quantity of materials at the right time. This reserve of stock is known as **buffer stock**.

3.4 EXAMPLE: STOCK VALUATION

(a) Suppose, for example, that you have 50 litres of a chemical in stock. You buy 2,000 litres to allow for the next batch of production. Both the opening stock and the newly-purchased stock cost £2 per litre.

	Litres	£
Opening stock	50	100
Purchases	2,000	4,000
	2,050	4,100

(b) You actually use 1,600 litres, leaving you with 450 litres. You know that each of the 1,600 litres used cost £2, as did each of the 450 litres remaining. There is no costing problem here.

(c) Now suppose that in the following month you decide to buy 1,300 litres, but have to pay £2.10 per litre because you lose a 10p discount if buying under 1,500 litres.

	Litres	Cost per litre £	Total cost £
Opening stock	450	2.00	900
Purchases	1,300	2.10	2,730
	1,750		3,630

For the next batch of production you use 1,600 litres, as before. What did the 1,600 litres used cost, and what value should you give to the 150 litres remaining?

3.5 SOLUTION

If we could identify which litres were used there would be no problem. Some would cost £2 per litre but most would cost £2.10. It may not, however, be possible to identify litres used. For instance, the chemical may not be perishable, and new purchases be simply mixed in with older stock in a central tank. There would thus be no way of knowing which delivery the 1,600 litres used belonged to. Even if the chemical were stored in tins with date stamps it would be a tedious chore to keep track of precisely which tins were used when (and since they are all the same, the exercise has no virtue from the point of view of the quality of the final product.)

It may not therefore be possible or desirable to track the progress of each individual litre. However we need to know the cost of the litres that we have used so that we know how much to charge for the final product and so that we can compare this cost with the equivalent cost in earlier or future periods. We also need to know the cost of closing stock both because it will form part of the usage figure in the next period and for financial accounting purposes. Closing stock is often a significant figure in the financial statements and it appears in both the profit and loss account and the balance sheet.

We therefore have to use a consistent method of pricing the litres which provides a reasonable approximation of the costs of the stock.

ASSESSMENT ALERT

The December 1999 Central Assessment asked candidates to give a reason why the company might wish to keep a buffer stock.

3.6 There are a number of different methods of valuing stock.

(a) **FIFO - First in, first out**

This method values **issues at the prices of the oldest items in stock at the time the issues were made.** The remaining **stock will thus be valued at the price of the most recent purchases.** Say, for example ABC Ltd's stock consisted of four deliveries of raw material in the last month:

	Units		
1 September	1,000	at	£2.00
8 September	500	at	£2.50
15 September	500	at	£3.00
22 September	1,000	at	£3.50

If on 23 September 1,500 units were issued, 1,000 of these units would be priced at £2 (the cost of the 1,000 oldest units in stock), and 500 at £2.50 (the cost of the next oldest 500). 1,000 units of closing stock would be valued at £3.50 (the cost of the 1,000 most recent units received) and 500 units at £3.00 (the cost of the next most recent 500).

(b) **LIFO - Last in, first out**

This method is the opposite of FIFO. **Issues will be valued at the prices of the most recent purchases; hence stock remaining will be valued at the cost of the oldest items.** In the example in (a) it will be 1,000 units of **issues** which will be valued at £3.50, and the other 500 units issued will be valued at £3.00. 1,000 units of **closing stock** will be valued at £2.00, and 500 at £2.50.

(c) **Cumulative weighted average pricing**

With this method we calculate an average cost of all the litres in stock whenever a new delivery is received. Thus the individual price of the units issued *and* of the units in closing stock will be (22 September being the date of the last delivery):

$$\frac{\text{Total cost of units in stock at 22 September}}{\text{Units in stock at 22 September}}$$

The average price per unit will be $\dfrac{£8,250}{3,000} = £2.75$.

(d) **Replacement cost**

This method values issues and stock at the cost to the business of replacing that stock. If replacement cost is used, this should stop a business paying out to shareholders when it really needs the money to replace its assets to keep operating.

(e) **Standard cost**

Under the standard costing method, all issues are at a predetermined standard price. We shall look at standard costing in more detail in Chapter 9.

3.7 EXAMPLE: FIFO, LIFO AND CUMULATIVE WEIGHTED AVERAGE PRICING

Let's go back to the example in Paragraph 3.4.

(a) **FIFO**

	Litres	*Cost* £	£
Opening stock	450	2.00	900
Purchases	1,300	2.10	2,730
	1,750		3,630
Usage	(450)	2.00	(900)
	1,300		2,730
Usage (1,600 – 450)	(1,150)	2.10	(2,415)
Closing stock	150		315

Total cost of usage is £900 + £2,415 = £3,315 and the value of closing stock is £315.

(b) **LIFO**

	Litres	Cost £	£
Opening stock	450	2.00	900
Purchases	1,300	2.10	2,730
	1,750		3,630
Usage	(1,300)	2.10	(2,730)
	450		900
Usage (1,600 – 1,300)	(300)	2.00	(600)
	150		300

Total cost of usage is £2,730 + £600 = £3,330 and the value of closing stock is £300.

(c) **Cumulative weighted average pricing**

	Litres	Cost £	£
Opening stock	450	2.000	900
Purchases	1,300	2.100	2,730
Stock at (£3,630/1,750)	1,750	2.074	3,630
Usage	(1,600)	2.074	(3,318)
	150		312

Usage costs £3,318 under this method and closing stock is valued at £312.

3.8 For FIFO, LIFO and cumulative weighted average pricing, note that the total of usage costs plus closing stock value is the same (£3,630) whichever method is used. In other words, the total expenditure of £3,630 is simply split between the expenses for the period and the remaining asset (stock) value in different proportions. The total expense will eventually be charged as usage costs but, according to the method used, different amounts will be charged in different periods.

3.9 The different results in this example are not very marked because we are dealing with fairly small quantities and the price fluctuation was not very significant. If we had been dealing in hundreds of thousands of litres or that the cost of the chemical had gone up by 50p, the differences would be, as you can imagine, far more significant.

ASSESSMENT ALERT

One of the tasks in both the June 1999 and the December 1999 Central Assessments included completing a stores ledger account using the **Last In First Out** (LIFO) method to cost issues and value stock of an item. Similar tasks in the future might require the use of the First In First Out (FIFO) method or cumulative weighted average pricing.

Activity 2.7

The following transactions took place during May 20X1. You are required to calculate the value of all issues and of closing stock using each of the following methods of valuation.

(a) FIFO
(b) LIFO
(c) Cumulative weighted average pricing

TRANSACTIONS DURING MAY 20X1

	Quantity	Unit cost	Total cost
	Units	£	£
Opening balance, 1 May	100	2.00	200
Receipts, 3 May	400	2.10	840
Issues, 4 May	200		
Receipts, 9 May	300	2.12	636
Issues, 11 May	400		
Receipts, 18 May	100	2.40	240
Issues, 20 May	100		
Closing balance, 31 May	200		
			1,916

Which method is correct?

3.10 This is a trick question, because there is no one correct method. Each method has **advantages** and **disadvantages.**

3.11 The advantages and disadvantages of the **FIFO** method are as follows.

   (a) **Advantages**

   (i) It is a logical pricing method which probably represents what is physically happening: in practice the oldest stock is likely to be used first.

   (ii) It is easy to understand and explain to managers.

   (iii) The closing stock value can be near to a valuation based on the cost of replacing the stock.

   (b) **Disadvantages**

   (i) FIFO can be cumbersome to operate because of the need to identify each batch of material separately.

   (ii) Managers may find it difficult to compare costs and make decisions when they are charged with varying prices for the same materials.

3.12 The advantages and disadvantages of the **LIFO** method are as follows.

   (a) **Advantages**

   (i) Stocks are issued at a price which is close to current market value. This is not the case with FIFO when there is a high rate of inflation.

   (ii) Managers are continually aware of recent costs when making decisions, because the costs being charged to their department or products will be current costs.

   (b) **Disadvantages**

   (i) The method can be cumbersome to operate because it sometimes results in several batches being only part-used in the stock records before another batch is received.

   (ii) LIFO is often the opposite to what is physically happening and can therefore be difficult to explain to managers.

   (iii) As with FIFO, decision making can be difficult because of the variations in prices.

3.13 The advantages and disadvantages of **average pricing** are as follows.

(a) **Advantages**

   (i)   Fluctuations in prices are smoothed out, making it easier to use the data for decision making.

   (ii)   It is easier to administer than FIFO and LIFO, because there is no need to identify each batch separately.

(b) **Disadvantages**

   (i)   The resulting issue price is rarely an actual price that has been paid, and can run to several decimal places.

   (ii)   Prices tend to lag behind a little behind current market values when there is gradual inflation.

Activity 2.8

(a)   What is the main disadvantage of the FIFO method of stock valuation?

(b)   What is the main advantage of the LIFO method?

(c)   What is the main advantage and the main disadvantage of the cumulative weighted average method?

4   STOCK CONTROL

KEY TERM

Stock control is the regulation of stock levels, one aspect of which is putting a value to the amounts of stock issued and remaining. The stock control system can also be said to include ordering, purchasing and receiving goods and keeping track of them while they are in the warehouse.

4.1   This section deals with the costs of stock holding and the location of stock. Section 5 deals with using computers to control stocks. Section 6 deals with the other aspect of stock control, namely reordering decisions.

Why hold stock?

4.2   The costs of purchasing stock are usually one of the largest costs faced by an organisation and, once obtained, stock has to be carefully controlled and checked.

4.3   The main reasons for holding stocks can be summarised as follows.

- To ensure sufficient goods are available to meet expected demand
- To provide a buffer between processes
- To meet any future shortages
- To take advantage of bulk purchasing discounts
- To absorb seasonal fluctuations and any variations in usage and demand
- To allow production processes to flow smoothly and efficiently
- As a necessary part of the production process (such as when maturing cheese)
- As a deliberate investment policy, especially in times of inflation or possible shortages

Holding costs

4.4 **Holding costs** are associated with high stock levels. The reasons they occur are as follows.

(a) **Costs of storage and stores operations**. Larger stocks require more storage space and possibly extra staff and equipment to control and handle them.

(b) **Interest charges**. Holding stocks involves the tying up of capital (cash) on which interest must be paid.

(c) **Insurance costs**. The larger the value of stocks held, the greater insurance premiums are likely to be.

(d) **Risk of obsolescence**. When materials or components become out-of-date and are no longer required, existing stocks must be thrown away and written off to the profit and loss account.

(e) **Deterioration**. When materials in store deteriorate to the extent that they are unusable, they must be thrown away (with the likelihood that disposal costs would be incurred) and again, the value written off stock plus the disposal costs will be a charged to the profit and loss account.

(f) **Theft**.

Costs of obtaining stock

4.5 **Ordering costs** are associated with low stock levels. The following costs are included in ordering costs.

(a) **Clerical and administrative costs** associated with purchasing, accounting for and receiving goods

(b) **Transport costs**

(c) **Production run costs**

Locating stock

4.6 You can probably picture a warehouse - a large room with rows and rows of high shelving, perhaps moveable ladders and maybe barrows or fork-lift trucks. Very modern 'highbay' warehouses have automatic guided vehicles (AGVs), stacker cranes and conveyors, all controlled by computer. All of this implies organisation: when they are brought into the warehouse stocks are not simply dumped in the nearest available space. There is a place for everything and everything is in its place. There is no point in keeping stock at all if you don't know where to find it when it is needed.

4.7 Suppose, for example, that a warehouse were arranged as shown below, A to F representing rows of shelving and 1 to 7 the access bays between them. Suppose the shelves were 4m high, 10m long and 1m wide and you needed to locate five 10 mm washers in stainless steel. (To put it another way, suppose you had a haystack and you were looking for a needle!) How would you go about organising the warehouse so that you could always find what you were looking for?

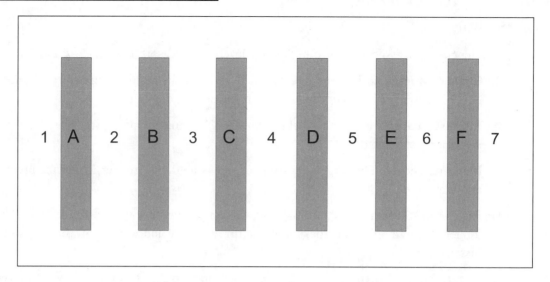

4.8   The solution is fairly obvious. You need to divide up the shelf-racks and give each section a code. A typical warehouse might organise its shelving as shown below.

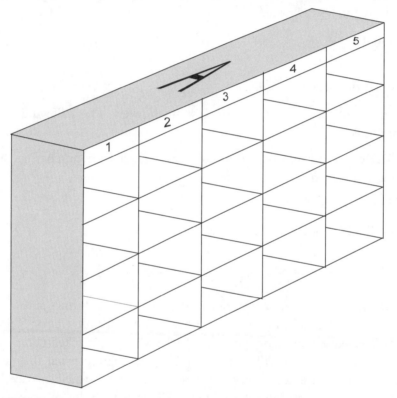

If you are reminded of a library, this is intentional: it is helpful to think of a warehouse as a library of materials.

You also need to keep a record which shows the whereabouts in the warehouse of all the different types of stock, including the 10mm washers in stainless steel. Suppose that the washers are listed as being kept in location A234.

4.9   The reference A234 would take you to Row A, bay 2, bin 3, shelf 4. Shelf 4 might contain a series of drawers containing washers of various sizes, each drawer being labelled with a precise part number (A234/1279, say) and a description of the item. (Coding is discussed in more detail later on in this chapter.)

4.10 The term **bin** as it is used above may be new to you, but you need to get used to it meaning something other than the receptacle by your desk full of screwed up paper and apple cores! **Bin** simply means a receptacle. In warehouse terms it normally means a division of shelving (or simply one shelf) or some other container which can be located by a code letter or number. The term is in general usage but it does not have a precise meaning.

4.11 In the light of this you should understand what a **bin card** is. **In a manual stock control system the bin card is kept with the actual stock and is updated whenever items are removed or added** to provide an accurate record of the quantity in stock for each stores item.

	BIN CARD							
Description .... Bin No:								
				Code No:				
Normal Quantity to order .... Maximum:								
				Minimum:				
				Re-order Level:				
Receipts			Issues			Balance	Remarks	
Date	G.R.N No.	Quantity	Date	Req. No.	Quantity	Quantity		

Note that the bin card does not need to show any information about the cost of materials.

4.12 Organisations will also maintain what are known as **stores ledger accounts,** an example of an account being shown below.

	STORES LEDGER ACCOUNT										
Material: .... Maximum Quantity:											
Code: .... Minimum Quantity:											
Date	Receipts				Issues				Stock		
	G.R.N. No.	Quantity	Unit Price £	Amount £	Stores Req. No.	Quantity	Unit Price £	Amount £	Quantity	Unit Price £	Amount £

Details from GRNs and materials requisition notes (see later) are used to update stores ledger accounts, which then provide a record of the quantity and value of each line of stock in the stores. The stores ledger accounts are normally kept in the cost department or in the stores office whereas the bin cards are written up and actually kept in the stores. There are two advantages to this procedure.

(a) The accounting records can be maintained more accurately and in a better condition by a cost clerk or an experienced stores clerk than by a stores assistant.

BPP PUBLISHING

(b) A control check is provided. The balances on the bin cards in the stores can be compared with the balances on the stores ledger accounts.

4.13 The use of bin cards and stores ledger accounts ensures that every issue and receipt of stock is recorded as it occurs so that there is a continuous clerical record of the balance of each item of stock. This is known as a **perpetual inventory system.**

4.14 You may be thinking that the system we have described is rather over-complicated. Why not, for example, start at one end of the room and end at the other numbering each separate location in sequence and numbering each stock item accordingly? The reasons are for practicality and flexibility.

It is much more practical to have large heavy items near to each other (to prevent fork-lift trucks from being driven from one end of the warehouse to the other all day!). In addition, frequently-used items should be kept near to the issue point so that the minimum time is spent locating them.

4.15 The last point is worth developing a little. Storekeeping involves a good deal of commonsense and a considerable knowledge of the types of stock held, and an effective storekeeping system should take the following points into account.

(a) Heavy items should not be stored on high shelves (in case the shelves collapse and to make handling as safe and unstrenuous as possible).

(b) Dangerous items (for example items with sharp edges) should not be stored above eye level.

(c) Items liable to be damaged by flood (for example paper stock) should not be stored on low shelves.

(d) Special arrangements should be made for the storage and handling of chemicals and flammable materials.

(e) Some stocks are sensitive to temperature and should be stored accordingly.

(f) Other stocks may have special hygiene or 'clean air' requirements.

Coding of materials

4.16 Each item held in stores must be unambiguously identified and this can best be done by numbering them with stock codes. The advantages of this are as follows.

(a) **Ambiguity is avoided**. Different people may use different descriptions for materials. This is avoided if numbers are used.

(b) **Time is saved**. Descriptions can be lengthy and time-consuming, particularly when completing written forms.

(c) **Production efficiency is improved**. If the correct material can be accurately identified from a code number, production hold-ups caused by the issue of incorrect material can be avoided.

(d) **Computerised processing** is made easier.

(e) Numbered code systems can be designed to be **flexible**, and can be **expanded** to include more stock items as necessary.

The digits in a code can stand for the type of stock, supplier, location and so forth. For example stock item A234/1279 might refer to the item of stock kept in row A, bay 2, bin 3, shelf 4. The item might be identified by the digits 12 and its supplier might be identified by the digits 79.

Issuing materials

4.17 The sole point of holding stocks is so that they can be used to make products. This means that they have to be issued from stores to production. This transaction will be initiated by production who will complete a **materials requisition note** and pass it to the warehouse.

MATERIALS REQUISITION						
Material Required for: (Job or Overhead Account) Department:					No. Date:	
Quantity	Description	Code No.	Weight	Rate	£	Notes
Foreman:						

4.18 The stores department will locate the stock, withdraw the amount required and update the bin card as appropriate. The stores ledger account will also be updated.

4.19 If the amount of materials required is overestimated the excess should be put back into store accompanied by a **materials returned note**. The form in our illustration is almost identical to a requisition note. In practice it would be wise to colour code the two documents (one white, one yellow, say) to prevent confusion.

MATERIALS RETURNED NOTE						
Material not needed for: (Job or Overhead Account) Department:					No. Date:	
Quantity	Description	Code No.	Weight	Rate	£	Notes
Foreman:						

4.20 There may be occasions when materials already issued but not required for one job can be used for another job in progress. In this case there is no point in returning the materials to the warehouse. Instead a **materials transfer note** can be raised. This prevents one job being charged with too many materials and another with too little.

4.21 You will note that all of the forms shown above have spaces for cost information (that is, monetary values). This will be inserted either by the stores department or in costing, depending upon how the system is organised. We have already described the various bases which may be used to put a value on stock - FIFO, LIFO or an average figure.

Stocktaking

4.22 Stocktaking involves counting the physical stock on hand at a certain date and then checking this against the balance shown in the clerical records. There are two methods of carrying out this process.

> **KEY TERMS**
>
> - **Periodic stocktaking**. This is usually carried out annually and the objective is to count all items of stock on a specific date.
>
> - **Continuous stocktaking**. This involves counting and checking a number of stock items on a regular basis so that each item is checked at least once a year, and valuable items can be checked more frequently. This has a number of advantages over periodic stocktaking. It is less disruptive, less prone to error, and achieves greater control.

Stock discrepancies

4.23 There will be occasions when stock checks disclose **discrepancies between the physical amount of an item in stock and the amount shown in the stock records**. When this occurs, the cause of the discrepancy should be investigated, and appropriate action taken to ensure that it does not happen again. Possible causes of discrepancies are as follows.

(a) Suppliers deliver a different quantity of goods than is shown on the goods received note. Since this note is used to update stock records, a discrepancy will arise. This can be avoided by ensuring that all stock is counted as it is received, and a responsible person should sign the document to verify the quantity.

(b) The quantity of stock issued to production is different from that shown on the materials requisition note. Careful counting of all issues will prevent this.

(c) Excess stock is returned from production without documentation. This can be avoided by ensuring that all movements of stock are accurately documented - in this case, a materials returned note should be raised.

(d) Clerical errors may occur in the stock records. Regular checks by independent staff should detect and correct mistakes.

(e) Breakages in stores may go unrecorded. All breakages should be documented and noted on the stock records.

(f) Employees may steal stock. Regular checks or continuous stocktaking will help to prevent this, and only authorised personnel should be allowed into the stores.

4.24 If the stock discrepancy is found to be caused by clerical error, then the records should be rectified immediately. If the discrepancy occurs because units of stock appear to be missing, the lost stock must be written off. If actual stock is greater than recorded stock, extra units of stock are added to the stock records. The accounting transaction will be recorded by a stores credit note, where items of stock have been lost, or a stores debit note, when there is more actual stock than recorded.

4.25 A stores credit note may have the following format.

STORES CREDIT NOTE			
Quantity	Item code	Description	£
Continuous stocktaking report number .... Credit note authorised by .... Date			

Activity 2.9

Give five reasons why stocktaking may identify discrepancies between physical stock held and stock records.

---

5 COMPUTERS AND STOCK CONTROL

5.1 Although the basic principles of stock control are not difficult in themselves, you will appreciate by now that an effective system requires a good deal of administrative effort, even if only a few items of stock are involved. There is therefore a good deal to be gained from computerisation of this function.

Computerised stock files

5.2 A typical computerised stock file would contain a record for each item, each record having fields (individual pieces of data) as follows.

(a) **Stock code:** a unique stock code to identify each item. This could be in bar code form for large organisations.

(b) **Description:** a brief description is helpful when perusing stock records and probably essential when printing out lists of stock for stock-taking purposes. Ideally the system will generate purchase orders which also require brief narrative details.

(c) **Supplier code**: this would match the code for the supplier in the purchase ledger.

(d) **Supplier's reference number:** again this information would be needed for purchase orders.

(e) **Quantity per unit:** this would specify how many individual items there were per 'unit'. This is sometimes called the 'factor'.

(f) **Cost price per item.**

(g) **Control levels:** there would be a field for each of the four control levels (minimum and maximum stock, reorder level and reorder quantity, which we look at in Section 6).

(h) **Location:** a location code could be included if it were not part of the stock code itself.

(i) **Movements history:** there could be fields for issues per day, per week, during the last month, in the last year and so on.

(j) **Job code:** there might be a field allowing costs to be linked to specific jobs. Stocks could be 'reserved' for jobs due to be started in the next week, say.

Stock reports

5.3 A system with fields such as those above might be able to generate the following reports.

(a) **Daily listing:** a daily list of all items ordered, received, issued or placed on reserve. This might have 'exception reports' for unusual movements of stock and for items that had reached the reorder level.

(b) **Stock lists:** lists could be produced for stocktaking purposes, with stock codes, descriptions and locations. This could be restricted to certain types of stock, such as high value items or stocks with high turnover.

(c) **Stock movements:** a report of stock movements over time would help in setting control levels and in identifying 'slow-moving stock' that is not really required.

(d) **Stock valuations:** this would show current balances and place a value on stocks according to which calculation method (FIFO, LIFO, and so on) was in use.

(e) **Supplier analysis:** this would list all the items of stock purchased from the same supplier, and might be useful for placing orders (several items could be ordered at the same time, cutting delivery costs).

Bill of materials

5.4 Many computerised stock control systems have a **bill of materials facility**. This allows assembly records (sometimes called explosion records) to be compiled, containing details of the various assemblies that make up the final product. A tape deck, for example may have three main assemblies - the motor mechanism, the electronics and the outer casing.

5.5 Each individual assembly could be further broken down into its constituent materials and components.

6 REORDERING STOCK

6.1 As noted earlier, the ideal is for businesses not to have any stocks on the premises unless they are about to be used in production which can be sold immediately. In practice many businesses would regard this approach as too risky or impractical because they are unable to predict either their own levels of demand or the reliability of their suppliers or both. They therefore set various **control levels**, the purpose of which is to ensure the following.

(a) The business **does not run out of stock** and **suffer disruption to production** as a result.

(b) The business **does not carry an excessive amount of stocks** which take up space, incur storage costs and possibly deteriorate with age.

6.2 The problems of when to reorder stock and how much to reorder are the most significant practical problems in stock management. To illustrate the problems in detail and the way in which they may be solved, we shall consider an example.

6.3 EXAMPLE: STOCK CONTROL LEVELS

(a) A new manufacturing business is being set up to make a single product. The product is to be made by moulding plastic. Jonathan, the manager, expects to make 10 units per day and has found that each unit will require 5kg of plastic. He decides to obtain enough materials to last a week (5 days). How much should he order?

(b) This is not difficult. Jonathan should order 5 days × 10 units × 5kg = 250kg.

The materials are placed in the stores ready for the commencement of production on the following Monday.

(c) The following week everything goes as planned, causing great celebration over the weekend. The following Monday however, Jonathan realises that he has no materials left. (This is called a '**stock-out**'). He rings up a number of suppliers but to his dismay none can deliver in less than 2 days. There is therefore no production for the whole of Monday and Tuesday.

(d) Jonathan doesn't want this to happen again so he orders four weeks worth of materials, even though this means increasing his overdraft at the bank by £4,000. The materials duly arrive on Wednesday morning but of the 1,000kg delivered (20 × 10 × 5 = 1,000) Jonathan finds he only has room to store 500kg. To accommodate the remainder he has to rent space in the factory next door at a cost of £20.

(e) Twenty days go by and production goes as planned. Jonathan doesn't want to get caught out again, so two days before he is due to run out of materials he places a fresh order, this time for only 500kg.

(f) Unfortunately, this time the suppliers are unable to deliver in 2 days as promised, but take 4 days. Another 2 days production is lost.

(g) As Jonathan's product establishes itself in the market, demand starts to increase. He starts to produce 15 units a day but again he is caught out because, obviously, this means that the materials are used up more quickly. He often runs out before the next delivery has arrived.

(h) So it goes on for the whole of Jonathan's first year in business. By the end of this time he works out that he has lost nearly three weeks production due to materials shortages. In despair he contacts a management consultant for advice.

6.4 SOLUTION

(a) Jonathan is told to calculate a number of figures from his records.

    (i)   The maximum daily usage

    (ii)   The maximum lead time. (**Lead time** is the time it takes between ordering stocks and having them delivered.)

    (iii) The average daily usage

    (iv) The average lead time

    (v)   The minimum daily usage and minimum lead time

    (vi) The cost of holding one unit of stock for one year (holding cost)

    (vii) The cost of ordering a consignment of stock

    (viii) The annual demand for materials

(b) Jonathan has kept careful records and some of these figures cause him little bother.

Maximum usage	100kg per day
Average usage	75kg per day
Minimum usage	50kg per day
Annual demand	19,500kg ($52 \times 5 \times 75$kg)
Maximum lead time	4 days
Average lead time	3 days
Minimum lead time	2 days

(c) The calculation of the **holding cost** is quite complicated. Jonathan has to work out a number of figures.

    (i) Materials can only be bought in 5kg boxes and therefore 'one unit' of stock is 5kg, not 1kg.

    (ii) The total cost of having one box in stock is made up of a number of separate costs.

        (1) Interest paid on the money borrowed to buy one box

        (2) Rental of the floor space taken up by one box

        (3) The warehouse keeper's wages

        (4) Administrative costs of taking deliveries, issuing materials, and keeping track of them

        (5) The cost of insuring the stock

    Eventually Jonathan works out that the figure is £0.62 per 'unit' of 5kg. He is shocked by this and wonders whether he should order smaller quantities more frequently. (Fortunately for Jonathan, there is little risk of obsolescence or deterioration of boxes. Many organisations have to include the cost of obsolescence or deterioration in holding costs, however.)

(d) **Ordering costs** are also quite difficult to calculate. Jonathan has to take into account:

    (i) the cost of stationery and postage;
    (ii) the cost of phoning round to suppliers; and
    (iii) the time taken up by doing this.

He is surprised to find that the figure works out to £19.87 per order and now wonders whether he should make fewer larger orders to keep these costs down.

(e) Now that Jonathan has these figures the consultant tells him how to calculate four stock control levels that will help him to avoid running out of stock and to keep down the costs of holding and ordering stock.

    (i) **Reorder level**. Jonathan already realises that stocks have to be reordered before they run out completely. This number tells him how low stocks can be allowed to fall before an order should be placed. It assumes that maximum usage and maximum lead time, the two worst events from the point of view of stock control, coincide.

KEY TERM

Reorder level = maximum usage × maximum lead time

Reorder level = 100kg × 4 days
               = 400kg

(ii) **Reorder quantity**

KEY TERM

The **reorder quantity** is the quantity of stock which is to be re-ordered when stock reaches the reorder level.

Jonathan has never known what the best amount to order would be. He is beginning to understand that there must be some way of juggling the costs of holding stock, the costs of ordering stock and the amount of stock needed but he does not know how to work it out. His consultant fortunately does and she gives him the following formula.

KEY TERM

The **economic order quantity (Q)**, or **EOQ** is the best amount to order and is calculated as follows.

$$Q = \sqrt{\frac{2cd}{h}}$$

where h is the cost of holding one unit of stock for one year
       c is the cost of ordering a consignment
       d is the annual demand
       Q is the 'economic order quantity' (EOQ), that is, the best amount to order

Remembering that a 'unit' of stock is 5kg and therefore annual demand is 19,500kg/5kg = 3,900 units, we can calculate the reorder quantity as follows.

$$Q = \sqrt{\frac{2 \times 19.87 \times 3,900}{0.62}}$$

= 500 units (approximately)
= 2,500kg

(f) Jonathan is not entirely convinced by the EOQ calculation but promises to try it out since it seems like a reasonable amount to order. He then asks what the other two control levels are, since he seems to have all the information he needs already. The consultant points out that the calculations done so far don't allow for other uncertain factors like a severe shortage of supply or unexpected rises or falls in demand. As a precaution Jonathan needs a **minimum stock level** below which stocks should never be allowed to fall, and a **maximum stock level** above which stock should not be able to rise. There is a risk of stock-outs if stock falls below the minimum level and a risk of stock being at a wasteful level if above the maximum level.

KEY TERM

Minimum stock level   =   reorder level – (average usage × average lead time)

Minimum stock level   =   400kg – (75kg × 3 days)
                      =   175kg

BPP PUBLISHING

KEY TERM

Maximum stock level = reorder level + reorder quantity −
(minimum usage × minimum lead time)

Maximum stock level = 400kg + 2,500kg − (50kg × 2 days)
= 2,800kg

6.5 The story has a happy ending. Jonathan finds that the EOQ works very well in practice. His costs are reduced and he suffers no stock-outs in the following year. The derivation of the EOQ formula is quite complicated and we suggest that you, too, simply accept it.

6.6 An easier way of working out a reorder quantity is to take the reorder level (400 kg for Jonathan) and assume that the usage and the lead time will be as little or short as possible. This means that if an order is placed when stock levels reach reorder level, by the time the next delivery is received Jonathan would have 400 − (2 days × 50 kg) = 300 kg in stock. The quantity to be delivered must not be so much that it takes stock over the maximum level (2,800 kg). The **maximum** reorder quantity in Jonathan's case is therefore 2,500 kg. This happens to coincide with the economic order quantity, although it need not do so.

Activity 2.10

Watkins Ltd uses 4,000 kg of a raw material in a year. It costs £10 to hold 1 kg for one year, and the costs of ordering each consignment of raw materials are £200.

Watkins Ltd uses between 100 kg and 600 kg a month, and the company's suppliers can take between 1 and 3 months to deliver materials that have been ordered.

Task

Calculate the following.

(a) The reorder quantity
(b) The reorder level
(c) The maximum level of stock the company should hold

Activity 2.11

You are given the following information about material Zenith which is used by Zeta Beta Ltd in the production of a number of their products.

(a) Budgeted average demand for material Zenith is 400 kilos per week and production is maintained for 50 weeks in the year.

(b) The ordering cost is £150 per order.

(c) The standard material cost of Zenith is £6 per kilo and holding costs are 33 1/3% of that figure per annum for each kilo.

(d) The maximum usage in any one week is 600 kilos and the minimum 400.

(e) On average the orders take anything from one to three weeks to be delivered after they have been placed.

(f) The cost accountant has calculated the optimum order quantity to be 1,732 kgs.

Task

Calculate the following.

(a) The reorder level for material Zenith
(b) The minimum level of stock that should be held
(c) The maximum level of stock that should be held

Key learning points

- Materials can be **classified** according to the substances that make them up, how they are measured, or their physical properties.

- **Raw materials** are goods purchased for incorporation into products for sale.

- **Work in progress** is a term which represents an intermediate stage between the manufacturer purchasing the materials that go to make up the finished product, and the finished product. It is another name for part-finished goods.

- A **finished good** is a product ready for sale or despatch.

- **FIFO (first in, first out)** prices materials issues at the prices of the oldest items in stock, and values closing stock at the value of the most recent purchases.

- **LIFO (last in, last out)** prices materials issues at the prices of the most recent purchases, and values closing stock at the value of the oldest items.

- **Cumulative weighted average pricing** calculates an average cost of all stock items whenever a new delivery is received. The price for materials issues and the value for closing stock will be the same.

- Under the **standard costing method** all issues are at a predetermined standard price.

- **Stock control** is the regulation of stock levels, which includes putting a value to the amounts of stock issued and remaining. Stock control also includes ordering, purchasing, receiving and storing goods.

- Materials held in stock are generally **coded** in order that each item is clearly identified.

- **Periodic stocktaking** is usually carried out annually, when all items of stock are counted on a specific date.

- **Continuous stocktaking** involves counting and checking a number of stock items on a regular basis so that each item is checked at least once a year.

- **Stock control levels** can be calculated in order to maintain stocks at the optimum level. The four critical control levels are **reorder level, reorder quantity, minimum stock level** and **maximum stock level.**

- The **economic order quantity** is the ordering quantity which minimises stock costs (holding costs and ordering costs).

Quick quiz

1   What are the three main ways of classifying materials?

2   What are raw materials?

3   What is work in progress?

4   Generally, are items which are ready for sale or despatch known as work in progress?

5   List the five documents which you are likely to use when buying materials.

6   The goods received note is matched with two other documents in the buying process. What are they?

7   How would you calculate the cost of a unit of material using cumulative weighted average pricing?

8   What are the advantages of FIFO?

9   What is a bin card in warehouse terms?

10 Which purchasing documents are used to update the stores ledger account?

11 What is the main point of holding stocks?

12 What does stocktaking involve?

13 What are the two methods of stocktaking that are commonly used?

14   What are the main reasons for a company setting control levels with regard to stock?

15   What is the formula for the economic order quantity?

16   How would you calculate the minimum and maximum stock levels?

Answers to quick quiz

1   According to the substances that make them up, how they are measured and their physical properties.

2   Goods purchased for incorporation into products for sale.

3   A term used to represent an intermediate stage between the purchase of raw materials and the completion of the finished product.

4   No. Finished goods.

5   • Purchase requisition form
    • Order form
    • Despatch note
    • Delivery note
    • Goods received note (GRN)

6   The purchase order and the invoice.

7   $\dfrac{\text{Total cost of units in stock}}{\text{Number of units in stock}}$

8   • It is a logical pricing method
    • It is easy to understand
    • The closing stock can be near to a valuation based on the cost of replacing the stock

9   A division of shelving or some other container which can be located by a code letter or number.

10   Goods received notes and materials requisition notes.

11   In order for them to be used to make products.

12   Counting physical stock on hand at a certain date, and checking this against the accounting records.

13   Periodic stocktaking and continuous stocktaking.

14   To ensure it doesn't run out of stock, and to ensure that it does not carry too much stock.

15   $Q = \sqrt{\dfrac{2cd}{h}}$

16   Minimum stock level   =   reorder level – (average usage × average lead time)
     Maximum stock level   =   reorder level + reorder quantity – (minimum usage × minimum lead time)

Answers to activities

Answer 2.1

(a)   Metal, rubber, plastic, glass, fabric, oil, paint, glue

(b)   Cereals, plastic, cardboard, glue. You might have included sugar and preservatives and so on, depending upon what you eat for breakfast

(c)   Sand, gravel, cement, bricks, plaster, wood, metal, plastic, glass, slate

(d)   You will have to mark your own answer. If you work for a service organisation like a firm of accountants, you could view the paper (and binding) of sets of accounts sent out to clients as raw materials, although in practice such materials are likely to be regarded as indirect costs

Answer 2.2

Direct materials can be traced directly to specific units of production, where as indirect materials cannot.

Answer 2.3

(a)   Direct
(b)   Direct
(c)   Indirect
(d)   Direct
(e)   Direct
(f)   Indirect (negligible value)
(g)   Indirect (negligible value)

Answer 2.4

Raw materials are goods purchased for incorporation into products for sale, but not yet issued to production. Work in progress is the name given to the materials while they are in the course of being converted to the final product. Finished goods are the end products when they are ready to be sold.

Answer 2.5

You would know what area of roof needed to be covered and what size and thickness of slates you wanted to use, so you could work out how many slates you needed. There is no way of knowing whether '1 tonne of slates' is adequate because slates of the same size and thickness are not necessarily all the same weight.

Answer 2.6

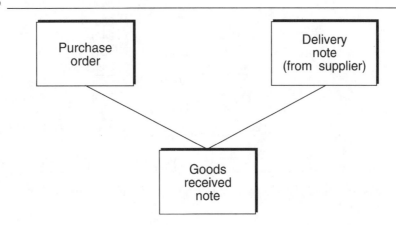

Answer 2.7

(a)   FIFO

Date of issue	Quantity issued Units	Value £	£	Cost of issues
4 May	200	100 at £2.00 100 at £2.10	200 210	
				410
11 May	400	300 at £2.10 100 at £2.12	630 212	
				842
20 May	100	100 at £2.12		212
				1,464
Closing stock value	200	100 at £2.12 100 at £2.40	212 240	
				452
				1,916

The cost of materials issued plus the value of closing stock equals the cost of purchases plus the value of opening stock (£1,916).

(b)   LIFO

Date of issue	Quantity issued Units	Value	£	Cost of issues £
4 May	200	200 at £2.10		420
11 May	400	300 at £2.12	636	
		100 at £2.10	210	
				846
20 May	100	100 at £2.40		240
				1,506
Closing stock value	200	100 at £2.10	210	
		100 at £2.00	200	
				410
				1,916

The cost of materials issued plus the value of closing stock equals the cost of purchases plus the value of opening stock (£1,916).

(c)   Cumulative weighted average

Date	Received Units	Issued Units	Balance Units	Total stock value £	Unit cost £	Price of issue £
Opening stock			100	200	2.00	
3 May	400			840	2.10	
			500*	1,040	2.08	
4 May		200		(416)	2.08	416
			300	624	2.08	
9 May	300			636	2.12	
			600*	1,260	2.10	
11 May		400		(840)	2.10	840
			200	420	2.10	
18 May	100			240	2.40	
			300*	660	2.20	
20 May		100		(220)	2.20	220
Cost of issues						1,476
Closing stock		200		440	2.20	440
						1,916

*   A new unit stock value is calculated whenever a new receipt of materials occurs.

The cost of materials issued plus the value of closing stock equals the cost of purchases plus the value of opening stock (£1,916).

Answer 2.8

(a)   FIFO has the disadvantage that if stocks are quite old they may be issued to production at a price which is well below the current market price. This gives the wrong message to production managers.

(b)   LIFO has the advantage that stock will be issued to production at a cost close to market value, thereby helping production managers gain a realistic idea of costs.

(c)   The weighted average method involves less cumbersome calculations than the other methods, but the issue price rarely represents an actual price that could be found in the market.

Answer 2.9

(a)   Stock quantities delivered may not have matched the quantity shown on the Goods Received Note, which is used to update the stock records.

(b)   The quantity of stock issued to production may not have matched the requisition.

(c)   Stock may have been returned without documentation.

(d)   There may be other errors in the stock records (for example casting errors).

(e)   Stock may have been destroyed or broken without a record being made.

(f)   Stock may have been stolen.

Answer 2.10

(a) Reorder quantity $= \sqrt{\dfrac{2cd}{h}}$

$= \sqrt{\dfrac{2 \times \text{ordering costs} \times \text{annual demand}}{\text{Stockholding costs}}}$

$= \sqrt{\dfrac{2 \times 200 \times 4{,}000}{10}}$

$=$ 400 kg

(b) Reorder level $=$ maximum usage $\times$ maximum lead time

$=$ 600×3

$=$ 1,800 kg

(c) Maximum stock level $=$ reorder level + reorder quantity − (minimum usage $\times$ minimum lead time)

$=$ $400 + 1{,}800 - (100 \times 1)$

$=$ 2,100 kg

Answer 2.11

(a) Reorder level $=$ maximum usage $\times$ maximum lead time

$=$ 600 kilos $\times$ 3 weeks

$=$ 1,800 kilos

(b) Minimum stock level $=$ reorder level − (average usage $\times$ average lead time)

$=$ 1,800 kilos − (500 kilos $\times$ 2 weeks)

$=$ 800 kilos

(c) Maximum stock level $=$ reorder level + reorder quantity − (minimum usage $\times$ minimum lead time)

$=$ 1,800 kilos + 1,732 kilos − (400 kilos $\times$ 1 week)

$=$ 3,132 kilos

Chapter 3   Labour costs

Chapter topic list

1   Determining labour costs

2   Recording labour costs

3   Overtime, bonuses and absences

4   Labour turnover

5   Analysis of labour efficiency and utilisation rates

Learning objectives

On completion of this chapter you will be able to:

	Performance criteria	Range statement
• identify and calculate direct labour costs in accordance with organisational policies and procedures	6.1.1, 6.1.3	6.1.1
• establish indirect labour costs in accordance with organisational procedures	6.2.2	6.2.1
• ensure that information relating to direct labour costs is clearly and correctly coded, analysed and recorded	6.1.2	6.1.1
• ensure that data and information relating to indirect and labour costs is accurately and clearly coded, analysed and recorded	6.2.1, 6.2.3	6.2.1
• deal with queries about direct and indirect labour	6.1.6, 6.2.8	6.1.1, 6.2.1

BPP PUBLISHING

1 DETERMINING LABOUR COSTS

What are labour costs?

1.1 Labour costs could be said to include any or all of the following items.

- The gross amount due to an employee
- Employer's national insurance
- Amounts paid to recruit labour
- Amounts paid for staff welfare
- Training costs
- The costs of benefits like company cars

The list could be extended, but we shall not go any further because in this chapter we are only concerned with the first item, the employee's gross salary.

1.2 The word **labour** is generally associated with strenuous physical effort but in the context of cost accounting it is not confined to manual work. **Labour costs** are the amounts paid to any employee, including supervisors, office staff, managers and tea ladies. We shall distinguish between **direct labour** and **indirect labour**, but even then you must not assume that this is necessarily a manual/clerical distinction (hopefully you are beginning to realise that direct costs and indirect costs differ in that they are accounted for differently).

Determining labour costs

1.3 There are three ways in which labour costs can be determined.

(a) According to some prior agreement

(b) According to the amount of time worked

(c) According to the amount and/or quality of work done (piecework or performance based remuneration).

1.4 Payment for most jobs is by a combination of methods (a) and (b). There will be a **basic wage** or **salary** which is agreed when the appointment is made. There will be a set number of hours per week during which the employee is expected to be available for work. There will be extra payments for time worked over and above the set hours, or deductions for time when the employee is not available beyond an agreed limit.

1.5 There may be periods when an organisation might wish to increase productivity, even though it does not have adequate resources to do so. In such situations, an organisation might wish to use **sub-contractors** to carry out any additional work. Alternatively, **agency staff** may be hired to work with the workforce on site in order to increase the labour resources (for a fixed period) of the organisation.

2 RECORDING LABOUR COSTS

2.1 You can see from the previous section that records of labour costs fall into three categories.

- Records of agreed basic wages and salaries
- Records of time spent working
- Records of work done

2.2 There are a number of ways in which this can be organised, but basically the information flow will be as follows.

48

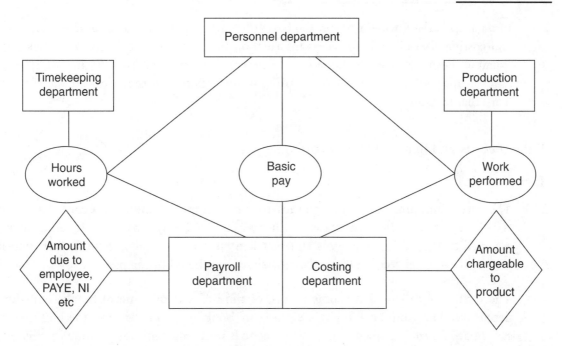

2.3   In practice, timekeeping would probably be a sub-function of production or of personnel. Alternatively, personnel may keep records of hours on the premises and available for work, while the production department keeps records of time spent doing different tasks. The system used will depend upon the nature of the job and the bases chosen for paying employees on the one hand and for costing products on the other.

2.4   Information flows back to the personnel department so that employees can be considered for promotion or disciplined if appropriate.

2.5   All the information may, in practice, be given first to payroll, who would then pass it on for costing analysis, or vice versa. (Remember that in some organisations payroll administration is contracted out to a third party.) The main point is that both payroll and costing need the same information, but they analyse it differently: payroll asks **who**, and costing asks **what**.

Basic pay

2.6   Levels of basic pay are ultimately decided by senior management who will take into account what other employers are paying for similar work, what they consider the work to be worth, how easy it is to recruit labour and any agreements with trade unions.

2.7   The basic pay due to an individual worker will be mentioned in his or her letter of appointment and included in his or her **contract of employment**. The main on-going record, however, will probably be kept on an **employee record card** held in the personnel department. This will also show subsequent increases in the wage rate or salary level and much other information. An example of an employee record card is shown on the following page.

2.8   Much of the information on the employee record card is confidential and there is no need for staff in the payroll department or the costing department to know about it.

Ideally, therefore, details of basic pay for all employees are compiled on separate lists which are given to payroll and costing. A fresh list should be issued whenever the pay rates are revised.

BPP PUBLISHING

2.9 In a **computerised wage system**, the basic rates are usually part of a **database**, and payroll and costing are only able to access information that is relevant to their tasks. Costing, for example, does not need to know the names of individual employees: in fact it is more efficient for workers to be coded according to the department they work in and the type of work that they do.

Time records and performance records

Attendance time

2.10 The bare minimum record of employees' time is a **simple attendance record** showing days absent because of holiday, sickness or other reason. Such a system is usually used when it is assumed that all of the employees' time is taken up doing one job and no further analysis is required. A typical record of attendance is shown on the following page.

2.11 The next step up is to have some **record of time of arrival, time of breaks and time of departure**. The simplest form is a **'signing-in' book** at the entrance to the building with, say, a page for each employee. Unless someone is watching constantly, however, this system is open to abuse and many employers use a **time recording clock** which stamps the time on a **clock card** inserted by the employee. A clock card is illustrated on Page 53. More modern systems involve the use of a plastic card like a credit card which is 'swiped' through a device which makes a computer record of the time of arrival and departure.

2.12 The next step is to analyse the hours spent at work according to what was done during those hours. The method adopted depends upon the size of the organisation and the nature of the work.

Detailed analysis of time: continuous production

2.13 Where routine, repetitive work is carried out it might not be practical to record the precise details. For example if a worker stands at a conveyor belt for seven hours his work can be measured by keeping a note of the number of units that pass through his part of the process during that time. If a group of employees all contribute to the same process, the total units processed per day (or week or whatever) can be divided by the number of employees.

2.14 EXAMPLE: LABOUR COST OF CONTINUOUS PRODUCTION

Team A comprises four members who are all paid £5 per hour and work a 35 hour week. During a particular week they processed 280 units. Calculate the following.

(a) The number of units Team A processes per hour
(b) The time it takes Team A to process one unit
(c) The labour cost of one unit

2.15 SOLUTION

(a) $\dfrac{\text{Total units processed}}{\text{Total hours}} = \dfrac{280}{35}$ = 8 units per hour

(b) $\dfrac{\text{Total minutes}}{\text{Total units processed}} = \dfrac{35 \times 60 \text{ minutes}}{280} = \dfrac{2,100}{280} = 7^{1}/_{2}$ minutes per unit

PERSONNEL RECORD CARD

NAME OTHER, A.N.

PERSONAL DETAILS

NUMBER

SURNAME	OTHER
FORENAMES	ALBERT NEIL

SEX	Nationality	British
(M) F	Social Security Number	WD 48 47 41C

Date of Birth	1 June 19Y9
Marital Status	Single (Married) Separated Divorced Widowed
Dependants	None
Disabilities	None
Pension Scheme	
Eligible	20W1 January
Joined	20W1 January

ADDRESS
94 Bootsale House
Antique Street
Old Salum
MERSEY ME5

Telephone 01973 89521

ADDRESS 1ST CHANGE
17 Newton Close
Brookeside
MERSEY ME1

Telephone 01973 12221

ADDRESS 2ND CHANGE

Telephone

Professional Qualifications

Certified Accountant 19X9

Educational Details

Higher Education

A levels	Economics (C)
BTec	Computer Services
GCSE	n/a
O levels	3
CSEs	4
Other	City & Guilds Photography

IN EMERGENCY CONTACT

Name Other, Noreen Olga   Wife
Address
17 Newton Close
Brookeside
MERSEY ME1

Telephone (h) 01973 12221
Telephone (wk) 01973 51443

EMPLOYMENT HISTORY

Years of Service (12 months to 31 December)

1 2 3 4 5 6 7 8 9 10 11 12 13 14 15 16 17 18 19 20 21 22

FROM	TO	TITLE	DEPT	REASON	PAY
1/1/X8	31/3/X8	Junior Clerk	Sls Ledger	1st job here	£6,500
1/4/X8	30/6/X8			Probation period over	£7,000
1/7/X8				Annual payrise 5%	£7,350
1/X9		Senior Clerk	Pur Ledger	Got ACCA Quals & promoted	£9,000
7/X9				10% pay rise	£9,900
7/Y0				10% (8% + 2% merit)	£10,890
12/Y0		Asst Technician	Payroll	Transfer	£10,890

Training History

Course Code	
0713/I	Induction to new employees

Special Details

Leave Entitlement   20 days

51

BPP
PUBLISHING

NAME: A.N. OTHER   DEPT: 072   NI REF: WD 4847 41C   LEAVE ENTITLEMENT: 20

	1	2	3	4	5	6	7	8	9	10	11	12	13	14	15	16	17	18	19	20	21	22	23	24	25	26	27	28	29	30	31
JAN																															
FEB																															
MAR																															
APR																															
MAY																															
JUNE																															
JULY																															
AUG																															
SEPT																															
OCT																															
NOV																															
DEC																															

Illness: I	Leave: L	Training: T	*Note overleaf:* (1) The reasons for special leave (eg bereavement).
Industrial Accident: IA	Unpaid Leave: UL	Jury Service: J	(2) Ensure training is noted on personnel card.
Maternity: M	Special Leave: SL		

RECORD OF ATTENDANCE

No				Ending	
Name					

	HOURS	RATE	AMOUNT	DEDUCTIONS	
Basic				Income Tax	
O/T				NI	
Others				Other	
				Total deduction	

Total		
Less deductions		
Net due		

	Time	Day	Basic time	Overtime
	1230	T		
	0803	T		
	1700	M		
	1305	M		
	1234	M		
	0750	M		

Signature ....

BPP PUBLISHING

(c) $\dfrac{\text{Total wages}}{\text{Total units processed}} = \dfrac{4 \times 35 \times £5}{280} = \dfrac{700}{280} = £2.50 \text{ per unit}$

Detailed analysis of time: job costing

2.16 When the work is not of a repetitive nature the records required might be one or more of the following.

(a) **Daily time sheets**. These are filled in by the employee to indicate the **time spent on each job**. The total time on the time sheet should correspond with time shown on the attendance record. Times are recorded daily and so there is less risk that they will be forgotten. This system does produce considerable paperwork.

(b) **Weekly time sheets**. These are similar to daily time sheets but are passed to the cost office at the end of the week. Paperwork is reduced and weekly time sheets are particularly suitable where there are few job changes in a week.

(c) **Job cards**. Cards are prepared for each job (or operation forming part of a complete job) unlike time sheets which are made out for each employee. When an employee works on a job he or she records on the job card the time spent on that job. Job cards also carry instructions to the operator on how the job is to be carried out. Such records reduce the amount of writing to be done by the employee and therefore the possibility of error.

(d) **Route cards**. These are similar to job cards, except that they follow the product through the works and carry details of all operations to be carried out. They thus carry the cost of all operations involved in a job and are very useful for control purposes.

2.17 It is important to note the following.

- Wages are calculated on the basis of the hours noted on the attendance card.
- Production costs are obtained from the time sheets/job cards/route cards.

2.18 The manual recording of times on time sheets or job cards is, however, liable to error or even deliberate deception, and may be unreliable. A **time clock** or **automated time recording system** is more accurate.

2.19 Time sheets and job or route cards can take many different forms, some of which involve computerised systems of time-recording. The following examples may help to indicate the basic principles of recording labour costs of production work.

Time Sheet No.							
Employee Name................ Clock Code................ Dept							
Date .... Week No.							
Job No.	Start Time	Finish Time	Qty	Checker	Hrs	Rate	Extension

```
                              JOB CARD

 Department _ _ _ _ _ _ _ _ _ _ _ _ _ _    Job no _ _ _ _ _ _ _ _ _ _ _ _ _ _ _ _ _ _ _ _

 Date _ _ _ _ _ _ _ _ _ _ _ _ _ _ _ _ _    Operation no _ _ _ _ _ _ _ _ _ _ _ _ _ _ _ _ _


 Time allowance _ _ _ _ _ _ _ _ _ _ _ _    Time started _ _ _ _ _ _ _ _ _ _ _ _ _ _ _ _ _ _

                                           Time finished _ _ _ _ _ _ _ _ _ _ _ _ _ _ _ _ _

                                           Hours on job   _ _ _ _ _ _ _ _ _ _ _ _ _ _ _ _ _
```

Description of job	Hours	Rate	Cost

```
 Employee no _ _ _ _ _ _ _ _ _ _ _ _ _ _   Certified by _ _ _ _ _ _ _ _ _ _ _ _ _ _ _ _

 Signature _ _ _ _ _ _ _ _ _ _ _ _ _ _ _ _
```

2.20 The **time sheet** will be filled in by the employee, for **hours worked** on each job (job code) or **area of work** (cost code). The cost of the hours worked will be entered at a later stage in the accounting department.

A **job card** will be given to the employee, showing the work to be done and the expected time it should take. The employee will record the time started and time finished for each job. Breaks for tea and lunch may be noted on the card, as standard times. The hours actually taken and the cost of those hours will be calculated by the accounting department.

Salaried labour

2.21 You might think there is little point in salaried staff filling in a detailed timesheet about what they do every hour of the day, as their basic pay is a flat rate every month but, in fact, in many enterprises they are required to do so. There are a number of reasons for this.

(a) Such timesheets aid the creation of **management information** about product costs, and hence **profitability**.

(b) The timesheet information may have a direct impact on the **revenue the enterprise receives** (see below).

(c) Timesheets are used to record hours spent and so **support claims for overtime payments** by salaried staff.

2.22 Below is shown the type of time sheet which can be found in large firms in the service sector of the economy. Examples of such firms are solicitors, accountants, and management consultants.

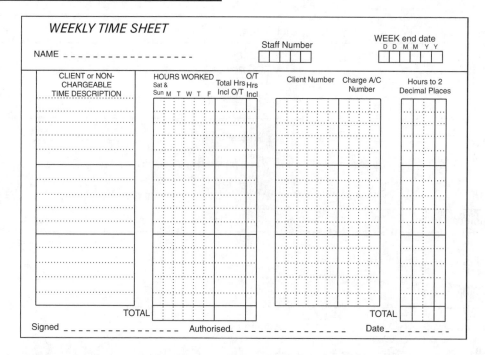

2.23 **Service firms are chiefly in the business of selling the time and expertise of their employees to clients.** This means that if an employee spends an hour at a particular client, the client will be billed for one hour of the employee's time. A time sheet is necessary so that clients will be charged for the correct amount of time that has been spent doing their work.

Activity 3.1

Below is shown Peter's payslip for April 20X1. Peter spent the whole of April working on Job 472 without assistance. What is the direct labour cost of Job 472?

Employee: TORK, P Staff No: 017		Employer: SLEEPY JEANS LTD	
NI No: NA 123456C Tax Code: 344L Pay By: Cheque		Date: 30/4/X1 Tax Period: 1	
DESCRIPTION		AMOUNT	THIS YEAR
BASIC BONUS (19X7)	*DIRECT LABOUR COST*	1,327.42 145.83	
	TOTAL PAY >>>	1,473.25	1,473.25
OTHER DEDUCTIONS	INCOME TAX NATIONAL INSURANCE	282.41 93.44	282.41 93.44
	NET PAY >>>	1,097.40	
OTHER ITEMS ADD EXPENSES REIMBURSED		301.28	
(HOL PAY ACCRUED 0.00)	TOTAL NET PAY >>>	1,398.68	

Idle time

2.24 In many jobs there are times when, through no fault of their own, employees cannot get on with their work. A machine may break down or there may simply be a temporary shortage of work.

2.25 **Idle time** has a cost because employees will still be paid their basic wage or salary for these unproductive hours and so there should be a record of idle time. This may simply comprise an entry on time sheets coded to 'idle time' generally, or separate idle time cards may be prepared. A supervisor might enter the time of a stoppage, its cause, its duration and the employees made idle on an **idle time record card**. Each stoppage should have a separate reference number which can be entered on time sheets or job cards as appropriate.

Measurement by output

2.26 (a) **Piecework** is a method of labour payment where workers are paid according to the amount of production completed.

(b) The labour cost of work done by pieceworkers is determined from what is known as a **piecework ticket** or an **operation card**. The card records the total number of items (or **pieces**) produced and the number of rejects. Payment is only made for 'good' production.

OPERATION CARD				
Operator's Name		Total Batch Quantity		
Clock No		Start Time		
Pay week No .... Date		Stop Time		
Part No		Works Order No		
Operation		Special Instructions		
Quantity Produced	No Rejected	Good Production	Rate	£
Inspector		Operative		
Foreman		Date		
PRODUCTION CANNOT BE CLAIMED WITHOUT A PROPERLY SIGNED CARD				

(c) A **disadvantage of the piecework method** is that workers may be so concerned with the volume of output that they produce, that the quality of the goods might suffer as a result of this.

Activity 3.2

(a) Walter Wally is chief foreman in a medium-sized factory which is working on about thirty different jobs at any one time. He spends most of his day on his feet, dealing with personnel and technical problems as and when they arise.

How might Walter's time be analysed?

(b) Peter Pratt is a bank clerk.

How might Peter's time be analysed?

Activity 3.3

Does the payroll department tell the costing department what the monthly labour costs should be or vice versa?

Coding of job costs

2.27 By now you will appreciate that to analyse labour costs effectively it is necessary to be able to link up different pieces of information in various ways. Most organisations therefore develop a series of codes to facilitate analysis for each of the following.

(a) **Employee number** and perhaps a team number

(b) **Pay rate**, for example 'A' for £5 per hour, 'B' for £6 per hour and so on

(c) **Department** and/or **location** if the organisation has different branches or offices

(d) **Job** or **batch type**, for example different codes for audit, accounts preparation and tax in a firm of accountants, or for bodywork and mechanical repairs in a garage

(e) **Job** or **batch number** to enable each successive example of the same type of work to be allocated the next number in sequence

(f) **Client number** so that all work done for the same client or customer can be coded to the same number

2.28 You might like to think of different ways in which different pieces of information could be grouped together. For example, combining (b), (c) and (d) would show you whether the workers in one location could do a certain type of work more cheaply than the workers in another location.

Activity 3.4

Below are shown some extracts from the files of Penny Lane Ltd. You are required to calculate the labour cost of jobs 249 and 250.

Personnel files

	George	Paul	Ringo	John
Grade	A	B	C	D

Payroll - Master file

Grade	Basic rate per hour
A	£8.20
B	£7.40
C	£6.50
D	£5.30

Production report - labour

Job	Employee	Hours
249	George	14
249	Paul	49
250	George	2
250	John	107
250	Ringo	74

Activity 3.5

The labour force of Limpsfield Ltd is divided into a team of six processing workers and four finishing workers. During a particular week 10,000 units were finished and 12,000 were processed. Processors work a 40 hour week, but finishers only work 35 hours. Their rates of pay are as follows.

	£ per hour
Processors	3.20
Finishers	4.50

Tasks

Calculate how many units each team processes or finishes per hour, how long each team takes to process one unit and the labour cost of one unit for each team. You should present the information in a form that would be generally understood and appreciated.

3 OVERTIME, BONUSES AND ABSENCES

3.1 This section is concerned with two things.

- What happens when more or less work is done than the basic amount agreed.
- The consequences of not coming to work.

Overtime

3.2 Before considering overtime payments, let us consider one of the most common forms of **time work**, namely a **day-rate system**, in which wages are calculated by the following formula.

Wages = Hours worked × rate of pay per hour

3.3 Day-rate systems may be summarised as follows.

(a) They are easy to understand

(b) They do not lead to very complex negotiations when they are being revised

(c) They are most appropriate when the quality of output is more important than the quantity, or where there is no basis for payment by performance

(d) There is no incentive for employees who are paid on a day-rate basis to improve their performance

3.4 If an employee works for more hours than the basic daily requirement many organisations pay an extra amount.

3.5 The overtime payment may simply be at the **basic rate**. If an employee earns £5 an hour he will get an extra £5 for every hour worked in addition to the basic hours. If he earns £10,000 a year an hourly rate can be calculated by multiplying the basic hours per day by the normal number of days worked per week by the 52 weeks in the year. For example 7 hours × 5 days × 52 weeks = 1,820 hours and the hourly rate is approximately £5.49.

3.6 Usually, however, overtime is paid at a **premium rate**. You will hear expressions like 'time and a third', ' time and a half' and so on. This means that the hourly rate for overtime hours is $(1 + 1/3) \times$ basic rate or $(1 + 1/2) \times$ basic rate.

3.7 EXAMPLE: OVERTIME PREMIUM

Pootings Ltd pays overtime at time and a quarter. Jo's basic hours are 9 to 5 with an hour for lunch, but one particular Friday she worked until six o'clock. She is paid a basic wage of £5 per hour. How much did she earn on the Friday in question, and how much of this is overtime premium?

3.8 SOLUTION

The most obvious way of calculating the amount earned is as follows.

	£
Basic time (7 × £5)	35.00
Overtime (1¼ × £5)	6.25
Total pay	41.25

3.9 It is wrong, however, to say that the overtime premium is £6.25. For costing purposes all of the hours worked, whether in basic time or outside it, are costed at the basic rate. The premium is the extra amount paid on top of the basic rate for the hours worked over and above the basic hours.

	£
Basic pay (8 × £5)	40.00
Overtime premium (¼ × £5)	1.25
	41.25

3.10 The **overtime premium** is thus £1.25. This is an important point because overtime premium is usually treated as an **indirect cost**. This is quite reasonable if you think about it. If you and your colleague use identical calculators it is reasonable to suppose that they cost the same amount to produce. It might be that one was assembled at 10 o'clock in the morning and the other at 10 o'clock at night but this doesn't make the calculators different from each other. They should therefore have the same cost and so **most organisations treat overtime premium as an overhead** and do not allocate it to the products manufactured outside basic hours.

3.11 There are two exceptions to this rule.

(a) If overtime is worked at the specific request of a customer to get his order completed, the premium is a **direct cost of the order**.

(b) If overtime is worked regularly by a production department in the normal course of operations, the overtime paid to direct workers could be incorporated into an **average direct labour hourly rate** (though it does not need to be).

ASSESSMENT ALERT

If you have trouble remembering how to deal with overtime premiums, think how you would feel if you had to pay more for your new car radio than all of the others in the shop, simply because it was made after 5.30 pm.

Incentives and bonuses

3.12 **Overtime premiums** are paid to encourage staff to work longer hours than normal (or at least to recognise and reward the personal sacrifice of doing so). **Incentives and bonuses** are paid to encourage staff to work harder whatever the time of day.

3.13 Incentive schemes include the following.

- Piecework
- Time-saved bonus
- Discretionary bonus
- Group bonus scheme
- Profit-sharing scheme

Piecework

3.14 **Pieceworking** can be seen as an incentive scheme since the more output you produce the more you are paid. If you are paid 5p per unit produced and you want to earn £300 gross a week you know you have to produce 6,000 units that week.

3.15 The system can be further refined by paying a different rate for different levels of production (**differential piecework**). For example the employer could pay 3p per unit for output of up to 3,500 a week, 5p per unit for every unit over 3,500.

3.16 In practice, persons working on such schemes normally receive a guaranteed minimum wage because they may not be able to work because of problems outside their control.

3.17 EXAMPLE: PIECEWORK

An employee is paid £5 per piecework hour produced. In a 35 hour week he produces the following output.

	Piecework time allowed per unit
3 units of product A	2.5 hours
5 units of product B	8.0 hours

Task

Calculate the employee's pay for the week.

3.18 SOLUTION

Piecework hours produced are as follows.

Product A	3×2.5 hours	7.5 hours
Product B	5×8 hours	40.0 hours
Total piecework hours		47.5 hours

Therefore employee's pay = $47.5 \times £5 = £237.50$ for the week.

Activity 3.6

Using the information on piecework rates, complete the operation card shown below and calculate Mr Shah's gross wages for pay week number 17.

Piecework rates

Up to 100 units a day	20p per unit on all units produced
101 to 120 units a day	30p per unit on all units produced
121 to 140 units a day	40p per unit on all units produced
Over 140 units a day	50p per unit on all units produced

 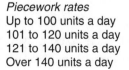

OPERATION CARD

Operator's Name ....Shah, L......................		Total Batch Quantity ....⁻..............		
Clock No		Start Time		
Pay week No. 7142...........................		Stop Time ....⁻..........................		
.....17......... Date W/E XX/XX/XX		.......⁻..........		

Part No ....713/V........................		Works Order No........14.AB..........		
Operation ....Drilling.....................		Special Instructions ....⁻...............		

Quantity Produced	No Rejected	Good Production	Rate	£
Monday 173	14	159	0-50	79-50
Tuesday 131	2	129	0-40	51-60
Wednesday 92	-	92	0-20	18-40
Thursday 120	7	113	0-30	33-90
Friday 145	5	140	0-40	56-00

Inspector..........ND............	Operative ....LS..............	239.40
Foreman	Date	
..............AN..................	..........XX/XX/XX............	

PRODUCTION CANNOT BE CLAIMED WITHOUT A PROPERLY SIGNED CARD

Time-saved bonus

3.19 Suppose that a garage has calculated that it takes an average of 45 minutes for an engineer to perform an MOT test, but the job could be done competently in 30 minutes. It could encourage its engineers to do such work at the faster rate by paying **a bonus for every minute saved** on the job up to a maximum of 15 minutes.

3.20 There are problems with this approach. In the first place it is necessary to establish a standard time for all types of work, and this may not be easy. In the second place a less than competent engineer may rush the job and not do it properly.

Discretionary bonuses

3.21 It is not uncommon, especially in smaller businesses, for **employers to give their employees bonuses simply because they think they deserve one**. This is a possible approach if it is difficult to measure an employee's output. Many office workers fall into this category. If, however, there is no obvious correspondence between what a person does and whether or not a bonus is paid, the scheme is likely to be perceived as unfair.

Group bonus schemes

3.22 Sometimes it is not possible to measure individual effort because overall performance is not within any one person's control (for example railway workers). In such cases, however, it is possible to measure overall performance and **a bonus can therefore be paid to all those who contributed**.

Profit-sharing schemes

3.23 In a **profit-sharing scheme** employees receive **a certain proportion of their company's year-end profits** (the size of their bonus might also be related to level of responsibility and length of service).

Activity 3.7

List five ways in which a company might reward extra effort by its employees.

Absence from work

3.24 An employee may be absent from work for a variety of reasons, the commonest being as follows.

- Holidays
- Sickness
- Maternity
- Training

3.25 The costs relating to absence through sickness, maternity and training are usually treated as an overhead rather than a direct cost of production. Although some organisations treat holiday pay as an overhead, the normal treatment is to regard it as a direct cost by charging an inflated hourly rate. Suppose an employee is normally paid £4 an hour for a 35 hour week and is entitled to four weeks' annual holiday. He will therefore receive £560 (£4 × 35 × 4) holiday pay. Assuming that the employee works the remaining 48 weeks, his attendance time will total 1,680 (48 × 35) hours. Dividing £560 by 1,680 hours gives an addition of approximately 33p per hour to the employee's hourly rate to ensure that holiday pay is recovered.

3.26 Time absent because of holidays is paid at the normal basic rate, as is absence on training courses as a rule. There are statutory minimum levels for maternity pay and sickness pay, but above these employers can be as generous (or otherwise) as they wish.

Activity 3.8

(a) What is differential piecework?
(b) Why might a company operate a group bonus scheme?

---

4 LABOUR TURNOVER

The reasons for labour turnover

4.1 There are many reasons why employees will leave their job. It may be because they wish to go to work for another company or organisation. Alternatively it may be for one of the following unavoidable reasons.

- Illness or accidents
- A family move away from the locality
- Marriage, pregnancy or difficulties with child care provision
- Retirement or death

4.2   In addition to the above examples, other causes of labour turnover are as follows.

- Paying a lower wage rate than is available elsewhere.
- Requiring employees to work in unsafe or highly stressful conditions.
- Requiring employees to work uncongenial hours.
- Poor relationships between management and staff.
- Lack of opportunity for career enhancement.
- Requiring employees to work in inaccessible places (eg no public transport).
- Discharging employees for misconduct, bad timekeeping or unsuitability.

Measuring labour turnover

> ### KEY TERMS
>
> - **Labour turnover** is a measure of the number of employees leaving/being recruited in a period of time (say one year) expressed as a percentage of the total labour force.
>
> - **Labour turnover rate** = $\dfrac{\text{Replacements}}{\text{Average number of employees in period}} \times 100\%$

4.3   EXAMPLE: LABOUR TURNOVER

(a)   Florence plc had a staff numbering 800 at the beginning of 20X1 and 1,200 at the end of that year. Four hundred employees resigned on 30 June, and were immediately replaced by 400 new employees on 1 July. 400 extra employees were also recruited at that time.

What is the labour turnover rate?

$$\text{Rate} = \frac{400}{(800+1,200) \div 2} \times 100\% = 40\%$$

(b)   Rome plc had a staff of 2,000 at the beginning of 20X1 and, owing to a series of redundancies caused by the recession, 1,000 at the end of the year. Voluntary redundancy was taken by 1,500 staff at the end of June, 500 more than the company had anticipated, and these excess redundancies were immediately replaced by new joiners.

The labour turnover rate is calculated as follows.

$$\text{Rate} = \frac{500}{(2,000+1,000) \div 2} \times 100\% = 33\%$$

> ### ASSESSMENT ALERT
>
> One of the tasks in the June 1999 Central Assessment required candidates to give a ratio that would express labour turnover.

The costs of labour turnover

4.4   The costs of labour turnover can be large and management should attempt to keep labour turnover as low as possible so as to minimise these costs. The **cost of labour turnover** may be divided into the following.

- Preventative costs
- Replacement costs

4.5 **Replacement costs**. These are the costs incurred as a result of **hiring new employees** and they include the following.

    (a)   Cost of selection and placement.

    (b)   Inefficiency of new labour; productivity will be lower.

    (c)   Costs of training; training costs will include formal training courses plus the costs of on-the-job instructors diverted from their own work to teach new recruits.

    (d)   Loss of output due to delay in new labour becoming available.

    (e)   Increased wastage and spoilage due to lack of expertise among new staff.

    (f)   The possibility of more frequent accidents at work.

    (g)   Cost of tool and machine breakages.

4.6 **Preventative costs** are costs incurred in order to **prevent employees leaving** and they include the following.

- Cost of personnel administration incurred in maintaining good relationships
- Cost of medical services including check-ups, nursing staff and so on
- Cost of welfare services, including sports facilities, laundry services and canteen meals
- Pension schemes providing security to employees

The prevention of high labour turnover

4.7 Labour turnover will be reduced by the following actions.

- Paying satisfactory wages
- Offering satisfactory hours and conditions of work
- Creating a good informal relationship between fellow workers and supervisors
- Offering good training schemes and a well-understood career or promotion ladder
- Improving the content of jobs to create job satisfaction
- Proper planning so as to avoid redundancies
- Investigating the cause of high labour turnover rates

5 ANALYSIS OF LABOUR EFFICIENCY AND UTILISATION RATES

Labour efficiency

5.1 Labour costs are often a large proportion of the total costs incurred by many organisations. It is important therefore that the performance of the labour force is continually measured.

5.2 Labour efficiency is one such performance measurement. Labour efficiency is generally measured by comparing actual results for an organisation with budgets. We mentioned budgets in Chapter 1 of this Interactive Text. You will remember that for now you can think of a budget as a plan for the future (in money terms) and therefore as the result that we expect to get.

Efficiency, capacity and production volume ratios

5.3 Three ways of measuring labour activity include the following.

- Efficiency ratio (or productivity ratio)
- Capacity ratio
- Production volume ratio, or activity ratio

KEY TERMS

- **Efficiency ratio** $=$ $\dfrac{\text{Expected hours to make output}}{\text{Actual hours taken}}$

- **Capacity ratio** $=$ $\dfrac{\text{Actual hours worked}}{\text{Hours budgeted}}$

- **Production volume ratio** $=$ $\dfrac{\text{Output measured in expected or standard hours}}{\text{Hours budgeted}}$

These ratios are usually expressed as percentages.

5.4 EXAMPLE: RATIOS

Barney Rubble Ltd budgets to make 25,000 standard units of output (in four hours each) during a budget period of 100,000 hours.

Actual output during the period was 27,000 units which took 120,000 hours to make.

Task

Calculate the efficiency, capacity and production volume ratios.

5.5 SOLUTION

(a) Efficiency ratio $\dfrac{(27,000 \times 4) \text{ hours}}{120,000} \times 100\% = 90\%$

(b) Capacity ratio $\dfrac{120,000 \text{ hours}}{100,000 \text{ hours}} \times 100\% = 120\%$

(c) Production volume ratio $\dfrac{(27,000 \times 4) \text{ hours}}{100,000} \times 100\% = 108\%$

5.6 These ratios may be used, therefore, to measure the performance of the labour force. At a later stage in your studies you will come across variances, in particular labour variances which are another means of measuring labour efficiency.

Labour utilisation

5.7 It is possible to monitor the efficient use of labour by calculating **labour utilisation rates** or ratios. These ratios consider how actual working time is utilised, that is to say whether the time is **productive** or **non-productive.** We shall now consider some of the ways in which labour utilisation can be measured.

Idle time

5.8 We considered idle time earlier on in this chapter. A useful ratio for the control of idle time is the **idle time ratio.**

KEY TERM

$$\text{Idle time ratio} = \frac{\text{Idle hours}}{\text{Total hours}} \times 100\%$$

This ratio is useful because it shows the proportion of available hours which were lost as a result of idle time.

Absenteeism

5.9 When staff are absent from work, this is another reason why productive time may be reduced. We can also calculate ratios which might provide useful measures of absenteeism. These ratios include the following.

(a) $\dfrac{\text{Number of hours / days absent from work (in a given period)}}{\text{Total number of hours / days paid (in a given period)}}$

(b) $\dfrac{\text{Number of hours / days absent from work (in a given period)}}{\text{Total number of hours / days worked (in a given period)}}$

5.10 It is important to keep a check on absenteeism and management should be aware of any patterns which may begin to emerge within an organisation.

Sickness

5.11 Similarly, levels of sickness may also be measured by means of ratios which are similar to those used for measuring absenteeism.

5.12 The types of ratio which might provide a useful measure of sickness within an organisation include the following.

(a) $\dfrac{\text{Number of days off work due to sickness (in a given period)}}{\text{Total number of days paid (in a given period)}}$

(b) $\dfrac{\text{Number of days off work due to sickness (in a given period)}}{\text{Total number of days worked (in a given period)}}$

5.13 As with absenteeism, it is important that sickness rates are monitored by management. It is possible that during the winter time sickness rates may seasonally be very high, possibly because of flu epidemics, colds or other illnesses which are rife during this period.

Overtime levels

5.14 The amount of overtime worked, and the costs of overtime to an organisation may also be measured by calculating ratios.

5.15 The management of an organisation may be interested to know whether the amount of overtime worked in an organisation occurs at any particular time of the year, and whether they may be justified in hiring extra staff during these periods.

5.16 The following ratios may be used to indicate the overtime levels in an organisation.

(a) $\dfrac{\text{Hours of overtime worked}}{\text{Total hours worked}}$

(b) $\dfrac{\text{Overtime labour costs}}{\text{Total labour costs}}$

5.17 It is worth noting that overtime levels may be seasonal. For example, staff working in department stores around Christmas may work many hours of overtime; many stores have late-night shopping and are generally open for longer hours than usual during this period.

Key learning points

- **Labour costs** can be determined according to some prior agreement, the amount of time worked or the quality of work done.

- **Labour attendance time** is recorded on an attendance record or a clockcard. **Jobtime** may be recorded on daily time sheets, weekly time sheets, jobcards or route cards depending on the circumstances.

- **Idle time** may occur when employees are not able to get on with their work, though this is through no fault of their own. Idle time has a cost and must therefore be recorded.

- The labour cost of work done by **pieceworkers** is recorded on a **piecework ticket/ operation card.**

- There are five main types of **incentive scheme,** piecework, time-saved bonus, discretionary bonus, group bonus scheme and profit-sharing scheme.

- **Labour turnover** is the rate at which employees leave a company and this rate should be kept as low as possible. The cost of labour turnover can be divided into **preventative** and **replacement** costs.

Quick quiz

1   What are the three categories which records of labour costs fall into?

2   Which two documents are used to record attendance time?

3   Which four documents may be used to record the amount of time spent on a job?

4   Give three reasons why salaried staff may be required to fill in detailed timesheets.

5   What is idle time, and why may it occur?

6   List five types of incentive scheme.

7   What is the formula used to calculate the labour turnover rate?

8   List five methods used to reduce labour turnover.

Answers to quick quiz

1   Agreed basic wages and salaries, time spent, work done.

2   A record of attendance and a clockcard.

3   Daily time sheets, weekly time sheets, job cards and route cards.

4   (a)   Timesheets assist in the creation of management information about product costs and profitability.

    (b)   Timesheet information may have a direct impact on the revenue an organisation receives.

    (c)   Timesheet information may support overtime claims made by salaried staff.

5   Time during which employees cannot get on with their work (though it is not their fault). It occurs when a machine breaks down or when there is a temporary shortage of work.

6   Piecework, time-saved bonus, discretionary bonus, group bonus scheme, profit-sharing scheme.

7   Labour turnover rate = $\dfrac{\text{Replacements}}{\text{Average number of employees in period}} \times 100\%$

8   • Paying satisfactory wages
     • Offering satisfactory hours and conditions of work
     • Offering good training schemes
     • Improving job content to create job satisfaction
     • Proper staff planning so as to avoid redundancies (see para 4.7 far full list)

Answers to activities

Answer 3.1

The direct labour cost is the gross basic wage, £1,327.42.

Answer 3.2

(a)   From the information given, the only way of analysing Walter's time is as so many hours of 'general foreman duties'. In other words his work is so diverse that it is not possible to trace it as a direct cost to individual jobs.

It would be more appropriate to ensure that details of the individual jobs were recorded in such a way that Walter's time could be equitably split between them. For example a job requiring 20 men is likely to require twice as much of Walter's attention as a job requiring 10 men.

(b)   Peter's time may at first seem to be as difficult to analyse as Walter's, but in fact it is probable that he could fill in a daily or weekly time sheet, splitting out his time between the various types of work that he does. For example he may spend 3 hours at the counter in the morning, and 1 hour filing and 2 hours dealing with correspondence in the afternoon.

Answer 3.3

The answer is neither or both! Payroll is interested in any work that employees have done that might earn them bonuses or give rise to deductions, and it may be the job of costing to provide this information. Costing in turn is interested in the basic rates due to different types of worker and this information is more likely to be held in the payroll department.

In other words the two departments are interdependent and require a common pool of information.

Answer 3.4

Job 249

Employee		Rate	Total
	Hours	£	£
George	14	8.20	114.80
Paul	49	7.40	362.60
			477.40

Job 250

Employee		Rate	Total
	Hours	£	£
George	2	8.20	16.40
John	107	5.30	567.10
Ringo	74	6.50	481.00
			1,064.50

Answer 3.5

Units per hour	Processors	Finishers
Total units	12,000	10,000
Total hours	40	35
Units per hour	300	286

Time per unit		
Total hours	40	35
Total units	12,000	10,000
Time for one unit	12 seconds	12.6 seconds

Cost per unit		
Total wages	40 × 6 × £3.20	35 × 4 × £4.50
Total units	12,000	10,000
Cost per 100 units	£6.40	£6.30

(*Tutorial note.* If you expressed time per unit in terms of hour per unit consider that a figure like '0.02 of an hour' means very little to most people, because we think of time in the units in which it is generally measured. Likewise £0.064 or even 6.4p is less meaningful than the figure for 100 units because 6.4p cannot be made up from coins of the realm. If you said '64p for 10 units', this is fine.)

Answer 3.6

OPERATION CARD					
Operators Name Shah, L			Total Batch Quantity -		
Clock No 7142			Start Time -		
Pay week No 17 Date W/E XX/XX/XX			Stop Time -		
Part No 713/V			Works Order No 14 AB		
Opertion Drilling			Special Instructions -		
Quantity Produced	No Rejected	Good Production		Rate	£
Monday 173	14	159		50p	79.50
Tuesday 131	2	129		40p	51.60
Wednesday 92	-	92		20p	18.40
Thursday 120	7	113		30p	33.90
Friday 145	5	140		40p	56.00
Insector ND			Operative LS		
Foreman AN			Date XX/XX/XX		
PRODUCTION CANNOT BE CLAIMED WITHOUT A PROPERLY SIGNED CARD					

		£
Gross wage	=	79.50
		51.60
		18.40
		33.90
		56.00
		239.40

Answer 3.7

(a) Overtime
(b) Piecework
(c) Bonus for saving time
(d) Discretionary bonus to individuals
(e) Group bonus
(f) Profit sharing schemes

WEEKLY TIME SHEET

Name ....   Staff number [ ][ ][ ][ ][ ]   Week ending [ ][ ][ ][ ][ ][ ]

	S/S	M	T	W	T	F	TOTAL	CODE
Chargeable time								[ ][ ][ ][ ][ ]
								[ ][ ][ ][ ][ ]
								[ ][ ][ ][ ][ ]
								[ ][ ][ ][ ][ ]
Changeable total								
Administration								[ ][ ][ ][ ][ ]
								[ ][ ][ ][ ][ ]
Total admin								
Training and courses								[ ][ ][ ][ ][ ]
								[ ][ ][ ][ ][ ]
Total training								
Holidays, sickness								[ ][ ][ ][ ][ ]
								[ ][ ][ ][ ][ ]
Total leave								
TOTAL								
O/T Memorandum								

Signed ....   Authorised ....

Answer 3.8

(a) Piecework is a system of payments according to the amount of work performed. Differential piecework involves paying a different rate for different levels of production.

(b) A group bonus scheme is appropriate where each individual's contribution to overall performance is highly diverse and overall performance is not within any one person's control. Group bonuses are likely to encourage team effort. They are simpler to administer than individual bonuses.

Chapter 4   Expenses

Chapter topic list

1   Expense distinctions

2   Types of expense

3   Depreciation and obsolescence

4   Recording and coding expenses

Learning objectives

On completion of this chapter you will be able to:

	Performance criteria	Range statement
• identify and calculate direct revenue expenditure in accordance with organisational policies and procedures	6.1.1, 5.1.3	6.1.1
• establish indirect expenses in accordance with organisational procedures	6.2.2	6.2.1
• ensure that information relating to direct expenses is clearly and correctly coded, analysed and recorded	6.1.2	6.1.1
• ensure that data and information relating to indirect expenses is accurately and clearly coded, analysed and recorded	6.2.1, 6.2.3	6.2.1
• deal with queries about direct and indirect expenses	6.1.6, 6.2.8	6.1.1, 6.2.1

 BPP PUBLISHING

1 EXPENSE DISTINCTIONS

1.1 We have now looked at materials costs and labour costs in some detail in Chapters 2 and 3. Any other costs that might be incurred by an organisation are generally known as **expenses.**

1.2 Like materials and labour costs, expenses can be also divided up into different categories. You should not find too much difficulty in distinguishing between the following.

- Direct expense costs
- Indirect expense costs
- Fixed expense costs
- Variable expense costs

Revenue and capital expenditure

1.3 Expenses may also be classified as either **revenue** expenditure or as **capital expenditure.**

> **KEY TERMS**
>
> - **Capital expenditure** is expenditure which results in the acquisition of fixed assets.
>
> - **Fixed assets** are assets which are acquired to provide benefits in more than one accounting period and are not intended to be resold in the normal course of trade.

1.4 Capital expenditure is not charged to the profit and loss account as an expense. A **depreciation charge** is instead charged to the profit and loss account in order to write the capital expenditure off over a period of time. The depreciation charge is therefore an expense in the profit and loss account.

1.5 EXAMPLE: DEPRECIATION CHARGES

If an asset is bought for £20,000 and it is expected to last for 5 years, then for five years, £4,000 (£20,000 ÷ 5 years) will be charged to the profit and loss account.

1.6 The costs incurred in purchasing fixed assets result in the fixed assets appearing in the balance sheet.

> **KEY TERM**
>
> **Revenue expenditure** is expenditure which is incurred for one of the following reasons.
>
> - For the purpose of the trade of the business, including administration expenses, selling and distribution expenses and finance charges.
>
> - In order to maintain the existing earning capacity of fixed assets.

1.7 **Revenue expenditure** is charged to the profit and loss account in the period to which it relates.

Revenue and capital expenditure compared

1.8 Let us look at an example which should help you to distinguish between **revenue items** and **capital items.**

1.9 EXAMPLE: REVENUE ITEMS AND CAPITAL ITEMS

Suppose that Bevan Ltd purchases a building for £30,000. A few years later it adds an extension to the building at a cost of £10,000. The building needs to have a few broken windows mended, its floors polished, and some missing roof tiles replaced. These cleaning and maintenance jobs cost £900.

Which items of expenditure are revenue expenditure and which are capital expenditure?

1.10 SOLUTION

The original purchase (£30,000) and the cost of the extension (£10,000) are capital expenditure because they are incurred to acquire and then improve a fixed asset. The other costs of £900 are revenue expenditure because they are maintaining the existing earning capacity of the building.

1.11 Revenue and capital items are therefore distinguished by the ways they are accounted for in the profit and loss account and the balance sheet.

Revenue and capital expenditure and costing

1.12 Revenue expenditure is of more relevance to the costing of products than capital expenditure. Capital expenditure is only of relevance when it is turned into revenue expenditure in the form of depreciation.

Activity 4.1

Distinguish between capital expenditure and revenue expenditure and give an example of each.

Direct expenses and indirect expenses

1.13 A second major distinction that must be made is between **direct** and **indirect** expenses.

> **KEY TERMS**
>
> • A **direct cost** is a cost that can be traced in full to the product, service, or department that is being costed.
>
> • **Direct material** is all material becoming part of the product (unless used in negligible amounts and/or having negligible cost).
>
> • **Direct wages** are all wages paid for labour (either as basic hours or as overtime) expended on work on the product itself.
>
> • **Direct expenses** are any expenses which are incurred on a specific product other than direct material cost and direct wages.

1.14 **Direct expenses** are charged to the product as part of the **prime** cost. Examples of direct expenses are as follows.

- The cost of **special** designs, drawings or layouts
- The **hire of tools** or equipment for a particular job
- **Maintenance costs** of tools, fixtures, fittings and so on

Direct expenses are also referred to as **chargeable expenses.**

1.15 **Indirect expenses** are also known as overheads and are studied in detail in the next chapter.

Fixed costs and variable costs

1.16 We have already come across the terms fixed cost and variable cost.

> **KEY TERMS**
>
> - A **fixed cost** is a cost which is incurred for a particular period of time and which, within certain activity levels, is unaffected by changes in the level of activity.
>
> - A **variable cost** is a cost which tends to vary with the level of activity.

1.17 Some examples of fixed costs and variable costs are as follows.

(a) Direct material costs are **variable costs** because they rise as more units of a product are manufactured.

(b) Sales commission is often a fixed percentage of sales turnover, and so is a **variable cost** that varies with the level of sales.

(c) Telephone call charges are likely to increase if the volume of business expands, and so they are a **variable overhead cost.**

(d) The rental cost of business premises is a constant amount, at least within a stated time period, and so it is a **fixed cost.**

Mixed costs

1.18 In practice, some costs are known as **mixed costs** (or **semi-variable** costs or **semi-fixed** costs). Semi-variable costs are incurred when output is nil, and also increase when output rises.

> **KEY TERM**
>
> A **semi-variable/semi-fixed/mixed cost** is a cost which contains both fixed and variable components and so is partly affected by changes in the level of activity.

1.19 Examples of mixed costs include the following.

(a) **Electricity and gas bills**

- Fixed cost = standing charge
- Variable cost = charge per unit of electricity used

(b) **Saleman's salary**

- Fixed cost = basic salary

- Variable cost = commission on sales made

(c) **Costs of running a car**

- Fixed cost = road tax, insurance
- Variable costs = petrol, oil, repairs (which vary with miles travelled)

Stepped costs

1.20 Another type of cost which you come across is known as a **stepped cost.** This type of cost is only fixed over a certain range, for example the cost of storing stock will be fixed up until a certain point. Beyond this point, extra storage space will be required thus incurring extra (fixed) costs.

Product costs and period costs

> **KEY TERMS**
>
> - **Product costs** are costs identified with a finished product. Such costs are initially identified as part of the value of stock. They become expenses (in the form of cost of goods sold) *only* when the stock is sold.
> - **Period costs** are costs that are deducted as expenses during the current period without ever being included in the value of stock held.

Controllable costs and uncontrollable costs

> **KEY TERMS**
>
> - A **controllable cost** is a cost which can be influenced by management decisions and actions.
> - An **uncontrollable cost** is any cost that cannot be affected by management within a given time span.

2 TYPES OF EXPENSE

2.1 Revenue expenditure other than materials and labour costs can arise for a number of different reasons.

(a) **Buildings costs**. The main types are rent, business rates and buildings insurance.

(b) **The costs of making buildings habitable**. Gas and electricity bills and water rates, repairs and maintenance costs and cleaning costs.

(c) **People-related costs**. These include expenditure on health and safety, the cost of uniforms, and the cost of staff welfare provisions like tea and coffee, canteen costs and staff training.

(d) **Machine operating costs**. Machines need fuel or power and they need to be kept clean and properly maintained. Machines also need to be insured. A proportion of the capital cost of the machines becomes revenue expenditure in the form of depreciation. Some machines are hired.

(e) **Information processing costs.** Associated with information processing are the costs of telephone, postage, fax, computer disks and stationery, as well as subscriptions to information sources, like trade journals.

(f) **Finance costs**. If there is a bank loan there will be interest and bank charges to pay, and if equipment is leased there will be lease interest. Dividends paid to shareholders, however, are not a cost, they are an appropriation of some of the income earned in excess of all costs.

(g) **Selling and distribution costs.** Selling expenses include advertising, the salaries and commissions of salesmen, and the costs of providing consumer service and after sales service. The organisation's finished product also has to be stored and then delivered to customers. Distribution expenses would therefore include warehouse charges, upkeep and running of delivery vehicles and carriage outwards.

(h) Finally there are the **costs of dealing with the outside world**. Fees paid to professionals like external auditors, surveyors or solicitors and the costs of marketing (such as market research) would all be collected under this heading.

2.2 A typical detailed profit and loss account might, therefore, have the following headings.

	£	£
Sales		X
Less cost of sales:		
opening stock	X	
materials	X	
labour	X	
depreciation	X	
power and fuel	X	
	X	
Less closing stock	(X)	
Cost of sales		(X)
Gross profit		X
Less costs of administration, distribution and selling:		
wages and salaries	X	
rent and rates	X	
insurance	X	
heat and light	X	
depreciation of office equipment	X	
repairs and maintenance	X	
cleaning	X	
telecommunications	X	
printing, postage and stationery	X	
hire of computer equipment	X	
advertising	X	
warehouse charges	X	
carriage outwards	X	
audit and accountancy fees	X	
bank charges	X	
interest	X	
		(X)
Profit before tax		X

2.3   The following paragraphs describe some of these expenses in more detail.

Rent

2.4   Rent is usually an annual charge payable quarterly in advance.

2.5   Rent is normally subject to a tenancy agreement and it may be fixed for a period of so many years, or reviewable annually, or there may be some other agreement.

Business rates

2.6   These are charges levied by local authorities in Britain, on non-domestic properties in their area. They are based upon a rateable value multiplied by a uniform rate. They are usually payable in two instalments in April and October each year. Most countries have expenses which are similar to business rates, though they may have different names.

Insurance costs

2.7   These comprise **premiums** paid to an insurance company to cover the risk, say, of damage to buildings or their contents by fire, flood, explosions, theft and so on. Buildings insurance is usually based on the cost of rebuilding the property with adjustments to take account of the property's particular location. It is an annual sum, payable either whenever the renewal date occurs or in instalments.

2.8   Other types of insurance are charged on a similar basis. Examples include employer's liability insurance (against the risk of harming employees), and vehicle insurance.

Electricity, gas and telecommunications

2.9   Electricity, gas and telecommunications charges normally have two elements, a fixed amount called a standing charge, generally payable quarterly, and a variable amount based on consumption. There are a number of rates depending on the status of the user (domestic/commercial/industrial) and the time of day the power is consumed or the calls are made.

Subscriptions

2.10   Subscriptions are generally paid annually, though not necessarily by calendar year. This category includes both subscriptions to publications like trade journals or information services and subscriptions for membership of Chambers of Commerce or professional or trade bodies and the like.

Professional fees

2.11   Such charges are usually made on the basis of time spent attending to the client's business.

Hire charges

2.12   Hire charges are sometimes payable on a time basis. For example a cement mixer may be hired for, say, £10 a day. Sometimes an additional charge is made for usage. A photocopier, for example, might have a meter on it showing how many copies had been made. The meter would be read periodically by the hire company and the invoice would include a charge for the number of copies made in the period.

Discretionary costs

2.13 Discretionary costs are, as you might expect, costs that are incurred at somebody's discretion. Whereas an organisation has to pay a certain amount for, say, electricity simply so that the business can function, other costs are not crucial to the short-term continuance of operations. The main examples are research and development costs, staff training and advertising.

Activity 4.2

State whether each of the following items should be classified as 'capital' or 'revenue' expenditure.

(a) Purchase of leasehold premises

(b) Annual depreciation of leasehold premises

(c) Solicitors' fees in connection with the purchase of leasehold premises

(d) Costs of adding extra storage capacity to a mainframe computer used by the business

(e) Computer repairs and maintenance costs

(f) Cost of new machinery

(g) Customs duty charged on the machinery when imported into the country

(h) 'Carriage' costs of transporting the new machinery from the supplier's factory to the premises of the business purchasing the machinery

(i) Cost of installing the new machinery in the premises of the business

(j) Wages of the machine operators

2.14 Before we go on to consider the way in which expenses are recorded and coded, we are going to look at one further type of expense.

3 DEPRECIATION AND OBSOLESCENCE

Depreciation

3.1 We mentioned depreciation at the beginning of this chapter and described it as a method of writing off capital expenditure.

There are two principal methods of depreciating an asset, the **straight line method** and the **reducing balance method**.

(a) The **straight line method** charges an equal amount of depreciation each period.

(b) The **reducing balance method** charges the largest amount of depreciation at the beginning of an asset's life. As the asset grows older the amount charged each period gets steadily smaller.

ASSESSMENT ALERT

Methods of depreciating an asset is a common Unit 6 Central Assessment topic. Make sure you understand how the two main methods differ

3.2 EXAMPLE: DEPRECIATION METHODS

Two assets are purchased for £8,000 each. One is depreciated over four years using the straight line method and the other is depreciated at the rate of 25% per annum on the reducing balance. What is the value of each asset after four years and how much per year is charged to the profit and loss account?

3.3 SOLUTION

	Asset A		Asset B	
	Balance sheet	Profit and loss account	Balance sheet	Profit and loss account
	£	£	£	£
Capital cost	8,000		8,000	
Year 1 charge	(2,000)	2,000	(2,000)	2,000
c/f	6,000		6,000	
Year 2 charge	(2,000)	2,000	1,500	1,500
c/f	4,000		4,500	
Year 3 charge	(2,000)	2,000	(1,125)	1,125
c/f	2,000		3,375	
Year 4 charge	(2,000)	2,000	(844)	844
c/f	-		2,531	

3.4 The profit and loss account charge for asset A is calculated by splitting the £8,000 capital cost into four. For asset B it is calculated by taking 25% of the opening balance each year. In theory asset B could continue to be depreciated for evermore.

3.5 In order to decide which method is most appropriate we need to think a little more about why we are depreciating the asset at all.

The objectives of depreciation accounting

3.6 If an asset is purchased for £8,000 at the beginning of the year and sold for £6,000 at the end of the year then it is reasonable to conclude that the cost of owning the asset for a year is £2,000. This £2,000 is a real cost and it is in addition to the costs of using the asset, like fuel and repairs costs.

3.7 If the business had not owned the asset it would not have been able to make its product. It is therefore reasonable that the £2,000 cost should be charged as a cost of the product (although we won't say how to do this, for now).

3.8 One of the objectives of depreciation accounting is therefore **to find some way of calculating this cost of ownership.**

3.9 Consider, however, the use of a machine that is constructed to do a specific job for a specific firm. It may last 20 years and yet be of no use to anybody else at any time in which case its resale value would be nil on the same day that it was bought. It is, however, hardly fair to charge the whole cost of the machine to the first product that it makes, or even to the first year's production. Very probably the products it is making in year 19 will be just as well made as the products made in year 1.

3.10 Thus a second objective of depreciation accounting is **to spread out the capital cost of the asset over as long a period as the asset is used.** In the example given there is a good case for spreading this cost in equal proportions over the whole 20 years.

81

3.11 The answer to the question 'which method is best?' therefore depends upon the following.

    (a)   The asset in question.

    (b)   The way it is used.

    (c)   The length of time it is used.

    (d)   The length of time it is useful in the light of changes in products, production methods and technology.

Depreciation in practice

3.12 This sounds as if there are a lot of things to take into account, but in practice you may find that the method most often used is the straight line method because it is simple and gives a reasonable approximation (given that depreciation is at best an estimate).

3.13 Typical depreciation rates under the straight line method are as follows.

Freehold land	Not depreciated
Freehold buildings	2% per annum (50 years)
Leasehold buildings	Over the period of the lease
Plant and machinery	10% per annum (10 years)
Fixtures and fittings	10% per annum (10 years)
Motor vehicles	25% per annum (4 years)

Note that these are not rules. Businesses can choose whatever method or rate they think is most appropriate. Motor vehicles, for example, are often depreciated using the reducing balance method since it is well known that in reality they lose the largest proportion of their value in their first few years.

3.14 Sometimes you may encounter depreciation methods that try to measure the fall in value/cost of use more accurately. A typical example is the machine-hour method which is illustrated below.

3.15 EXAMPLE: THE MACHINE-HOUR METHOD

A machine costs £100,000 and it is estimated that it will be sold as scrap for £5,000 at the end of its useful life. Experience has shown that such machines can run for approximately 10,000 hours before they wear out. What is the depreciation charge for the first year if the machine was used for 1,500 hours?

3.16 SOLUTION

The machine hour rate is calculated as follows.

$$\frac{\text{Cost} - \text{residual value}}{\text{Useful life}}$$

$$\frac{£(100,000 - 5,000)}{10,000 \text{ hours}} = £9.50 \text{ per machine hour}$$

The depreciation charge for the first year is therefore

$$1,500 \times £9.50 = £14,250$$

This method is all very well if there are only a few such assets and careful records are kept of operating times but it would be quite an administrative burden if there were many such machines with different values, different lives and different usage.

Obsolescence

> **KEY TERM**
>
> **Obsolescence** is the loss in value of an asset because it has been superseded, for example due to the development of a technically superior asset or changes in market conditions.

3.17 As the loss in value is due to quite another reason than the **wear and tear** associated with depreciation and because obsolescence may be rapid and difficult to forecast, it is not normal practice to make regular charges relating to obsolescence. Instead, **the loss resulting from the obsolescence should be charged direct to the costing profit and loss account.**

Activity 4.3

(a) It has been calculated that a fork-lift truck is used 65% of the time in the warehouse and the rest of the time in the production department.

Does this have any significance for costing purposes?

(b) At the end of its first year of use the meter on a leather stamping machine read 9728. It cost £4,000 and the suppliers are willing to buy it back for 20% of its cost at any time so that it can be used for parts. The sales literature claimed that it was capable of producing at least 100,000 stampings. The machine is used exclusively on one product, which will be discontinued in three years' time.

    RESIDUAL VALUE.

(i) Is the depreciation charge for the machine a direct expense or an indirect expense? ✓

(ii) What is the depreciation charge for the first year? *STRAIGHT LINE   4000 - 800 = 3200*

$$\frac{3200}{4} = 800.$$

Activity 4.4

A machine was purchased three years ago for £75,000. Due to a change in government regulations, the component the machine produces can only be used for a further two years. At the end of two years, however, the machine can be sold for scrap for £5,000.

    70,000   STRAIGHT LINE = 14000 / YEAR

Task

Calculate the depreciation charge for the five years the machine is owned using both a straight line method and at a rate of 30% per annum on the reducing balance.

4 RECORDING AND CODING EXPENSES

4.1 In this chapter we are only going to deal with the initial stages of recording expenses. Much more detail will be found in the following chapter which explains how overhead costs are attributed to the total costs of individual units of product.

Direct expenses

4.2 **Direct expenses** (such as plant hire for a specific job or solicitor's fees for drawing up a contract to provide a service) can simply be coded to the appropriate job or client when the bill arrives and recorded together with other direct costs.

Indirect expenses

> **KEY TERM**
>
> **Allocation** is the process by which whole cost items are charged direct to a cost unit or cost centre.

4.3   **Indirect expenses** are initially allocated to the appropriate cost centres. We met cost centres briefly in Chapter 1 but in case you have forgotten a cost centre is something (location, function, activity or item of equipment, say) which incurs costs that can be attributed to units of production (cost units). That something may be any of the following.

Cost centre type	Examples	
	Production	Service
Location	Factory A	Top floor
Function	Finishing department	Accounts department
Activity	Painting	Invoicing
Item of equipment	Spray-gun	Computer

4.4   The decision as to which cost centre is the appropriate one for an expense depends upon the type of expense. Some expenses will be solely related to production or to administration or to selling and distribution and can easily be allocated to the appropriate cost centre. Other costs, however, will be shared between these various functions and so such costs cannot be allocated directly to one particular cost centre. Cost centres therefore have to be established for the **initial allocation** of such shared expenses. Examples of shared expenses include: rent, rates, heating and lighting, buildings maintenance and so on.

4.5   **EXAMPLE: OVERHEAD ALLOCATION**

The coding, analysis and recording of indirect expenses and other overheads at the initial stage may be demonstrated by the following example.

The weekly costs of Medlycott Ltd include the following.

Wages of foreman of Department A	£1,000
Wages of foreman of Department B	£1,200
Indirect materials consumed in Department A	£400
Rent of premises shared by Departments A and B	£1,500

Medlycott Ltd's cost accounting system includes the following cost centres.

Code
101   Department A
102   Department B
201   Rent

Show how the costs will be initially coded.

4.6 SOLUTION

(a)

	£	Code
Wages of foreman of Department A	1,000	101
Wages of foreman of Department B	1,200	102
Indirect materials consumed in Department A	400	101
Rent of premises shared by Departments A and B	1,500	201

(b) You may think that this is so obvious as not to be worth explaining. You will certainly not be surprised to be told that the next stage is to share the rent paid between the two departments. Why, you might ask, do we not split the cost of rent straightaway and not bother with cost centre 201?

(c) To answer this question consider the following extract from the cost accounts of Medlycott Ltd, several months after the previous example. Cost centre 201 is no longer used because nobody could see the point of it.

	Cost centre	
	101	*102*
	£	£
Wages	1,172.36	1,415.00
Materials	73.92	169.75
Rent	638.25	1,086.75

You have just received a memo telling you that starting from this month (to which the above figures relate), Department A is to pay 25% of the total rent for the premises shared with Department B and Department B is to be split into 2 departments, with the new department (C) paying 37% of the remaining rent charge. The manager of Department B is standing over you asking you how much his department's new monthly rent charge will be.

(d) The answer is £815.06. More importantly the first thing you have to do to calculate the answer is to recreate the total cost information that used to be allocated to cost centre 201. This is not very difficult in the present example, but imagine that there were 10 cost centres sharing premises and the cost information was recorded in a bulky ledger. Do you think it would have been easy to spot that the monthly rent had increased to £1,725?

Documentation

4.7 There are several ways in which this initial allocation could be documented. A common method is to put a stamp on the invoice itself with boxes to fill in, as appropriate.

%	A/C	£	P
25%	101	431	25
47.25%	102	815	06
27.75%	103	478	69
TOTAL	201	1725	00
Approved		Date	
Authorised		Date	
Posted		Date	

BPP PUBLISHING

4.8   The dividing up of the total cost into portions (**apportionment**) is described in more detail in the next chapter.

Activity 4.5

Listed below are fifteen entries in the cash book of Beancounters, a small firm of accountants. You are required to code up the invoices according to the sort of expense you think has been incurred.

Nominal codes	Nominal account
0010	Advertising
0020	Bank charges
0030	Books and publications
0040	Cleaning
0050	Computer supplies
0060	Heat and light
0070	Motor expenses
0080	Motor vehicles
0090	Office equipment
0100	Printing, postage and stationery
0110	Rates
0120	Rent
0130	Repairs and maintenance
0140	Staff training
0150	Staff welfare
0160	Subscriptions
0170	Telephone
0180	Temporary staff
0190	Travel

		£	Code
Strange (Properties) Ltd	OTHER	4,000.00	0120
Yorkshire Electricity plc	OTHER	1,598.27	0060
Dudley Stationery Ltd	DEPTS	275.24	0100
Dora David (cleaner)	OTHER	125.00	0040
BPP Publishing Ltd	DEPTS	358.00	0030
AAT	DEPTS	1,580.00	0140
British Telecom	CLIENT/DEPTS	1,431.89	0170
Kall Kwik (Stationers)	DEPTS	312.50	0100
Interest to 31.3.X3	OTHER	2,649.33	0020
L & W Office Equipment	DEPTS	24.66	0090
Avis	DEPTS	153.72	0070
Federal Express	DEPTS	32.00	0100
Starriers Garage Ltd	DEPTS	79.80	0070

Activity 4.6

Beancounters is divided up into three departments: audit, business services and tax. Which of the expenses listed in Activity 4.5 do you think are chargeable in total directly to individual clients, which are chargeable in total directly to departments and which cannot be split except by some method of apportionment?

Apportionment and responsibility accounting

4.9   The last point raises another important question. It is unlikely that the managers of departments A, B and C have any control over the amount of rent that is paid for the building. They need to be made aware that their part of the building is not free but they are not responsible for the cost. The person responsible for controlling the amount of a cost such as this is more likely to be a separate manager, who looks after the interests of all of the company's buildings.

4.10 If cost centre 201 is maintained it can therefore be used to collect all the costs that are the responsibility of the premises manager. This approach is known as **responsibility accounting** and such cost centres can be called **responsibility centres.**

ASSESSMENT ALERT

The following notes have been extracted from the guidance for element 5.1.

'Expenses

- Procedures and documentation relating to expenses
- Allocation of expenses to cost centres
- Objectives of depreciation accounting'

Make sure that you are happy with all of the above since assessments are likely to include tasks relating to these areas.

Key learning points

- **Capital expenditure** is expenditure which results in the acquisition of fixed assets. Fixed assets are assets acquired to provide benefits in more than one accounting period. Capital expenditure is charged to the profit and loss account via a depreciation charge over a period of time.

- **Revenue expenditure** is expenditure which is incurred for the purpose of the trade of the business, or in order to maintain the existing earning capacity of fixed assets. It is charged to the profit and loss account in the period to which it relates.

- There are two principal methods of depreciating an asset, the **straight-line** method and the **reducing balance** method.

- **Obsolescence** is the loss in value of an asset because it has been superseded.

- **Direct expenses** are recorded by coding them to the appropriate job or client.

- **Indirect expenses** are initially **allocated** to appropriate cost centres and then spread out or **apportioned** to the cost centres that have benefited from the expense.

- In **responsibility accounting,** cost centres collect the costs that are the responsibility of the cost centre manager, and hence may be known as **responsibility centres.**

Quick quiz

1 What is capital expenditure?

2 What is revenue expenditure?

3 What is the main distinguishing feature of capital and revenue expenditure?

4 What are the two main methods of depreciating an asset?

5 What are the two main objectives of depreciation accounting?

6 What is obsolescence?

7 What is responsibility accounting?

Answers to quick quiz_____

1 Expenditure resulting in the acquisition of fixed assets. It is not charged to the profit and loss account as an expense. Instead a depreciation charge is made to the profit and loss account which writes off the capital expenditure over a period of time.

2   Revenue expenditure is expenditure incurred for the purpose of the trade of the business, or in order to maintain the existing earning capacity of fixed assets. It is charged to the profit and loss account in the period to which it relates.

3   The way that they are accounted for in the profit and loss account (see answers 1 and 2).

4   Straight line method and reducing balance method.

5   To find a way of calculating the cost of ownership of fixed assets and to spread out the capital cost of the asset over its lifetime.

6   The loss in value of an asset because it has been superseded.

7   When cost centre managers have responsibility for controlling the amount of the cost collected within certain cost centres, such cost centres are called responsibility centres.

Answers to activities

Answer 4.1

Capital expenditure is expenditure which results in the acquisition of fixed assets or an improvement in their ability to earn income. *Revenue* expenditure is expenditure which is incurred either for the purpose of the trade or to maintain the *existing* earning capacity of fixed assets.

For example:

Expense	Cost	Capital/revenue
Ford Transit van	£8,000	Capital
Sign-painting of company name, logo and telephone number on van	£500	Capital
Petrol for van	£500	Revenue
New engine, replacing old one which blew up	£1,000	Revenue

Answer 4.2

(a)   Capital expenditure

(b)   Depreciation of a fixed asset is revenue expenditure.

(c)   The legal fees associated with the purchase of a property may be added to the purchase price and classified as capital expenditure. The cost of the leasehold premises in the balance sheet of the business will then include the legal fees.

(d)   Capital expenditure (enhancing an existing fixed asset)

(e)   Revenue expenditure

(f)   Capital expenditure

(g)   If customs duties are borne by the purchaser of the fixed asset, they may be added to the cost of the machinery and classified as capital expenditure.

(h)   Similarly, if carriage costs are paid for by the purchaser of the fixed asset, they may be included in the cost of the fixed asset and classified as capital expenditure.

(i)   Installation costs of a fixed asset are also added to the fixed asset's cost and classified as capital expenditure.

(j)   Revenue expenditure

Answer 4.3

(a)   Yes. The annual depreciation charge for the forklift truck is an indirect revenue expense to be shared (65:35) between the warehouse and the production department. In other words it is a *cost* of these departments.

(b)   (i)   The machine is used exclusively for one product and therefore the whole of the depreciation charge is traceable *directly* to that product. Depreciation is thus a direct expense in this case.

(ii) At the current rate of usage it looks as though the machine will last ten years but it will not be needed after the fourth year of its life and so straight line depreciation over four years seems the most appropriate charge.

$$\text{Depreciation charge} \quad = \quad \frac{\text{Cost} - \text{residual value}}{\text{Useful life}} = \frac{£4,000 - £800}{4}$$

$$= \quad £800$$

Answer 4.4

Straight line method

$$\text{Depreciation per annum} \quad = \quad \frac{\text{Cost} - \text{residual value}}{\text{Expected life}}$$

$$= \quad £\frac{(75,000 - 5,000)}{5 \text{ years}}$$

$$= \quad \underline{£14,000}$$

Reducing balance method

	£
Capital cost	75,000
Year 1 charge (£75,000 × 30%)	22,500
	52,500
Year 2 charge (£52,500 × 30%)	15,750
	36,750
Year 3 charge (£36,750 × 30%)	11,025
	25,725
Year 4 charge (£25,725 × 30%)	7,718
	18,007
Year 5 charge (£18,007 × 30%)	5,402
	12,605

Answer 4.5

	£	Code
Strange (Properties) Ltd	4,000.00	0120
Yorkshire Electricity plc	1,598.27	0060
Dudley Stationery Ltd	275.24	0100
Dora David (Cleaner)	125.00	0040
BPP Publishing Ltd	358.00	0140
AAT	1,580.00	0160
British Telecom	1,431.89	0170
Kall Kwik (Stationers)	312.50	0100
Interest to 31.3.X3	2,649.33	0020
L & W Office Equipment	24.66	0100
Avis	153.72	0190
Federal Express	32.00	0100
Starriers Garage Ltd	79.80	0070

Answer 4.6

There is no definitive answer to this activity, but it is enough that you gave it some thought. The following expenses may be chargeable directly to clients.

	£	
Kall Kwik (Stationers)	312.50	Photocopying costs: say 200 sets of accounts to be sent to shareholders?
Avis	153.72	The cost of renting a car to travel on a client's business?

The following expenses *may* be chargeable directly to departments.

	£	
Dudley Stationery Ltd	275.24	If this type of stationery is used exclusively by one department.
L & W Office Equipment	24.66	If the item is used exclusively by one department.
Starriers Garage Ltd	79.80	The car is probably used by a specific employee.

Federal Express expenses could also fall into this category. The remaining items need to be split between departments. Training costs and AAT subscriptions could be split according to the specific staff involved, rent according to the floor area occupied and so on. (The next chapter goes into this in more detail.)

Part B
Overheads and absorption costing

Chapter 5 Overheads and absorption costing

Chapter topic list

1   What are overheads?

2   What is absorption costing?

3   Overhead apportionment

4   Overhead absorption

5   Blanket absorption rates and separate departmental absorption rates

6   Over and under absorption

7   Predetermined rates and actual costs

8   Fixed and variable overheads and capacity

9   Non-production overheads

10   Activity based costing

Learning objectives

On completion of this chapter you will be able to:

	Performance criteria	Range statement
• attribute actual overhead costs to cost centres in accordance with agreed methods of allocation, apportionment and absorption	5.2.4	5.2.1, 5.2.2
• adjust for under or over recovered overhead costs in accordance with established procedures	5.2.5	5.2.1, 5.2.2
• use different methods of apportionment	5.2.7	5.2.2
• follow procedures for establishing absorption rates	5.2.7	5.2.2
• review methods of allocation, apportionment and absorption	5.2.7	5.2.2

BPP PUBLISHING

1   WHAT ARE OVERHEADS?

KEY TERM

An **overhead** is the cost incurred in the course of making a product, providing a service or running a department, but which cannot be traced directly and in full to the product, service or department.

1.1   **Overheads** are the total of the following.

- Indirect materials
- Indirect labour
- Indirect expenses

(Note that in the previous chapter we were looking at **expenses**, and whether they were direct or indirect.)

1.2   Before we go any further let us look at one common way of categorising overheads.

(a)   Production overhead
(b)   Administration overhead
(c)   Selling overhead
(d)   Distribution overhead

KEY TERMS

- **Production (or factory) overhead** includes all indirect material costs, indirect wages and indirect expenses incurred in the factory from receipt of the order until its completion.

- **Administration overhead** is all indirect material costs, wages and expenses incurred in the direction, control and administration of an undertaking.

- **Selling overhead** is all indirect materials costs, wages and expenses incurred in promoting sales and retaining customers.

- **Distribution overhead** is all indirect material costs, wages and expenses incurred in making the packed product ready for despatch and delivering it to the customer.

1.3   Examples of production overhead include the following.

(a)   **Indirect materials** which cannot be traced in the finished product.

- Consumable stores, eg material used in negligible amounts

(b)   **Indirect wages**, meaning all wages not charged directly to a product.

- Salaries and wages of non-productive workers eg supervisors

(c)   **Indirect expenses** (other than material and labour) not charged directly to production.

- Rent, rates and insurance of a factory
- Depreciation, fuel, power and maintenance

1.4 Examples of administration overhead are as follows.

    (a) **Depreciation** of office administration overhead, buildings and machinery.

    (b) **Office salaries**, including salaries of administrative directors, secretaries and accountants.

    (c) Rent, rates, insurance, lighting, cleaning and heating of general offices, telephone and postal charges, bank charges, legal charges, audit fees.

1.5 Examples of selling overhead are as follows.

    (a) **Printing** and **stationery**, such as catalogues and price lists.

    (b) **Salaries** and **commission** of salesmen, representatives and sales department staff.

    (c) **Advertising** and **sales promotion**, market research.

    (d) Rent, rates and insurance of sales offices and showrooms, bad debts and collection charges, cash discounts allowed, after sales service.

1.6 Examples of distribution overhead are as follows.

    (a) Cost of packing cases.

    (b) Wages of packers, drivers and despatch clerks.

    (c) Freight and insurance charges, rent, rates, insurance and depreciation of warehouses, depreciation and running expenses of delivery vehicles.

1.7 There are a number of schools of thought as to the correct method of dealing with overheads.

- Absorption costing
- Activity based costing
- Marginal costing

We will be looking at absorption costing in detail, and we will consider activity based costing briefly in Section 10 of this chapter. Marginal costing is beyond the scope of Unit 6.

2 WHAT IS ABSORPTION COSTING?

2.1 **The objective of absorption costing is to include in the total cost of a product** (unit or job, say) **an appropriate share of the organisation's total overhead.** By an appropriate share we mean an amount that reflects the amount of time and effort that has gone into producing a unit or completing a job.

2.2 If an organisation had but one production department and produced identical units then the total overheads would be divided among the total units produced. Life is, of course, never that simple. **Absorption costing is a method of sharing overheads between a number of different products on a fair basis.**

The effect of absorption costing

2.3 Before describing the procedures by which overhead costs are shared out among products, it may be useful to consider the reasons why absorption costing is commonly used.

2.4 Suppose that a company makes and sells 100 units of a product each week. The direct cost per unit is £6 and the unit sales price is £10. Production overhead costs £200 per week and

BPP PUBLISHING

administration, selling and distribution overhead costs £150 per week. The weekly profit could be calculated as follows.

	£	£
Sales (100 units × £10)		1,000
Direct costs (100 × £6)	600	
Production overheads	200	
Administration, selling, distribution costs	150	
		950
Profit		50

2.5 **In absorption costing, overhead costs will be added to each unit of product manufactured and sold.**

	£ per unit
Direct cost per unit	6
Production overhead (£200 per week for 100 units)	2
Full factory cost	8

The weekly profit would be calculated as follows.

	£
Sales	1,000
Less factory cost of sales (100 × £8)	800
Gross profit	200
Less administration, selling, distribution costs	150
Net profit	50

2.6 It may already be apparent that the weekly profit is £50 no matter how the figures have been presented. This being so, how does absorption costing serve any useful purpose in accounting? Is it necessary?

Is absorption costing necessary?

2.7 The reasons for using absorption costing have traditionally been identified as follows.

(a) **Stock valuations**. Stock in hand must be valued for two reasons.

   (i) For the closing stock figure in the balance sheet

   (ii) For the cost of sales figure in the profit and loss account. The valuation of stocks will actually affect profitability during a period because of the way in which cost of sales is calculated.

   The cost of goods produced
   + the value of opening stocks
   − the value of closing stocks
   = the cost of goods sold.

   In our example above, closing stocks could be valued at direct cost (£6), but in absorption costing, they would be valued at a fully absorbed factory cost of £8 per unit.

(b) **Pricing decisions**. Many companies attempt to fix selling prices by calculating the full cost of production or sales of each product, and then adding a margin for profit. In our example, the company might have fixed a gross profit margin at 25% on factory cost, or 20% of the sales price, in order to establish the unit sales price of £10. '**Full cost plus pricing**' can be particularly useful for companies which do jobbing or contract work, where each job or contract is different, so that a standard unit sales price cannot be fixed. Without using absorption costing, a full cost is difficult to ascertain.

(c) **Establishing the profitability of different products.** This argument in favour of absorption costing is more contentious, but is worthy of mention here. If a company sells more than one product, it will be difficult to judge how profitable each individual product is, unless overhead costs are shared on a fair basis and charged to the cost of sales of each product.

Statement of standard accounting practice 9 (SSAP 9)

2.8 Of these three arguments, the problem of valuing stocks is perhaps the most significant, because **absorption costing is recommended in financial accounting by the statement of standard accounting practice on stocks and long-term contracts (SSAP 9).** SSAP 9 deals with financial accounting systems and not with cost accounting systems. The cost accountant is (in theory) free to value stocks by whatever method seems best, but where companies integrate their financial accounting and cost accounting systems into a single system of accounting records, the valuation of closing stocks will be determined by SSAP 9.

Costing procedures

2.9 The three stages of calculating the costs of overheads to be charged to manufactured output are **allocation**, **apportionment** and **absorption**. (Absorption costing is the name used since absorption is the ultimate aim of the other two procedures.)

2.10 **Allocation** is the process of assigning costs to cost centres. We studied the process of allocation in the previous chapter.

2.11 We shall now begin our study of absorption costing by looking at the process of **overhead apportionment**.

Activity 5.1

(a) What is absorption costing?
(b) Identify three reasons for using absorption costing.
(c) What are the three stages of absorption costing?

---

3 OVERHEAD APPORTIONMENT

> **KEY TERM**
>
> **Apportionment** is a procedure whereby indirect costs (overheads) are spread fairly between cost centres.

Stage one: sharing out common costs

3.1 Overhead apportionment follows on from overhead allocation. The first stage of overhead apportionment is to **identify all overhead costs** as production, administration, selling and distribution overhead. This means that the shared costs (such as rent and rates, heat and light and so on) initially allocated to a single cost centre must now be shared out between the other (functional) cost centres.

Bases of apportionment

3.2 It is important that overhead costs are shared out on a **fair basis** but this is much more easily said than done. It is rarely possible to use only one method of apportioning costs to the various cost centres of an organisation. The bases of apportionment for the most usual cases are given below.

Overhead to which the basis applies	Basis
Rent, rates, heating and light, repairs and depreciation of buildings	Floor area occupied by each cost centre
Depreciation, insurance of equipment	Cost or book value of equipment
Personnel office, canteen, welfare, wages and cost offices, first aid	Number of employees, or labour hours worked in each cost centre
Heating, lighting (see above)	Volume of space occupied by each cost centre
Carriage inwards (costs paid for the delivery of material supplies)	Value of material issues to each cost centre

3.3 Don't forget that some overhead costs can be allocated directly to the user cost centre without having to be apportioned, for example indirect wages and consumable supplies, because they relate solely to that cost centre.

3.4 EXAMPLE: OVERHEAD APPORTIONMENT

Kettle Ltd incurred the following overhead costs.

	£
Depreciation of factory	1,000
Factory repairs and maintenance	600
Factory office costs (treat as production overhead)	1,500
Depreciation of equipment	800
Insurance of equipment	200
Heating	390
Lighting	100
Canteen	900
	5,490

Information relating to the production and service departments in the factory is as follows.

	Department			
	Production	*Production*	*Service*	*Service*
	A	*B*	*X*	*Y*
Floor space (sq. metres)	1,200	1,600	800	400
Volume (cubic metres)	3,000	6,000	2,400	1,600
Number of employees	30	30	15	15
Book value of equipment	£30,000	£20,000	£10,000	£20,000

How should the overhead costs be apportioned between the four departments?

3.5 SOLUTION

Item of cost	Basis of apportionment	Total cost £	A £	B £	X £	Y £
Factory depreciation	(floor area)	1,000	300	400	200	100
Factory repairs	(floor area)	600	180	240	120	60
Factory office	(no. of employees)	1,500	500	500	250	250
Equipment depn	(book value)	800	300	200	100	200
Equipment insurance	(book value)	200	75	50	25	50
Heating	(volume)	390	90	180	72	48
Lighting	(floor area)	100	30	40	20	10
Canteen	(no. of employees)	900	300	300	150	150
Total		5,490	1,775	1,910	937	868

Total — To Department A B X Y

ASSESSMENT ALERT

Would you be able to explain the difference between allocated overheads and apportioned overheads if you were asked to do so in an assessment? This is exactly what candidates in the December 1999 Central Assessment had to do.

3.6 EXAMPLE: MORE OVERHEAD APPORTIONMENT

Friar Tuck Ltd is preparing its production overhead budgets and determining the apportionment of those overheads to products. Cost centre expenses and related information have been budgeted as follows.

	Total £	Machine shop A £	Machine shop B £	Assembly £	Canteen £	Mainten- ance £
Indirect wages	78,560	8,586	9,190	15,674	29,650	15,460
Consumable materials (inc. maintenance)	16,900	6,400	8,700	1,200	600	-
Rent and rates	16,700					
Buildings insurance	2,400					
Power	8,600					
Heat and light	3,400					
Depreciation of machinery	40,200					
Value of machinery	402,000	201,000	179,000	22,000	-	-
Other information:						
Power usage - technical estimates (%)	100	55	40	3	-	2
Direct labour (hours)	35,000	8,000	6,200	20,800	-	-
Machine usage (hours)	25,200	7,200	18,000	-	-	-
Area (sq ft)	45,000	10,000	12,000	15,000	6,000	2,000

How should the overheads be apportioned to the five cost centres?

3.7 SOLUTION

	Total	A	B	Assembly	Canteen	Mainten-ance	Basis of appor-tionment
	£	£	£	£	£	£	£
Indirect wages	78,560	8,586	9,190	15,674	29,650	15,460	Actual
Consumable materials	16,900	6,400	8,700	1,200	600	-	Actual
Rent and rates	16,700	3,711	4,453	5,567	2,227	742	Area
Insurance	2,400	533	640	800	320	107	Area
Power	8,600	4,730	3,440	258	-	172	Usage
Heat and light	3,400	756	907	1,133	453	151	Area
Depreciation	40,200	20,100	17,900	2,200	-	-	Value
	166,760	44,816	45,230	26,832	33,250	16,632	

Workings

1   *Rent and rates, insurance, heat and light*

Floor area is a sensible measure to use as the basis for apportionment.

	Area	Proportion total area	Share of rent & rates	Share of insurance	Share of heat & light
	Sq feet		£	£	£
Machine shop A	10,000	10/45	3,711	533	756
Machine shop B	12,000	12/45	4,453	640	907
Assembly	15,000	15/45	5,567	800	1,133
Canteen	6,000	6/45	2,227	320	453
Maintenance	2,000	2/45	742	107	151
	45,000		16,700	2,400	3,400

2   *Power*

	Metered units	Proportion of total	Share of cost
			£
Machine shop A	580,180	0.55	4,730
Machine shop B	421,949	0.40	3,440
Assembly	31,648	0.03	258
Maintenance	21,098	0.02	172
	1,054,875		8,600

3   *Depreciation*

In the absence of specific information about what fixed assets belong to which departments and what the depreciation rates in use are, this cost is shared out on the basis of the relative value of each department's machinery to the total. In practice more specific information would (or should) be available.

Stage two: apportioning service cost centre costs to production cost centres

3.8   The second stage of overhead apportionment concerns **the treatment of service cost centres**. A factory is divided into several production cost centres and also many service cost centres, but **only the production cost centres are directly involved in the manufacture of the units**. In order to be able to add production overheads to unit costs, it is necessary to have all the overheads charged to (or located in) the production cost centres. The next stage in absorption costing is therefore to apportion the costs of service cost centres to the production cost centres.

3.9   There are three methods by which the apportionment of service cost centre costs can be done.

(a) Apportion the costs of each service cost centre to production cost centres only (**direct**).

(b) Apportion the costs of each service cost centre not only to production cost centres, but also to other service cost centres which make use of its services, and eventually apportion all costs to the production cost centres alone by a gradual process of **repeated distribution**.

(c) Apportion the costs of each service cost centre, not only to production cost centres, but also to some (but not all) of the service cost centres that make use of its services. This is known as the **step-down** method.

We shall look at each of these methods in more detail below.

3.10 Whichever method is used, the basis of apportionment must be fair and a different apportionment basis may be applied for each service cost centre. This is demonstrated in the following table.

Service cost centre	Possible basis of apportionment
Stores	Number or cost value of material requisitions
Maintenance	Hours of maintenance and repair work done for each cost centre
Production planning	Direct labour hours worked for each production cost centre

3.11 EXAMPLE: DIRECT APPORTIONMENT

Maid Marion Ltd incurred the following overhead costs.

	Production departments		Stores department	Maintenance department
	P	*Q*		
	£	£	£	£
Allocated costs	6,000	4,000	1,000	2,000
Apportioned costs	2,000	1,000	1,000	500
	8,000	5,000	2,000	2,500

Production department P requisitioned materials to the value of £12,000. Department Q requisitioned £8,000 of materials. The maintenance department provided 500 hours of work for department P and 750 for department Q. What are the total production overhead costs of Departments P and Q?

3.12 SOLUTION

Service department	Basis of apportionment	Total cost	Dept P	Dept Q
		£	£	£
Stores	Value of requisitions	2,000	1,200	800
Maintenance	Direct labour hours	2,500	1,000	1,500
		4,500	2,200	2,300
Previously allocated and apportioned costs		13,000	8,000	5,000
Total overhead		17,500	10,200	7,300

3.13 EXAMPLE: DIRECT APPORTIONMENT AGAIN

Look back to the example solution in Paragraph 3.7. Using the bases of apportionment which you consider most appropriate from the information provided in Paragraph 3.6, calculate overhead totals for Friar Tuck Ltd's three production departments.

3.14 SOLUTION

	Total	A	B	Assembly	Canteen	Mainten-ance	Basis of appor-tionment
	£	£	£	£	£	£	£
Total overheads	166,760	44,816	45,230	26,832	33,250	16,632	
Reallocate	-	7,600	5,890	19,760	(33,250)	-	Dir labour
	-	4,752	11,880	-	-	(16,632)	Mac usage
Totals	166,760	57,168	63,000	46,592	-	-	

The repeated distribution/reciprocal allocation method of apportionment

3.15 **Apportionment** is a procedure whereby indirect costs are spread fairly between cost centres. It could therefore be argued that a fair sharing of service cost centre costs is not possible unless consideration is given to the work done by each service cost centre for other service cost centres.

3.16 For example, suppose a company has two production and two service departments (stores and maintenance). The following information about activity in a recent costing period is available.

	Production departments		Stores department	Maintenance department
	1	2		
Overhead costs	£10,030	£8,970	£10,000	£8,000
Cost of material requisitions	£30,000	£50,000	-	£20,000
Maintenance hours needed	8,000	1,000	1,000	-

The problem is that the stores department uses the maintenance department, and the maintenance department uses the stores.

(a) If service department overheads were apportioned directly to production departments, the apportionment would be as follows.

Service department	Basis of apportionment	Total cost	1	2
		£	£	£
Stores	(Material requisitions)	10,000	3,750	6,250
Maintenance	(Maintenance hours)	8,000	7,111	889
		18,000	10,861	7,139
Overheads of Departments 1 and 2		19,000	10,030	8,970
		37,000	20,891	16,109

(b) If, however, recognition is made of the fact that the stores and maintenance department do work for each other, and the basis of apportionment remains the same, we ought to apportion service department costs as follows.

	Production departments		Stores department	Maintenance department
	1	2		
Stores (100%)	30%	50%	-	20%
Maintenance (100%)	80%	10%	10%	-

This may be done using the **repeated distribution method of apportionment**, which is perhaps best explained by means of an example.

3.17 EXAMPLE: REPEATED DISTRIBUTION (RECIPROCAL ALLOCATION) METHOD OF APPORTIONMENT

	Production departments 1 £	2 £	Stores department £	Maintenance department £
Overhead costs	10,030	8,970	10,000	8,000
Apportion stores (see note (a))	3,000	5,000	(10,000)	2,000
			0	10,000
Apportion maintenance	8,000	1,000	1,000	(10,000)
			1,000	0
Repeat: Apportion stores	300	500	(1,000)	200
Repeat: Apportion maintenance	160	20	20	(200)
Repeat: Apportion stores	6	10	(20)	4
Repeat: Apportion maintenance	4	-	-	(4)
	21,500	15,500	0	0

Notes

(a) The first apportionment could have been the costs of maintenance, rather than stores; there is no difference to the final results.

(b) When the repeated distributions bring service department costs down to small numbers (here £4), the final apportionment to production departments is an approximate rounding.

3.18 You should note the difference in the final overhead apportionments to each production department using the different apportionment methods. Unless the difference is substantial, the first method might be preferred because it is clerically simpler to use.

Step-down method

3.19 The **step-down** method is very similar to the repeated distribution method. The main difference is that, unlike the reciprocal allocation method that we have just looked at, the final results will depend upon which apportionment was made first. Let us demonstrate this method by means of an example.

3.20 EXAMPLE: STEP-DOWN METHOD OF APPORTIONMENT

Using the information in the example in paragraph 3.17, apportion the overhead costs using the step-down method of apportionment, starting with the stores department.

	Production departments 1 £	2 £	Stores department £	Maintenance department £
Overhead costs	10,030	8,970	10,000	8,000
Apportion stores (30%/50%/20%)	3,000	5,000	(10,000)	2,000
			-	10,000
Apportion maintenance ($^8/_9$/$^1/_9$)	8,889	1,111	-	(10,000)
	21,919	15,081	-	-

If the first apportionment had been the maintenance department, then the overheads of £8,000 would have been apportioned as follows.

	Production departments		Stores	Maintenance
	1	*2*	*department*	*department*
	£	£	£	£
Overhead costs	10,030	8,970	10,000	8,000
Apportion maintenance				
(80%/10%/10%)	6,400	800	800	(8,000)
			10,800	-
Apportion stores ($^3/_8/^5/_8$)	4,050	6,750	(10,800)	
	20,480	16,520	-	-

Note

Notice how the final results differ, depending upon whether stores or maintenance are apportioned first.

Activity 5.2

Sandstorm Ltd is a jobbing engineering concern which has three production departments (forming, machines and assembly) and two service departments (maintenance and general).

The following analysis of overhead costs has been made from the year just ended.

	£	£
Rent and rates		8,000
Power		750
Light, heat		5,000
Repairs, maintenance:		
Forming	800	
Machines	1,800	
Assembly	300	
Maintenance	200	
General	100	
		3,200
Departmental expenses:		
Forming	1,500	
Machines	2,300	
Assembly	1,100	
Maintenance	900	
General	1,500	
		7,300
Depreciation:		
Plant		10,000
Fixtures and fittings		250
Insurance:		
Plant		2,000
Buildings		500
Indirect labour:		
Forming	3,000	
Machines	5,000	
Assembly	1,500	
Maintenance	4,000	
General	2,000	
		15,500
		52,500

Other available data are as follows.

	Floor area sq.ft	Plant value £	Fixtures & fittings £	Effective horse-power	Direct cost for year £	Labour hours worked	Machine hours worked
Forming	2,000	25,000	1,000	40	20,500	14,400	12,000
Machines	4,000	60,000	500	90	30,300	20,500	21,600
Assembly	3,000	7,500	2,000	15	24,200	20,200	2,000
Maintenance	500	7,500	1,000	5	-	-	-
General	500	-	500	-	-	-	-
	10,000	100,000	5,000	150	75,000	55,100	35,600

Service department costs are apportioned as follows.

	Maintenance %	General %
Forming	20	20
Machines	50	60
Assembly	20	10
General	10	–
Maintenance	–	10
	100	100

Task

Using the data provided prepare an analysis showing the distribution of overhead costs to departments.

4 OVERHEAD ABSORPTION

KEY TERM

Overhead absorption is the process whereby overhead costs allocated and apportioned to production cost centres are added to unit, job or batch costs. Overhead absorption is sometimes called **overhead recovery.**

4.1 Having allocated and/or apportioned all overheads, the next stage in the costing treatment of overheads is to add them to, or absorb them into, cost units. The cost unit of a business is the thing that it sells. For the biro manufacturer it is the biro, or a box of 100 biros if he only sells them in that quantity. For a solicitor it is an hour of his time and there are as many more examples as there are different types of business.

Overheads are usually added to cost units using a **predetermined overhead absorption rate**, which is calculated using figures from the budget.

4.2 An overhead absorption rate for the forthcoming accounting period is calculated as follows.

(a) An **estimate is made of the overhead** likely to be incurred during the coming period.

(b) An **estimate is made of the total hours, units, or direct costs** or whatever it is upon which the overhead absorption rates are to be based (the **activity level**).

(c) The **estimated overhead is divided by the budgeted activity level**. This produces the overhead absorption rate.

4.3 The overhead then gets into the cost unit by **applying** the rate that has been calculated to the information already established for the cost unit. If overhead is absorbed at, say £2 per labour hour, then a cost unit that takes 3 labour hours to produce absorbs 3 × £2 = £6 in overheads. Let's look at a very simple example. It might help to make things clearer.

4.4 EXAMPLE: THE BASICS OF ABSORPTION COSTING

Suppose total overhead of Athena Ltd is estimated to be £50,000 and total labour hours are expected to be 100,000 hours. The business makes two products, the Greek and the Roman. Greeks take 2 labour hours each to make and Romans take 5. What is the overhead cost per unit for Greeks and Romans respectively if overheads are absorbed on the basis of labour hours?

4.5 SOLUTION

(a) First calculate the absorption rate.

$$\text{Absorption rate} = \frac{\text{Total estimated overhead}}{\text{Total estimated activity level}} = \frac{£50,000}{100,000 \text{ hrs}}$$

$$= £0.50 \text{ per labour hour}$$

(b) Now apply it to the products.

	Greek	Roman
Labour hours per unit	2	5
Absorption rate per labour hour	£0.50	£0.50
Overhead absorbed per unit	£1	£2.50

Possible bases of absorption

4.6 The different bases of absorption (or 'overhead recovery rates') which can be used are as follows.

- A percentage of direct materials cost
- A percentage of direct labour cost
- A percentage of total direct cost (prime cost)
- A rate per machine hour
- A rate per direct labour hour
- A rate per unit
- A percentage of factory cost (for administration overhead)
- A percentage of sales or factory cost (for selling and distribution overhead)

4.7 Which basis should be used for production overhead depends largely on the organisation concerned. As with apportionment it is a matter of being fair.

4.8 Many factories tend to use the **direct labour hour rate** or **machine hour rate** in preference to a rate based on a percentage of direct materials cost, wages or prime cost. A **machine hour rate** would be used in departments where production is controlled or dictated by machines. In such a situation, where a small number of workers supervise a process that is performed almost entirely by machine, the distinction between direct and indirect labour may be difficult to identify, and labour costs may not be the principal costs of production. A **direct labour hour basis** is more appropriate in a labour intensive environment. We shall return to this point at the end of this chapter.

4.9 EXAMPLE: OVERHEAD ABSORPTION RATES

The budgeted production overheads and other budget data of Eiffel Ltd are as follows.

Budget	Production dept X	Production dept Y
Overhead cost	£36,000	£5,000
Direct materials cost	£32,000	
Direct labour cost	£40,000	
Machine hours	10,000	
Direct labour hours	18,000	
Units of production		1,000

What would the absorption rate be for each department using the various bases of apportionment?

4.10 SOLUTION

(a) Department X

   (i)   % of direct materials cost $\dfrac{£36,000}{£32,000} \times 100\% = 112.5\%$

   (ii)   % of direct labour cost $\dfrac{£36,000}{£40,000} \times 100\% = 90\%$

   (iii)   % of total direct cost $\dfrac{£36,000}{£72,000} \times 100\% = 50\%$

   (iv)   Rate per machine hour $\dfrac{£36,000}{10,000 \text{ hrs}} = £3.60$ per machine hour

   (v)   Rate per direct labour hour $\dfrac{£36,000}{18,000 \text{ hrs}} = £2$ per direct labour hour

(b) For department Y the absorption rate will be based on units of output.

$$\dfrac{£5,000}{1,000 \text{ units}} = £5 \text{ per unit produced}$$

4.11 EXAMPLE: OVERHEAD ABSORPTION RATES ONCE MORE

Using the information in Paragraph 3.6 and the example solution in Paragraph 3.14, determine budgeted overhead absorption rates for each of Friar Tuck Ltd's production departments using bases of absorption which you consider most appropriate from the information provided.

4.12 SOLUTION

Machine shop A: $\dfrac{£57,168}{7,200} = £7.94$ per machine hour

Machine shop B: $\dfrac{£63,000}{18,000} = £3.50$ per machine hour

Assembly: $\dfrac{£46,592}{20,800} = £2.24$ per direct labour hour

Activity 5.3

(a) List six possible bases of absorption.

(b) If overheads in total are expected to be £108,000 and direct labour hours (which are used as the absorption base) are planned to be 90,000 hours costing £5 per hour, what is the absorption rate:

(i)   per direct labour hour
(ii) as a percentage of direct labour cost?

The effect on total cost of applying different bases

4.13   The choice of the basis of absorption is significant in determining the cost of individual units, or jobs, produced. Using the Eiffel Ltd example in Paragraphs 4.11 and 4.12, suppose that in department X an individual product has a materials cost of £80, a labour cost of £85, and requires 36 labour hours and 23 machine hours to complete. The overhead cost of the product would vary, depending on the basis of absorption used by the company for overhead recovery.

(a)   As a percentage of direct material cost, the overhead cost would be

$$112.5\% \times £80 = £90.00$$

(b)   As a percentage of direct labour cost, the overhead cost would be

$$90\% \times £85 = £76.50$$

(c)   As a percentage of total direct cost, the overhead cost would be

$$50\% \times £165 = £82.50$$

(d)   Using a machine hour basis of absorption, the overhead cost would be

$$23 \text{ hrs} \times £3.60 = £82.80$$

(e)   Using a labour hour basis, the overhead cost would be $\quad 36 \text{ hrs} \times £2 \quad = £72.00$

4.14   In theory, each basis of absorption would be possible, but the company should choose a basis for its own costs which seems to be '**fairest**'. In our example, this choice will be significant in determining the cost of individual products, as the following summary shows, but the total cost of production overheads is the estimated overhead expenditure, no matter what basis of absorption is selected. It is the relative share of overhead costs borne by individual products and jobs which is affected by the choice of overhead absorption basis.

4.15   A summary of the product costs for the example beginning in Paragraph 4.9 is shown as follows.

	\multicolumn{5}{c}{*Basis of overhead recovery*}			
	Percentage of materials cost	*Percentage of labour cost*	*Percentage of prime cost*	*Machine hours*	*Direct labour hours*
	£	£	£	£	£
Direct material	80	80.0	80.0	80.0	80
Direct labour	85	85.0	85.0	85.0	85
Production overhead	90	76.5	82.5	82.8	72
Full factory cost	255	241.5	247.5	247.8	237

The arbitrary nature of absorption costing

4.16 Absorption costing may irritate you because, even if a company is trying to be 'fair', there is a great lack of precision about the way an absorption base is chosen.

4.17 This arbitrariness is one of the main criticisms of absorption costing, and if absorption costing is to be used (because of its other virtues) then it is important that the methods used are kept under regular review. Changes in working conditions should, if necessary, lead to changes in the way in which work is accounted for.

5   BLANKET ABSORPTION RATES AND SEPARATE DEPARTMENTAL ABSORPTION RATES

> **KEY TERM**
>
> A **blanket overhead absorption rate** is an absorption rate used throughout a factory for all jobs and units of output irrespective of the department in which they were produced.

5.1 Consider a factory in which total overheads were £500,000 and there were 250,000 direct machine hours, during the period under consideration. We could calculate a **blanket overhead absorption rate** of £2 per direct machine hour (£500,000 ÷ 250,000). This would mean that all jobs passing through the factory would be charged at the same rate of £2 per direct machine hour.

5.2 If a factory has a number of departments, and jobs do not spend an equal amount of time in each department, then the use of a blanket overhead absorption rate is not really appropriate.

5.3 The main argument against the use of blanket overhead absorption rates is the fact that some products will absorb a higher overhead charge than is fair. Likewise, other products may absorb less overhead charge than is fair.

5.4 If different departments use separate absorption rates, overheads should be charged to products on a fairer basis than when blanket overhead absorption rates are used. The overhead charged to products should then be representative of the costs of the efforts and resources put into making them.

5.5   EXAMPLE: SEPARATE ABSORPTION RATES

(a) Gibson Ltd has two production departments, for which the following budgeted information is available.

	Department Alpha	Department Beta	Total
Estimated overheads	£360,000	£200,000	£560,000
Estimated direct labour hours	200,000 hrs	40,000 hrs	240,000 hrs

If a single factory overhead absorption rate per direct labour hour is applied, the rate of overhead recovery would be:

$$\frac{£560,000}{240,000 \text{ hrs}} = £2.33 \text{ per direct labour hour}$$

(b) If separate departmental rates are applied, these would be:

$$Department\ Alpha = \frac{£360,000}{200,000\ hours} \qquad Department\ Beta = \frac{£200,000}{40,000\ hours}$$

$$= £1.80\ per\ direct\ labour\ hour \qquad = £5\ per\ direct\ labour\ hour$$

Department Beta has a higher overhead rate per hour worked than department Alpha.

Now let us consider two separate jobs.

(i) Job Xen has a total direct cost of £100, takes 30 hours in department Beta and does not involve any work in department Alpha.

(ii) Job Yen has a total direct cost of £100, takes 28 hours in department Alpha and 2 hours in department Beta.

What would be the factory cost of each job, using the following rates of overhead recovery?

(i) A single factory rate of overhead recovery
(ii) Separate departmental rates of overhead recovery

5.6 SOLUTION

	Job Xen		Job Yen
Single factory rate	£		£
Direct cost	100		100
Factory overhead (30 × £2.33)	70		70
Factory cost	170		170
Separate departmental rates	£		£
Direct cost	100		100.0
Factory overhead: department Alpha	0	(28 × 1.8)	50.4
department Beta (30 × 5)	150	(2 × 5)	10.0
Factory cost	250		160.4

5.7 Using a single factory overhead absorption rate, both jobs would cost the same. However, since job Xen is done entirely within department Beta where overhead costs are relatively higher, whereas job Yen is done mostly within department Alpha, where overhead costs are relatively lower, it is arguable that job Xen should cost more than job Yen. This will only occur if separate departmental overhead recovery rates are used to reflect the work done on each job in each department separately.

5.8 If all jobs do not spend approximately the same time in each department then, to ensure that all jobs are charged with their fair share of overheads, it is necessary to establish separate overhead rates for each department.

Activity 5.4

Pippin Ltd make two types of fruit juicer. One model is for domestic use selling for £400 and the other for industrial applications selling for £500. Unit costs are as follows.

	Domestic	Industrial
	£	£
Materials	28	40
Direct labour	180	80
Direct expenses	40	200

Direct labour is paid at the rate of £10 per hour. Direct expenses comprise machine running costs and these are incurred at the rate of £8 per hour.

Production overheads in the coming year are expected to be £1,040,000. Planned production volume is 20,000 of each product.

Task

Calculate the absorption rate and the total (direct and indirect) production cost per unit of each product if a single factory overhead absorption rate per direct labour hour is used.

Activity 5.5

Cott and Wool Ltd has two service departments serving two production departments. Overhead costs apportioned to each department are as follows.

Production 1	Production 2	Service 1	Service 2
£	£	£	£
97,428	84,947	9,384	15,823

Service 1 department is expected to work a total of 40,000 hours, divided as follows.

	Hours
Production 1	20,000
Production 2	15,000
Service 2	5,000

Service 2 department is expected to work a total of 12,000 hours divided up as follows.

	Hours
Production 1	3,000
Production 2	8,000
Service 1	1,000

Task

Reapportion the costs of the two service departments using the direct apportionment method.

Activity 5.6

The finance director of Cott and Wool Ltd has just seen your attempt to reapportion the service department costs. He commented 'Actually we use the repeated distribution method here' and walked away.

Task

Prove to the finance director that you know how to use the repeated distribution method.

Activity 5.7

When you show the finance director how you have reapportioned the costs of the two service departments, he says 'Did I say that we used the repeated distribution method? Well, I meant to say the step-down method.'

Task

Prove to the finance director that you know how to use the step-down method. (*Note.* Apportion the overheads of service department 1 first.)

6   OVER AND UNDER ABSORPTION

6.1   It was stated earlier that the usual method of accounting for overheads is to add overhead costs on the basis of a **predetermined recovery rate**. This rate is a sort of **standard cost** since it is based on figures representing what is supposed to happen (that is, figures from the budget). Using the predetermined absorption rate, the actual cost of production can be established as follows.

	Direct materials
plus:	direct labour
plus:	direct expenses
plus:	overheads (based on the predetermined overhead absorption rate)
equals:	actual cost of production

6.2 Many students become seriously confused about what can appear a very unusual method of costing (actual cost of production including a figure based on the budget). Study the following example. It will help clarify this tricky point.

6.3 EXAMPLE: USING THE PREDETERMINED RECOVERY RATE

Patrick Ltd budgeted to make 100 units of product called Jasmine at a cost of £3 per unit in direct materials and £4 per unit in direct labour. The sales price would be £12 per unit, and production overheads were budgeted to amount to £200. A unit basis of overhead recovery is in operation. During the period 120 units were actually produced and sold (for £12 each) and the actual cost of direct materials was £380 and of direct labour, £450. Overheads incurred came to £210.

What was the cost of sales of product Jasmine, and what was the profit? Ignore administration, selling and distribution overheads.

6.4 SOLUTION

The cost of production and sales is the actual direct cost plus the cost of overheads, absorbed at a predetermined rate as established in the budget. In our example, the overhead recovery rate would be £2 per unit produced (£200 ÷ 100 units).

The actual cost of sales is calculated as follows.

	£
Direct materials (actual)	380
Direct labour (actual)	450
Overheads absorbed (120 units × £2)	240
Full cost of sales, product Jasmine	1,070
Sales of product Jasmine (120 units × £12)	1,440
Profit, product Jasmine	370

6.5 You may already have noticed that the actual overheads incurred, £210, are not the same as the overheads absorbed (that is, included) into the cost of production and hence charged against profit, £240. Nevertheless, in normal absorption costing £240 is the 'correct' cost. The discrepancy between actual overheads incurred, and the overheads absorbed, which is an inevitable feature of absorption costing, is only reconciled at the end of an accounting period, as the **under absorption** or **over absorption** of overhead.

Why does under or over absorption occur?

6.6 The rate of overhead absorption is based on two estimates and so it is quite likely that either one or both of the estimates will not agree with what actually occurs. Overheads incurred will, therefore, probably be either greater than or less than overheads absorbed into the cost of production. Let's consider an example.

6.7 Suppose that the estimated overhead in a production department is £80,000 and the estimated activity is 40,000 direct labour hours. The overhead recovery rate (using a direct labour hour basis) would be £2 per direct labour hour.

Actual overheads in the period are, say £84,000 and 45,000 direct labour hours are worked.

	£
Overhead incurred (actual)	84,000
Overhead absorbed (45,000 × £2)	90,000
Over absorption of overhead	6,000

In this example, the cost of produced units or jobs has been charged with £6,000 more than was actually spent. An adjustment to reconcile the overheads charged to the actual overhead is necessary and the over-absorbed overhead will be written off as an adjustment to the profit and loss account at the end of the accounting period.

6.8 **The overhead absorption rate is predetermined from estimates of overhead cost and the expected volume of activity**. Under or over recovery of overhead will therefore occur in the following circumstances.

(a) Actual overhead costs are different from the estimates.

(b) The actual activity volume is different from the estimated activity volume.

(c) Both actual overhead costs and actual activity volume are different from the estimated costs and volume.

6.9 EXAMPLE: UNDER/OVER ABSORPTION

Watkins Ltd has a budgeted production overhead of £50,000 and a budgeted activity of 25,000 direct labour hours and therefore a recovery rate of £2 per direct labour hour. Calculate the under-/over-absorbed overhead, and the reasons for the under/over absorption, in the following circumstances.

(a) Actual overheads cost £47,000 and 25,000 direct labour hours are worked.
(b) Actual overheads cost £50,000 and 21,500 direct labour hours are worked.
(c) Actual overheads cost £47,000 and 21,500 direct labour hours are worked.

6.10 SOLUTION

(a)

	£
Actual overhead	47,000
Absorbed overhead (25,000 × £2)	50,000
Over-absorbed overhead	3,000

Here there is over absorption because although the actual and estimated direct labour hours are the same, actual overheads cost *less* than expected and so too much overhead has been charged against profit.

(b)

	£
Actual overhead	50,000
Absorbed overhead (21,500 × £2)	43,000
Under-absorbed overhead	7,000

Here there is under absorption because although estimated and actual overhead costs were the same, fewer direct labour hours were worked than expected and hence insufficient overheads have been charged against profit.

(c)

	£
Actual overhead	47,000
Absorbed overhead (21,500 × £2)	43,000
Under-absorbed overhead	4,000

The reason for the under absorption is a combination of the reasons in (a) and (b).

113

6.11 If you are still unsure about when the overhead is under absorbed and when it is over absorbed try looking at it from a different point of view.

(a) If the actual absorption rate that would have been calculated if the actual figures had been known turns out to be less than the estimated one used for absorption then too much overhead will have been absorbed and there will have been **over absorption**.

(b) If the actual rate is more than the estimated one then too little overhead will have been absorbed and there will have been **under absorption**.

The occurrence of under- and over-absorbed overheads can be summarised as follows.

Actual rate	*Absorption of overheads*
Less	Over
More	Under

6.12 EXAMPLE: ABSORPTION OF OVERHEADS

The total production overhead expenditure of Friar Tuck Ltd, the company we encountered earlier in the chapter, was £176,533 and its actual activity was as follows.

	Machine shop A	*Machine shop B*	*Assembly*
Direct labour hours	8,200	6,500	21,900
Machine usage hours	7,300	18,700	-

Using the information in Paragraph 3.6 and the example solution in Paragraph 4.14, calculate the under or over absorption of overheads.

6.13 SOLUTION

		£	£
Actual expenditure			176,533
Overhead absorbed			
Machine shop A	7,300 hrs × £7.94	57,962	
Machine shop B	18,700 hrs × £3.50	65,450	
Assembly	21,900 hrs × £2.24	49,056	
			172,468
Under-absorbed overhead			4,065

ASSESSMENT ALERT

The following equation should help you to calculate the under/over recovery of overheads quickly and easily.

ACTUAL OVERHEADS – ABSORBED OVERHEADS = POSITIVE / NEGATIVE VALUE

- If the result is **NEGATIVE (N)**, there is **OVER ABSORPTION (O)**

- If the result is **POSITIVE (P)**, there is **UNDER ABSORPTION (U)**

Remember **NOPU!**

Activity 5.8

Why does over- or under-absorption of overheads occur?

Activity 5.9

Brave & Hart Ltd has a budgeted production overhead of £214,981 and a budgeted activity of 35,950 hours of direct labour. Before settling on these estimates the company's accountant had a number of other possibilities for each figure, as shown below. Determine (preferably by inspection rather than full calculation) whether overheads will be over or under absorbed in each case if the alternatives turn out to be the actual figures.

Over or under?

(a) $\dfrac{215,892}{35,950}$

(b) $\dfrac{214,981}{36,005}$

(c) $\dfrac{213,894}{36,271}$

(d) $\dfrac{215,602}{35,440}$

7 PREDETERMINED RATES AND ACTUAL COSTS

7.1 Using a **predetermined overhead absorption rate** more often than not leads to under or over absorption of overheads because actual output and overhead expenditure will turn out to be different from estimated output and expenditure. You might well wonder why the complications of under or over absorption are necessary. Surely it would be better to use actual costs and outputs, both to avoid under or over absorption entirely and to obtain more 'accurate' costs of production?

7.2 Suppose that a company draws up a budget (a plan based on estimates) to make 1,200 units of a product in the first half of 20X1. Budgeted production overhead costs, all fixed costs, are £12,000. Due to seasonal demand for the company's product, the volume of production varies from month to month. Actual overhead costs are £2,000 per month. Actual monthly production in the first half of 20X1 is listed below, and total actual production in the period is 1,080 units.

The table below shows the production overhead cost per unit using the following.

(a) A predetermined absorption rate of $\dfrac{£12,000}{1,200}$ = £10 per unit

(b) An actual overhead cost per unit each month

(c) An actual overhead cost per unit based on actual six-monthly expenditure of £12,000 and actual six-monthly output of 1,080 units = £11.11 per unit

				Overhead cost per unit	
			(a)	*(b)*	*(c)*
			Predetermined	*Actual cost*	*Average actual cost*
	Expenditure	*Output*	*unit rate*	*each month*	*in the six months*
Month	*(A)*	*(B)*		*(A) ÷ (B)*	
	£	Units	£	£	£
January	2,000	100	10	20.00	11.11
February	2,000	120	10	16.67	11.11
March	2,000	140	10	14.29	11.11
April	2,000	160	10	12.50	11.11
May	2,000	320	10	6.25	11.11
June	2,000	240	10	8.33	11.11
	12,000	1,080			

7.3 Methods (a) and (c) give a constant overhead cost per unit each month, regardless of seasonal variations in output. Method (b) gives variable unit overhead costs, depending on the time of the year. For this reason, it is argued that method (a) or (c) would provide more useful (long-term) costing information.

7.4 In addition, if prices are based on full cost with a percentage mark-up for profit, method (b) would give seasonal variations in selling prices, with high prices in low-season and low prices in high-season. Methods (a) and (c) would give a constant price based on 'cost plus'.

7.5 With method (a), overhead costs per unit are known throughout the period, and cost statements can be prepared at any time. This is because **predetermined overhead rates are known in advance**. With method (c), overhead costs cannot be established until after the end of the accounting period. For example, overhead costs of output in January 20X1 cannot be established until actual costs and output for the period are known, which will be not until after the end of June 20X1.

7.6 For the reasons given above, **predetermined overhead rates are preferable to actual overhead costs**, in spite of being estimates of costs and in spite of the need to write off under-or over-absorbed overhead costs to the P & L account.

Activity 5.10

Give three reasons why the use of predetermined overheads is seen as being preferable to using actual overheads in costing.

8 FIXED AND VARIABLE OVERHEADS AND CAPACITY

8.1 When an organisation has estimated fixed and variable production overheads, it may calculate a separate absorption rate for each.

(a) A **fixed overhead absorption rate** is intended to share out a fixed cost for a given time period between items of production (or other activities).

(b) A **variable overhead absorption rate** is intended to charge a variable cost to the item of production (or other activity) that is responsible for incurring the cost. Extra activity adds to the total variable overhead cost, and the variable overhead absorption rate is intended to recognise this fact.

8.2 For example, suppose that a company expects its fixed overhead costs in period 9 to be £12,000 and its variable overhead costs to be £1 per direct labour hour.

(a) If the budget is for 4,000 direct labour hours, the absorption rate per hour would be as follows.

	£
Fixed overhead (£12,000 ÷ 4,000)	3
Variable overhead	1
Total	4

(b) If the budget is for 5,000 direct labour hours, the absorption rate per hour would be as follows.

	£
Fixed overhead (£12,000 ÷ 5,000)	2.4
Variable overhead	1.0
Total	3.4

The absorption rate, and so the fully absorbed cost of production, comes down as the budgeted volume of activity rises, but only for fixed overheads, not variable overheads. This is because the (constant) fixed overheads are being shared between a greater number of hours whereas the total variable overhead continues to rise with the volume of activity.

Overhead absorption rates, costs and capacity

8.3 **The importance of the volume of activity in absorption costing cannot be overstated,** not only because large differences between budgeted and actual volume create large amounts of under- or over-absorbed overheads, but also because higher budgeted output reduces absorption rates and costs.

8.4 A major criticism of absorption costing derives from this point. We saw when discussing materials that the modern view is that production should be tailored to demand. Under absorption costing however, managers are tempted to produce, not for the market, but to absorb allocated overheads and reduce unit costs. Production in excess of demand, however, really only increases the overheads (for example warehousing) that the organisation has to bear.

Full capacity, practical capacity and budgeted capacity

8.5 In connection with capacity you may come across a number of terms, as follows.

> ### KEY TERMS
>
> - **Full capacity** is the maximum number of hours that could be worked in ideal conditions.
>
> - **Practical capacity** is full capacity less an allowance for hours lost unavoidably because conditions are not ideal.
>
> - **Budgeted capacity** is the number of hours that a business plans to work.

As a simple example, budgeted capacity would be 60% of practical capacity if a business planned to work a 3 day week rather than a 5 day week. Full capacity would be a 7 day week.

Activity 5.11

What do you understand by the term 'capacity'? What are 'full capacity', 'practical capacity' and 'budgeted capacity'?

---

9 NON-PRODUCTION OVERHEADS

9.1 For **external reporting** (eg statutory accounts) it is not necessary to allocate non-production overheads to products.

9.2 For **internal reporting** purposes and for a number of industries which base the selling price of their product on estimates of *total* cost or even actual cost (such industries usually use a job costing system), a total cost per unit of output may be required. Builders, law firms and garages often charge for their services by adding a percentage profit margin to actual cost. For product pricing purposes and for internal management reports it may therefore be appropriate to allocate non-production overheads to units of output.

117

Bases for apportioning non-production overheads

9.3 A number of non-production overheads such as delivery costs or salespersons' salaries are clearly identified with particular products and can therefore be classified as direct costs. The majority of non-production overheads, however, cannot be directly allocated to particular units of output.

9.4 Two possible methods of allocating such non-production overheads are as follows.

Method 1

9.5 **Choose a basis for the overhead absorption rate** which most closely matches the non-production overhead such as direct labour hours, direct machine hours and so on.

The problem with such a method is that most non-production overheads are unaffected in the short term by changes in the level of output and tend to be fixed costs.

Method 2

9.6 **Allocate non-production overheads on the ability of the products to bear such costs.** One possible approach is to use the production cost as the basis for allocating non-production costs to products.

The **overhead absorption rate** is calculated as follows.

$$\text{Overhead absorption rate} = \frac{\text{Estimated non-production overheads}}{\text{Estimated production costs}}$$

9.7 If, for example, budgeted distribution overheads are £200,000 and budgeted production costs are £800,000, the predetermined distribution overhead absorption rate will be 25% of production cost.

9.8 Other bases for absorbing overheads are as follows.

Types of overhead	Possible absorption base
Selling and marketing	Sales value
Research and development	Consumer cost (= production cost minus cost of direct materials) or added value (= sales value of product minus cost of bought in materials and services)
Distribution	Sales values
Administration	Consumer cost or added value

Administration overheads

9.9 The administration overhead usually consists of the following.

- Executive salaries
- Office rent and rates
- Lighting
- Heating and cleaning the offices

In cost accounting, administration overheads are regarded as periodic charges which are charged against the gross costing profit for the year (as in financial accounting).

Selling and distribution overheads

9.10 **Selling and distribution overheads** are often considered collectively as one type of overhead but they are actually quite different forms of expense.

(a) **Selling costs** are incurred in order to obtain sales

(b) **Distribution costs** begin as soon as the finished goods are put into the warehouse and continue until the goods are despatched or delivered to the customer

9.11 **Selling overhead** is therefore often absorbed on the basis of sales value so that the product lines generating the most income take a large proportion of overhead.

9.12 **Distribution overhead** is more closely linked to production than sales and from one point of view could be regarded as an extra cost of production. It is, however, more usual to regard production cost as ending on the factory floor and to deal with distribution overhead separately. It is generally absorbed on a percentage of production cost but special circumstances, such as size and weight of products affecting the delivery charges, may cause a different basis of absorption to be used.

10 ACTIVITY BASED COSTING

10.1 **Absorption costing** appears to be a relatively straightforward way of adding overhead costs to units of production using, more often than not, a volume-related absorption basis (such as direct labour hours or direct machine hours). **Absorption costing assumes that all overheads are related primarily to production volume.** This system was developed in a time when most organisations produced only a narrow range of products and when overhead costs were only a very small fraction of total costs, direct labour and direct material costs accounting for the largest proportion of the costs. Errors made in adding overheads to products were therefore not too significant.

10.2 Nowadays, however, with the advent of advanced manufacturing technology, overheads are likely to be far more important and in fact direct labour may account for as little as 5% of a product's cost. Moreover, there has been an increase in the costs of service support functions, such as setting-up, production scheduling, first item inspection and data processing, which assist the efficient manufacture of a wide range of products. These overheads are not, in general, affected by changes in production volume. They tend to vary in the long term according to the range and complexity of the products manufactured rather than the volume of output.

10.3 Because absorption costing tends to allocate too great a proportion of overheads to high volume products (which cause relatively little diversity), and too small a proportion of overheads to low volume products (which cause greater diversity and therefore use more support services), alternative methods of costing have been developed. **Activity based costing (ABC)** is one such development.

10.4 The major ideas behind **activity based costing** are as follows.

(a) **Activities cause costs.** Activities include ordering, materials handling, machining, assembly, production scheduling and despatching.

(b) Products create demand for the activities.

(c) Costs are assigned to products on the basis of a product's consumption of the activities.

Outline of an ABC system

10.5   An ABC costing system operates as follows.

Step 1.   Identify an organisation's major activities.

Step 2.   Identify the factors which determine the size of the costs of an activity/cause the costs of an activity. These are known as **cost drivers**. Look at the following examples.

Activity	Cost driver
Ordering	Number of orders
Materials handling	Number of production runs
Production scheduling	Number of production runs
Despatching	Number of despatches

Step 3.   Collect the costs of each activity into what are known as **cost pools** (equivalent to cost centres under more traditional costing methods).

Step 4.   Charge support overheads to products on the basis of their **usage of the activity**. A product's usage of an activity is measured by the number of the activity's cost driver it generates.

Suppose, for example, that the cost pool for the ordering activity totalled £100,000 and that there were 10,000 orders (the cost driver). Each product would therefore be charged with £10 for each order it required. A batch requiring five orders would therefore be charged with £50.

10.6   **Absorption costing** and **ABC** have many similarities. In both systems, **direct costs go straight to the product and overheads are allocated to production cost centres/cost pools.** The main difference is as follows.

(a)   **Absorption costing** uses usually two **absorption bases** (labour hours and/or machine hours) to charge overheads to products.

(b)   **ABC** uses many **cost drivers** as absorption bases (number of orders, number of despatches and so on) to charge overheads to products.

10.7   In summary, ABC has absorption rates which are more closely linked to the cause of the overheads.

Cost drivers

10.8   A **cost driver** is an activity which generates costs. Examples of cost drivers include the following.

- Sales levels as these **drive** the costs of sales commission
- Miles travelled as these **drive** the fuel costs
- Hours worked as these **drive** the costs of labour

10.9   **The principal idea of ABC is to identify cost drivers**. There are no clear-cut rules for selecting cost drivers, just as there are no rules for what to use as the basis for absorbing costs in absorption costing.

10.10 (a)   **Overheads which vary with output** should be traced to products using volume-related cost drivers eg **direct labour hours** or **direct machine hours**.

(b) **Overheads which do not vary with output** should be traced to products using **transaction based cost drivers** eg number of production runs, or number of orders received.

Activity 5.12

What is the difference between absorption costing and activity based costing? Which do you think is preferable?

Activity 5.13

D Vower & Co manufacture an assimilator with unit costs as follows.

	£
Direct labour (12 hours @ £7.50)	90
Materials	428
Direct expenses (22 machine hours @ £6)	132

Planned production for the coming year is 20,000 units and production overheads are expected to be £859,329. Total labour hours are expected to be 318,500 and total machine hours 637,000.

Task

Making any assumptions you think are appropriate, answer the following questions.

(a) Why are total labour hours different from total machine hours?

(b) What is the total production overhead absorbed by products other than the assimilator, if labour hours are used as an absorption base?

(c) What absorption base do you think would be most appropriate for the assimilator? Explain why.

(d) How much overhead is absorbed per unit of the assimilator using machine hours as the absorption base?

Activity 5.14

Blott Ltd have cornered the market in hi-tech mopping up machines. Two models are available, one for domestic use selling for £200 and the other for industrial applications selling for £250. Unit costs are as follows.

	Squeegess £	Imbibulator £
Materials	14	20
Direct labour	90	40
Direct expenses	20	100

Direct labour is paid at the rate of £5 per hour. Direct expenses comprise machine running costs and these are incurred at the rate of £4 per hour.

Production overheads in the coming year are expected to be £1,000,000. Planned production volume is 10,000 of each product.

Tasks

(a) Calculate the absorption rate and the total (direct and indirect) production cost per unit of each product if a single factory overhead absorption rate per direct labour hour is used.

(b) State whether you think the unit costs you have calculated for (a) are fair. If not, describe a fairer approach to overhead absorption at Blott Ltd. Assume that any other information you might need could be made available.

Activity 5.15

OH Incorporated is the US sister company of Blott Ltd. By an extraordinary coincidence, its direct costs, in dollars, happen to be exactly the same as those of Blott Ltd in sterling.

Production overheads for OH Incorporated are expected to be as follows for the two products.

	Squeegess $	*Imbibulator* $
	325,000	625,000

Tasks

(a) Calculate the absorption rate and the total production cost per unit of each product if separate rates per direct labour hour are used for each product.

(b) Calculate the absorption rate and the total production cost of an Imbibulator if the absorption basis is machine hours. Decide whether this is preferable to a labour hour basis for the Imbibulator.

Key learning points

- **Overhead** is the cost incurred in the course of making a product, providing a service or running a department, but which cannot be traced directly and in full to the product, service or department.

- The four main types of overhead are **production, administration, selling** and **distribution.**

- Overheads may be dealt with by **absorption** costing, **activity based** costing or **marginal** costing.

- The main reasons for using absorption costing are for **stock valuations, pricing decisions** and **establishing the profitability of different products.**

- **Allocation, apportionment** and **absorption** are the three stages of calculating the costs of overheads to be charged to manufactured output.

- **Apportionment** is a procedure whereby indirect costs (overheads) are spread fairly between cost centres.

- Service cost centres' costs may be apportioned to production cost centres by the **repeated distribution method,** or the **step-down method.**

- Overhead absorption is the process whereby costs of cost centres are added to unit, job or batch costs. Overhead absorption is sometimes called **overhead recovery.**

- **Predetermined overhead absorption** rates are calculated using budgeted figures.

- A **blanket overhead absorption rate** is an absorption rate used throughout a factory for all jobs and units of output irrespective of the department in which they were produced.

- The actual cost of production is made up of the following.

  o Direct materials
  o Direct labour
  o Direct expenses
  o Overheads (based on the predetermined overhead absorption rate)

- **Under** or **over absorption** of overheads occurs because the predetermined overhead absorption rates are based on forecasts (estimates).

- If an organisation has estimated fixed and variable production overheads, it may calculate a **separate absorption rate** for each.

- The three main types of capacity are **full** capacity, **practical** capacity and **budgeted** capacity.

- **Non-production overheads** may be allocated by choosing a basis for the overhead absorption rate which most closely matches the non-production overhead, or on the basis of a product's ability to bear costs.

- **Activity based costing** is an alternative to absorption costing. It involves the identification of the factors (**cost drivers**) which cause the costs of an organisation's major activities.

Quick quiz

1   What are the three main ways of dealing with overheads?

2   What is the main objective of absorption costing?

3   What are the three stages in charging overheads to units of output?

4   What is overhead apportionment?

5   What are the two stages of overhead apportionment?

6   What are the three methods by which the costs of service cost centres can be apportioned?

7   What is overhead absorption?

8   What is the main argument against the use of blanket overhead absorption rates?

9   What makes up the actual cost of production?

10   In which circumstances will under or over absorption of overheads occur?

11   What are the three types of capacity that you are likely to encounter in absorption costing, and how would you define them?

12   Suggest two possible methods for allocating non-production overheads to products.

13   What are the major ideas behind activity based costing?

Answers to quick quiz

1   Absorption costing, activity based costing and marginal costing.

2   To include an appropriate share of the organisation's total overhead in the total cost of a product.

3   Allocation, apportionment and absorption.

4   A procedure whereby indirect costs (overheads) are spread fairly between cost centres.

5   Sharing out common costs and apportioning service cost centre costs to production cost centres.

6   Direct, repeated distribution and step-down method.

7   The process whereby costs of cost centres are added to unit, job or process costs.

8   The fact that some products will absorb a higher or lower overhead charge than is fair.

9   Direct materials, direct labour, direct expenses and overheads (based on the predetermined overhead absorption rate).

10   •   If actual overhead costs are different from estimates.

        •   If actual activity volume is different from estimated activity volume.

        •   If both actual overhead costs and actual activity are different from estimated costs and activity.

11   •   Full capacity. The maximum number of hours that could be worked in ideal conditions.

        •   Practical capacity. Full capacity less hours lost unavoidably because conditions are not ideal.

        •   Budgeted capacity. The number of hours that a business plans to work.

12   By choosing a basis for the overhead absorption rate which most closely matches the non-production overhead or by allocating the non-production overheads on the product's ability to bear such costs.

13   •   Activities cause costs.
        •   Products create demand for activities.
        •   Costs are assigned to products on the basis of a product's consumption of the activities.

Answers to activities

Answer 5.1

(a) Absorption costing is a method of determining a product cost that includes a proportion of all production overheads incurred in the making of the product and possibly a proportion of other overheads such as administration and selling overheads.

(b) (i) To value stock and comply with SSAP 9
(ii) To fix selling prices
(iii) To compare the profitability of different products

(c) (i) Allocation of costs to cost centres

(ii) Apportionment of costs between cost centres (and reapportionment of service cost centre costs to production cost centres)

(iii) Absorption of costs into cost units

Answer 5.2

Analysis of distribution of actual overhead costs

	Basis	Forming £	Machines £	Assembly £	Machining £	General £	Total £
Directly allocated overheads:							
Repairs, maintenance		800	1,800	300	200	100	3,200
Departmental expenses		1,500	2,300	1,100	900	1,500	7,300
Indirect labour		3,000	5,000	1,500	4,000	2,000	15,500
Apportionment of other overheads:							
Rent, rates	1	1,600	3,200	2,400	400	400	8,000
Power	2	200	450	75	25	0	750
Light, heat	1	1,000	2,000	1,500	250	250	5,000
Dep'n of plant	3	2,500	6,000	750	750	0	10,000
Dep'n of F and F	4	50	25	100	50	25	250
Insurance of plant	3	500	1,200	150	150	0	2,000
Insurance of buildings	1	100	200	150	25	25	500
		11,250	22,175	8,025	6,750	4,300	52,500

Basis of apportionment:

1 floor area
2 effective horsepower
3 plant value
4 fixtures and fittings value

Apportionment of service department overheads to production departments, using the repeated distribution method.

	Forming £	Machines £	Assembly £	Maintenance £	General £	Total £
Overheads	11,250	22,175	8,025	6,750	4,300	52,500
	1,350	3,375	1,350	(6,750)	675	
					4,975	
	995	2,985	498	497	(4,975)	
	99	249	99	(497)	50	
	10	30	5	5	(50)	
	1	3	1	(5)		
	13,705	28,817	9,978	0	0	52,500

Answer 5.3

(a) Possible bases of absorption include the following.

(i) A percentage of direct materials costs
(ii) A percentage of direct labour costs
(iii) A percentage of total direct costs
(iv) A rate per machine hour
(v) A rate per direct labour hour
(vi) A rate per unit
(vii) A percentage of factory cost (for administration overhead)
(viii) A percentage of sales or of factory cost (for selling and distribution overhead)

Anything else that gives a fair share of the costs to cost units is also a possibility.

(b) (i) $\dfrac{£108,000}{90,000}$ = £1.20 per direct labour hour

(ii) $\dfrac{£108,000}{90,000 \times £5} \times 100\%$ = 24% of direct labour cost

Answer 5.4

	Domestic	Industrial
(a) Direct labour cost	£180	£80
Rate per hour	£10	£10
Hours per unit	18	8
Production volume	20,000	20,000
Total labour hours	360,000	160,000

$\dfrac{\text{Total overhead}}{\text{Total labour hours}} = \dfrac{1,040,000}{(360,000 + 160,000)}$ = £2.00 per hour

	Domestic £	Industrial £
Materials	28.00	40.00
Direct labour	180.00	80.00
Direct expenses	40.00	200.00
Direct cost	248.00	320.00
Production overhead (18 × £2.00)/(8 × £2.00)	36.00	16.00
	284.00	336.00

Answer 5.5

Direct apportionment method	Production 1 £	Production 2 £	Service 1 £	Service 2 £
	97,428	84,947	9,384	15,823
Apportion Service 1 costs (20 : 15)	5,362	4,022	(9,384)	–
	102,790	88,969	-	15,823
Apportion Service 2 costs (3 : 8)	4,315	11,508	-	(15,823)
	107,105	100,477	-	-

Answer 5.6

Repeated distribution method	Production 1 £	Production 2 £	Service 1 £	Service 2 £
	97,428	84,947	9,384	15,823
Apportion Service 1 costs (20:15:5)	4,692	3,519	(9,384)	1,173
	102,120	88,466	-	16,996
Apportion Service 2 costs (3:8:1)	4,249	11,331	1,416	(16,996)
	106,369	99,797	1,416	-
Reapportionment (20:15:5)	708	531	(1,416)	177
	107,077	100,328	-	177
Reapportionment (3:8:1)	44	118	15	(177)
	107,121	100,446	15	-
Reapportionment (20:15)	9	6	(15)	-
	107,130	100,452	-	-

Answer 5.7

Step-down method	Production 1 £	Production 2 £	Service 1 £	Service 2 £
	97,428	84,947	9,384	15,823
Apportion Service 1 costs (20:15:5)	4,692	3,519	(9,384)	1,173
	102,120	88,466	-	16,996
Apportion Service 2 costs (3:8)	4,635	12,361	-	(16,996)
	106,755	100,827	-	-

Answer 5.8

The absorption rate is calculated using estimates of both the total overhead likely to be incurred and the total quantity of the chosen basis.

$$\frac{\text{Total overhead}}{\text{Total basis}} = \text{Absorption rate}$$

If either figure turns out to be incorrectly estimated (as it almost certainly will) the estimated absorption rate will have been either too high or too low, and hence over- or under- absorption of overheads will have occurred.

Answer 5.9

You could try to answer this activity by considering how the value of a simple fraction like 4 divided by 2 would increase or decrease as the value of the denominator or numerator varied. Remember that if the actual rate is more than the estimated rate there will be under absorption and vice versa.

(a) Under (because actual production overheads are higher than standard).
(b) Over (because actual hours are higher than standard).
(c) Over (because actual production overheads are lower than standard).
(d) Under (because actual hours are lower than standard).

If you find it difficult to do this by inspection, there is nothing wrong with calculating the estimated rate (£5.98) and then the actual rate in each case (£6.00; £5.97; £5.90; £6.08), but having done this make sure that you can explain in non-numerical terms what has happened. For example, in (c) lower overheads and a higher number of active hours have led to over absorption.

Answer 5.10

(a) A predetermined rate gives a constant overhead cost per unit rather than a fluctuating rate. This is more useful costing information in the long term.

(b) If selling prices were based on full cost plus a percentage mark up, the fluctuating costs which would result from the use of an actual rate would lead to variations in selling prices from period to period. High prices would be charged when demand for the product was at its lowest (because overhead costs would be spread over a smaller number of units) and this would be likely to lead to an even greater fall off in demand. A predetermined rate avoids these problems.

(c) Actual overhead costs are not known in full until the end of a period, which may be too late for costing and price-setting purposes. Predetermined rates are, by nature, known in advance.

Answer 5.11

Capacity means the volume of production that an organisation is capable of achieving. It is usually qualified by an adjective and expressed in hours of production.

(a) Full capacity is the maximum number of hours that could be worked in ideal conditions.
(b) Practical capacity is full capacity less an allowance for hours lost unavoidably.
(c) Budgeted capacity is the number of hours an organisation plans to work in a period.

Answer 5.12

Activity based costing is similar to absorption costing in that it attempts to ascribe to cost units a proportion of overheads. However, it is fairer than absorption costing in that there is an attempt to do this on the basis of what actually caused the cost to be incurred rather than according to some arbitrarily chosen basis. In many circumstances for example overheads will not be reduced if fewer labour hours are worked since their level is not connected to the number of labour hours. They might be significantly reduced if production runs were longer (there would be fewer set ups) and this might entail longer working hours.

Answer 5.13

(a) There is no reason why the total labour hours should be the same as the total machine hours, even if labour's role is confined solely to operating machines. For example the totals could be arrived at as follows.

175 workers × 52 weeks × 5 days × 7 hours = 318,500 hours

350 machines × 52 weeks × 5 days × 7 hours = 637,000 hours

This is just one of an infinite number of possibilities. Labour time and machine time could be almost completely unrelated.

(b) $\dfrac{\text{Total overhead}}{\text{Total labour hours}} = \dfrac{£859,329}{318,500} = £2.70$ per hour

Total labour hours for the assimilator = 12 hours × 20,000 units = 240,000 hours

Therefore overheads absorbed by the assimilator = 240,000 × £2.70 = £648,000

Other products absorb the remainder of the overheads.

	£
Total overhead	859,329
Assimilator	(648,000)
Other products	211,329

(c) A machine hour rate would be more appropriate for the assimilator since it takes more machine hours than labour hours to produce an assimilator and the machine running cost is a larger proportion of the total cost.

(d) Rate per hour = $\dfrac{859,329}{637,000} = £1.35$ per hour

It takes 22 machine hours to make one assimilator.

22 × £1.35 = £29.70 per unit

Answer 5.14

		Squeegess	*Imbibulator*
(a)	Direct labour cost	£90	£40
	Rate per hour	£5	£5
	Hours per unit	18	8
	Production volume	10,000	10,000
	Total labour hours	180,000	80,000

$\dfrac{\text{Total overhead}}{\text{Total labour hours}} = \dfrac{£1,000,000}{(180,000 + 80,000)} = £3.85$ per hour

	Squeegess	Imbibulator
	£	£
Materials	14.00	20.00
Direct labour	90.00	40.00
Direct expenses	20.00	100.00
Direct cost	124.00	160.00
Production overhead (18 × £3.85)/(8 × £3.85)	69.30	30.80
	193.30	190.80

(b) The unit costs are probably not fair because the Squeegess's costs are mainly labour based whereas the Imbibulator's costs appear to be mainly machine based. Because a labour hour basis is used the Squeegess makes a much smaller profit than the Imbibulator. A separate absorption rate for each product would be fairer, but we would need to know what part of the total overhead incurred related to the Squeegess and what part to the Imbibulator.

Answer 5.15

(a) Using separate rates per direct labour hour the absorption rates will be as follows.

	Squeegess	Imbibulator
Total overhead	$325,000	$625,000
Total labour hours	180,000	80,000
Absorption rate per direct labour hour	$1.81	$7.81

The total production cost per unit will therefore be as before except with a different amount of overhead absorbed.

	Squeegess	Imbibulator
	$	$
Direct cost	124.00	160.00
Overhead (18 × $1.81)/(8 × $7.81)	32.58	62.48
	156.58	222.48

(b) On the face of it a machine hour rate is more appropriate since Imbibulator production is machine intensive, but the answer is the same (subject to rounding). Machine hours are $100 ÷ $4 = 25 hours.

10,000 units × 25 hours = 250,000 hours

$$\frac{\text{Total overhead}}{\text{Total machine hours}} = \frac{\$625,000}{250,000} = \$2.50 \text{ per hour}$$

	$
Direct cost	160.00
Overheads (25 × $2.50)	62.50
	222.50

The cost would be the same whatever basis was used because ultimately we are spreading the overhead costs over the same number of units of *one product*.

If the Imbibulator department produced two different sorts of Imbibulator, with different requirements for labour or machine hours, then different unit costs *would* arise, depending upon the absorption basis used.

Part C
Cost accounting principles

Chapter 6   *Cost behaviour*

Chapter topic list

1   Introduction to cost behaviour

2   Cost behaviour patterns

3   Cost behaviour and levels of activity

4   Determination of fixed and variable elements: the high-low technique

---

Learning objectives

On completion of this chapter you will be able to:

	Performance criteria	Range statement
• understand cost behaviour patterns	n/a	n/a
• describe how cost behaviour is affected by levels of activity	n/a	n/a
• use the high-low technique in order to determine fixed and variable elements of costs	n/a	n/a

BPP PUBLISHING

1 INTRODUCTION TO COST BEHAVIOUR

1.1 In Chapter 1, we introduced you to costs in general, and the subject of cost accounting. Since the opening chapter of this Interactive Text, we have met a number of different types of cost. You should now be able to divide costs into the following categories.

- Direct
- Indirect
- Fixed
- Variable

1.2 How would you go about dividing costs into variable costs and fixed costs? Well, you can hopefully remember the general rule which is that **variable costs vary directly with changes in activity levels,** whereas **fixed costs do not vary directly with changes in activity levels.**

1.3 We can demonstrate the ways in which costs behave by drawing graphs. This chapter aims to examine the different ways in which costs behave (this is known as **cost behaviour** analysis) and to demonstrate this behaviour graphically.

KEY TERM

Cost behaviour is the way in which costs are affected by changes in the volume of output (level of activity).

Level of activity

KEY TERM

The **level of activity** refers to the amount of work done, or the number of events that have occurred.

1.4 Depending on circumstances, the level of activity may refer to the volume of production in a period, or the number of items sold, or the value of items sold, the number of invoices issued, the number of invoices received, the number of units of electricity consumed, the labour turnover and so on.

Basic principles of cost behaviour

1.5 The basic principle of cost behaviour is that **as the level of activity rises, costs will usually rise**. It will cost more to produce 2,000 units of output than it will cost to produce 1,000 units; it will usually cost more to make five telephone calls than to make one call and so on.

1.6 This principle is common sense. The problem for the accountant, however, is to determine for each item of cost the way in which costs rise and by how much as the level of activity increases.

For our purposes here, the level of activity for measuring cost will generally be taken to be the volume of production.

2   COST BEHAVIOUR PATTERNS

Fixed costs

2.1   As you already know, a fixed cost is a cost which tends to be unaffected by increases or decreases in the volume of output. Fixed costs are a period charge, in that they relate to a span of time; as the time span increases, so too will the fixed costs (which are sometimes referred to as period costs for this reason).

2.2   A sketch graph of a fixed cost would look like this.

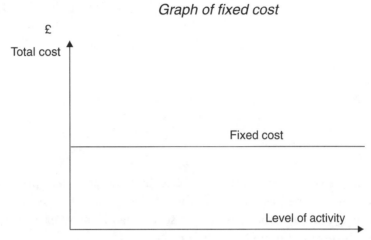

Graph of fixed cost

The following are fixed costs.

(a)   The salary of the managing director (per month or per annum)

(b)   The rent of a single factory building (per month or per annum)

(c)   Straight line depreciation of a single machine (per month or per annum)

Step costs

2.3   Many items of cost are a fixed cost in nature within certain levels of activity. For example the depreciation of a machine may be fixed if production remains below 1,000 units per month, but if production exceeds 1,000 units, a second machine may be required, and the cost of depreciation (on two machines) would go up a step. A sketch graph of a step cost would look like this.

Graph of step cost

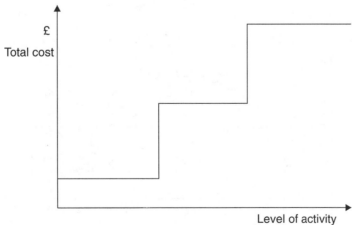

Other examples of step costs are as follows.

(a)   **Rent,** where accommodation requirements increase as output levels get higher.

(b)   **Basic wages.** Basic pay of employees is nowadays usually fixed, but as output rises, more employees (direct workers, supervisors, managers etc) are required.

Variable costs

2.4   A variable cost is a cost which tends to vary directly with the volume of output. The variable cost per unit is the same amount for each unit produced whereas *total* variable cost increases as volume of output increases. A sketch graph of a variable cost would look like this.

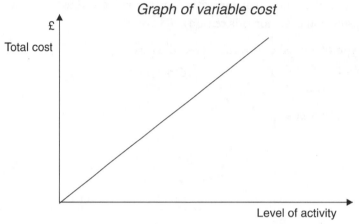

2.5   A constant variable cost per unit implies that the purchase price per unit of material purchased or cost per labour hour worked and so on is constant, and that the rate of material usage/labour productivity is also constant. In other words, **constant rate and efficiency levels are implied in variable costs.**

(a)   The most important variable cost is the cost of raw materials (where there is no discount for bulk purchasing. Bulk purchase discounts reduce the cost of purchases).

(b)   Direct labour costs are, for very important reasons, classed as a variable cost even though basic wages are usually fixed.

(c)   Sales commission is variable in relation to the volume or value of sales.

Mixed costs (or semi-variable costs or semi-fixed costs)

2.6   We had a brief look at mixed costs in Chapter 4. These are cost items which are **part fixed** and **part variable**, and are therefore partly affected by changes in the level of activity.

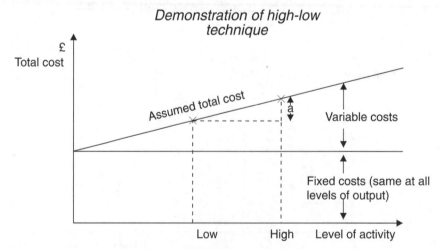

Examples of these costs include electricity and gas bills, both of which are costs where there is normally a standing basic charge plus a variable charge per unit of consumption.

Activity 6.1

Are the following likely to be fixed, variable or mixed costs?

(a) Mobile telephone bill
(b) Annual salary of the chief accountant
(c) The accounting technician's annual membership fee to AAT (paid by the company)
(d) Cost of materials used to pack 20 units of product X into a box
(e) Wages of warehousemen

Other cost behaviour patterns

2.7 Other cost behaviour patterns may be appropriate to certain cost items. Graphs (a) and (b) show the behaviour of the cost of materials after the deduction of a bulk purchase discount.

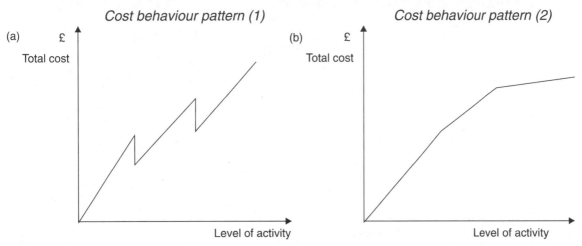

In graph (a) the bulk purchase discount applies retrospectively to all units purchased whereas in graph (b) the discount applies only to units purchased in excess of a certain quantity, the earlier units being paid for at a higher unit cost.

Graph (c) represents an item of cost which is variable with output up to a certain maximum level of cost; graph (d) represents a cost which is variable with output, subject to a minimum (fixed) charge.

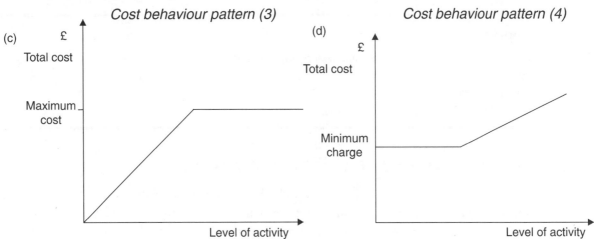

Cost behaviour and total and unit costs

2.8 The following table relates to different levels of production of the Randolph. The variable cost of producing a Randolph is £5. Fixed costs are £5,000.

	1 Randolph £	10 Randolphs £	50 Randolphs £
Total variable cost	5	50	250
Variable cost per unit	5	5	5
Total fixed cost	5,000	5,000	5,000
Fixed cost per unit	5,000	500	100
Total cost (fixed and variable)	5,005	5,050	5,250
Total cost per unit	5,005	505	105

By studying the table above, you should be able to see how different activity levels have an affect on the variable cost per unit, fixed cost per unit and the total cost per unit of a Randolph.

In summary, as activity levels rise:

* the variable cost per unit remains constant;
* the fixed cost per unit falls;
* the total cost per unit falls.

2.9 In sketch graph form this may be illustrated as follows.

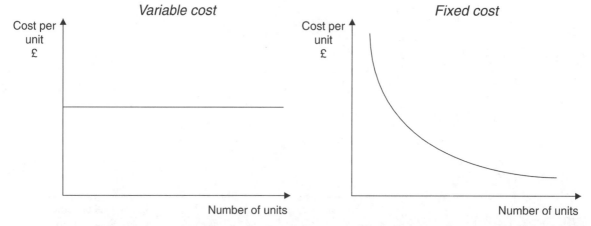

ASSESSMENT ALERT

Be prepared to sketch graphs showing how fixed and variable costs behave in general with changes in the level of production. Remember to use a ruler and a sharp pencil when drawing graphs in an assessment - you are much more likely to impress the assessor if you do so!

Activity 6.2

Draw graphs to illustrate the following cost behaviour patterns.

(a) Variable costs
(b) Fixed costs
(c) Step costs

3 COST BEHAVIOUR AND LEVELS OF ACTIVITY

3.1 The following example highlights how and why costs may be analysed into fixed, variable and stepped cost items. Make sure that you study it carefully and that you have a clear understanding of the cost behaviour principles involved.

3.2 EXAMPLE: COST BEHAVIOUR AND LEVELS OF ACTIVITY

Brandy Snap Ltd has a fleet of company cars for sales representatives. Running costs have been estimated as follows.

(a) Cars cost £12,000 when new, and have a guaranteed trade-in value of £6,000 at the end of two years. Depreciation is charged on a straight-line basis.

(b) Petrol and oil cost 15 pence per mile.

(c) Tyres cost £300 per set to replace; replacement occurs after 30,000 miles.

(d) Routine maintenance costs £200 per car (on average) in the first year and £450 in the second year.

(e) Repairs average £400 per car over two years and are thought to vary with mileage. The average car travels 25,000 miles per annum.

(f) Tax, insurance, membership of motoring organisations and so on cost £400 per annum per car.

Task

Calculate the average cost per annum of cars which travel 20,000 miles per annum and 30,000 miles per annum.

3.3 SOLUTION

Costs may be analysed into fixed, variable and stepped cost items, a stepped cost being a cost which is fixed in nature but only within certain levels of activity.

(a) *Fixed costs*

	£ per annum
Depreciation £(12,000 – 6,000) ÷ 2	3,000
Routine maintenance £(200 + 450) ÷ 2	325
Tax, insurance etc	400
	3,725

(b) *Variable costs*

	Pence per mile
Petrol and oil	15.0
Repairs (£400 ÷ 50,000 miles)	0.8
	15.8

(c) Step costs are tyre replacement costs, which are £300 at the end of every 30,000 miles.

   (i) If the car travels less than or exactly 30,000 miles in two years, the tyres will not be changed. Average cost of tyres per annum = £0.

   (ii) If a car travels more than 30,000 miles and up to (and including) 60,000 miles in two years, there will be one change of tyres in the period. Average cost of tyres per annum = £150 (£300 ÷ 2).

   (iii) If a car exceeds 60,000 miles in two years (up to 90,000 miles) there will be two tyre changes. Average cost of tyres per annum = £300. (£600 ÷ 2).

The estimated costs per annum of cars travelling 20,000 miles per annum and 30,000 miles per annum would therefore be as follows.

	20,000 miles per annum £	30,000 miles per annum £
Fixed costs	3,725	3,725
Variable costs (15.8p per mile)	3,160	4,740
Tyres	150	150
Cost per annum	7,035	8,615

4   DETERMINATION OF FIXED AND VARIABLE ELEMENTS: THE HIGH-LOW TECHNIQUE

4.1   It is generally assumed that costs are one of the following.

- Variable
- Fixed
- Semi-variable

4.2   There are several methods for identifying the fixed and variable elements of semi-variable costs. Each method is only an estimate, and each will produce different results. One of the principal methods is the **high-low technique.**

High-low technique

4.3   Follow the steps below to estimate the fixed and variable elements of semi-variable costs.

Step 1.   Review records of costs in previous periods. Select the following.

- The period with the **highest** activity level
- The period with the **lowest** activity level

Step 2.   Determine the following.

- Total cost at high activity level
- Total cost at low activity level
- Total units at high activity level
- Total units at low activity level

Step 3.   Calculate the following

$$\frac{\text{Total cost at high activity level} - \text{total cost at low activity level}}{\text{Total units at high activity level} - \text{total units at low activity level}} = \text{variable cost per unit (v)}$$

Step 4.   The fixed costs can be determined as follows.

(Total cost at high activity level) – (total units at high activity level × variable cost per unit)

4.4   The following graph demonstrates the high-low technique.

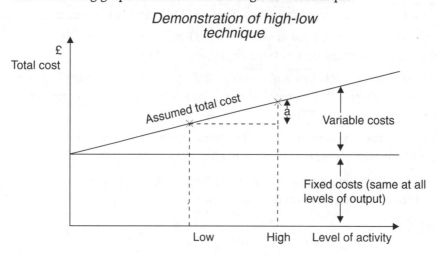

Demonstration of high-low technique

4.5   EXAMPLE: THE HIGH-LOW TECHNIQUE

Gin and Tonic Ltd has recorded the following total costs during the last five years.

Year	Output volume	Total cost
	Units	£
20X3	65,000	145,000
20X4	80,000	160,000
20X5	90,000	170,000
20X6	60,000	140,000
20X7	75,000	155,000

Task

Calculate the total cost that should be expected in 20X8 if output is 85,000 units.

4.6   SOLUTION

Step 1.

- Period with highest activity = 20X5
- Period with lowest activity = 20X6

Step 2.

- Total cost at high activity level = 170,000
- Total cost at low activity level = 140,000
- Total units at high activity level = 90,000
- Total units at low activity level = 60,000

Step 3.   Variable cost per unit (v) is calculated as follows.

$$= \frac{\text{Total cost at high activity level} - \text{total cost at low activity level}}{\text{Total units at high activity level} - \text{total units at low activity level}}$$

$$= \frac{170,000 - 140,000}{90,000 - 60,000} = \frac{30,000}{30,000} = £1 \text{ per unit}$$

Step 4.   Fixed costs (F) are calculated as follows.

F = (Total cost at high activity level) – (total units at high activity level × variable cost per unit)

= 170,000 – (90,000 × 1)

= 170,000 – 90,000

= £80,000

Therefore the costs in 20X8 for output of 85,000 units are as follows.

		£
Variable costs =	85,000 × £1 =	85,000
Fixed costs =		80,000
		165,000

4.7   Note that the step-by-step guide has been covered in order that you fully understand the process involved.

Activity 6.3

The costs of operating the Maintenance department of a computer manufacturer, Port and Lemon Ltd, for the last four months have been as follows.

Month	Output volume units	Total cost £
1	7,000	110,000
2	8,000	115,000
3	7,700	111,000
4	6,000	97,000

Task

What costs should be expected in month 5 when output is expected to be 7,500 units?

Key learning points

- **Cost behaviour patterns** demonstrate the way in which costs are affected by changes in the level of activity.

- Costs which are affected by the level of activity are **variable costs.**

- Costs which are not affected by the level of activity are **fixed costs** or **period costs.**

- **Step costs** are costs which are fixed in nature within certain levels of activity.

- **Mixed costs** (semi-variable/semi-fixed costs) are partly fixed and partly variable, and therefore only partly affected by changes in activity levels.

- The basic principle of cost behaviour is that as the level of activity rises, costs will usually rise.

- The level of activity is the amount of work done or the number of events that have occurred.

- In general as activity levels rise, the variable cost per unit remains constant, the fixed cost per unit falls and the total cost per unit falls.

- The **high-low technique** is used to estimate the fixed and variable elements of semi-variable costs.

Quick quiz

1   How do variable costs differ from fixed costs?

2   How would you describe cost behaviour?

3   What does the level of activity refer to?

4   What is the basic principle of cost behaviour?

5   What is a step cost?

6   How do mixed costs behave?

7   What is the formula used for estimating the variable cost per unit of a product using the high-low technique?

Answers to quick quiz

1   Variable costs vary directly with changes in activity levels, whereas fixed costs do not.

2   The way in which costs vary with the level of activity.

3   The amount of work done or the number of events that have occurred.

4   As the level of activity rises, costs will normally rise.

5   A cost which is fixed in nature within certain levels of activity.

6   They are only partly affected by changes in the level of activity (as they are part-fixed and part-variable costs).

7       $$\frac{\text{Total cost at high activity level - total cost at low activity level}}{\text{Total units at high activity level - total units at low activity level}}$$

Answers to activities

Answer 6.1

(a)   Mixed
(b)   Fixed
(c)   Fixed
(d)   Variable
(e)   Variable

Answer 6.2

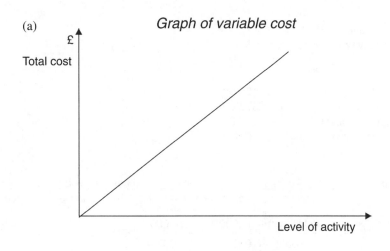

(a)   *Graph of variable cost*

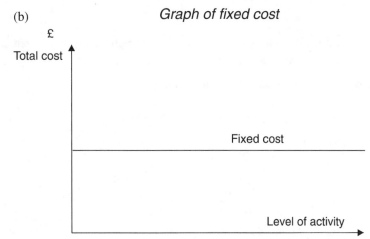

(b)   *Graph of fixed cost*

BPP
PUBLISHING

Graph of step cost

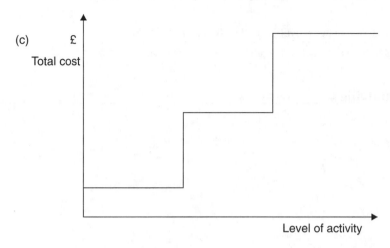

(c) £
Total cost

Level of activity

Answer 6.3

Step 1

Period with highest activity   =   month 2
Period with lowest activity   =   month 4

Step 2

Total cost at high activity level	=	£115,000
Total cost at low activity level	=	£97,000
Total units at high activity level	=	8,000
Total units at low activity level	=	6,000

Step 3

Variable cost per unit   = $\dfrac{\text{Total cost at high activity level} - \text{total cost at low activity level}}{\text{Total units at high activity level} - \text{total units at low activity level}}$

$$= \frac{£(115,000 - 97,000)}{8,000 - 6,000} = \frac{£18,000}{2,000} = £9 \text{ per unit}$$

Step 4

Fixed costs   =   (Total cost at high activity level) – (total units at high activity level × variable cost per unit)

        =   £115,000 – (8,000 × £9) = £115,000 – 72,000   = £43,000

Therefore, the costs in month 5 for output of 7,500 units are as follows.

	£
Variable costs (7,500 × £9)	67,500
Fixed costs	43,000
Total costs	110,500

Chapter 7 Bookkeeping entries for cost information

Chapter topic list

1 Cost information and ledger accounting

2 Getting costs into finished units

3 Control accounts

4 Cost bookkeeping systems

5 Journal entries

Learning objectives

On completion of this chapter you will be able to:

	Performance criteria	Range statement
• code and record cost information	6.1.2, 6.2.1	6.1.1, 6.2.1
• resolve queries or refer them to others as appropriate	6.1.6, 6.2.8	6.1.1, 6.2.1

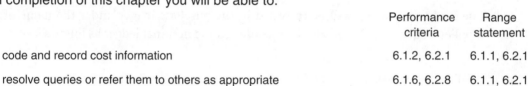

1 COST INFORMATION AND LEDGER ACCOUNTING

1.1 In previous chapters we have scrupulously avoided T accounts, debits and credits, ledgers and bookkeeping. The cost records we have described so far are quite adequate for individual products or jobs, and it is not essential to go beyond this.

1.2 However, unless records of **totals** are maintained and checks of these records are made, there is no way of knowing whether all the costs that should have been recorded really have been recorded. The solution to this problem is **to link the cost records to the cash and credit transactions that are summarised in the nominal ledger**. If you like you can think of recording cost information as dealing with debits. Let us look at an example to illustrate what we mean.

1.3 EXAMPLE: COST INFORMATION AND LEDGER ACCOUNTING

(a) Suppose you buy £100 of materials for cash and £100 on credit. What entries will you make in the ledgers?

(b) From the knowledge you have already acquired elsewhere you should have no difficulty in answering this question. The cash transaction will be recorded in the cash book, analysed as appropriate. It will also be recorded in the nominal ledger as follows.

		£	£
DEBIT	Purchases	100	
CREDIT	Cash		100

(c) The credit transaction will be recorded in the purchase ledger under the name of the supplier in question. It will also be recorded in the nominal ledger as follows.

		£	£
DEBIT	Purchases	100	
CREDIT	Creditors ledger control account		100

(d) Now consider this transaction from the point of view of what you have learnt in this book. The appropriate stores ledger and bin card will have been updated to show the acquisition of £200 worth of stock but the cash and credit side of the transactions have not entered any cost records. In other words, the cost records are only interested in the entry made in the nominal ledger under purchases.

1.4 We could go further and explain that just as the analysed cash book is a very detailed breakdown of the entries in the cash control account in the nominal ledger, and just as the creditors ledger shows the detailed information behind the creditors ledger control account, **the cost records are a detailed breakdown of the information contained in the purchases account, the wages and salaries account, and all the expense accounts in the nominal ledger.**

1.5 It is tempting to go no further than this. So long as you understand the basic principles of double entry bookkeeping, the cost accounting aspects of it should cause you no more difficulty than any other aspects.

1.6 All you really need to know, however, is the following.

(a) How to turn purchases, wages and so on into finished units of production.
(b) How to deal with under-/or over-absorbed overheads

2   GETTING COSTS INTO FINISHED UNITS

2.1   In your studies for other papers you may have come across **stock accounts,** and you may have got used to the idea that entries are only made in these accounts at the year end (the opening stock balance is written off to the profit and loss account and the closing stock balance is carried forward in its place). The following layout should be very familiar.

	P & L	
	£	£
Sales		3,600
Opening stock	500	
Materials	500	
Labour	500	
Production overheads	500	
	2,000	
Closing stock	(200)	
Cost of sales		(1,800)
Gross profit		1,800

2.2   The confusing thing here is that there are three figures that represent stock, but only two that are bold enough to advertise the fact! The figure called **cost of sales** is, of course, stock that has been sold.

2.3   We shall demonstrate how a single purchase of materials works through into the final accounts. The relevant double entries are as follows.

			£	£
(a)	DEBIT	Materials	X	
	CREDIT	Cash		X

   Being the buying of materials which are put into raw materials stock

(b)	DEBIT	Work in progress	X	
	CREDIT	Materials		X

   Being the issue of materials to production for use in work in progress

(c)	DEBIT	Finished goods	X	
	CREDIT	Work in progress		X

   Being the issue of units that are now finished to finished goods stock

(d)	DEBIT	Cost of sales	X	
	CREDIT	Finished goods		X

   Being the taking of units out of finished goods stock and selling them

(e)	DEBIT	Profit and loss account	X	
	CREDIT	Cost of sales		X

   Being the closing off of ledger accounts and the drawing up of financial statements

2.4   Entry (e) would only be made at the end of a period.

2.5   EXAMPLE: BASIC COST ACCOUNTING ENTRIES

Fred Flintstone Ltd begins trading with £200 cash. £200 is initially spent on timber to make garden furniture. £100 worth of timber is left in store, whilst the other £100 is worked on to make garden chairs and tables. Before long, £50 worth of timber has been converted into garden furniture and this furniture is sold for £150. How will these events and transactions be reflected in the books?

2.6   SOLUTION

CASH ACCOUNT

	£		£
Cash - opening balance	200	Purchase of materials	200
Sale of finished goods	150	Closing balance	150
	350		350

MATERIALS ACCOUNT

	£		£
Cash purchase	200	Transfer to WIP	100
		Closing balance	100
	200		200

WORK IN PROGRESS ACCOUNT

	£		£
Transfer from materials	100	Transfer to finished goods	50
		Closing balance	50
	100		100

FINISHED GOODS ACCOUNT

	£		£
Transfer from WIP	50	Transfer to cost of sales	50
	50		50

COST OF SALES ACCOUNT

	£		£
Transfer from finished goods	50	Shown in profit and loss account	50
	50		50

SALES ACCOUNT

	£		£
Shown in profit and loss account	150	Cash	150
	150		150

FRED FLINTSTONE LTD
PROFIT AND LOSS ACCOUNT

	£
Sales	150
Cost of sales	50
Profit	100

FRED FLINTSTONE LTD
BALANCE SHEET

	£	£
Cash		150
Stocks: materials	100	
WIP	50	
		150
		300
Capital: b/f		200
profit		100
		300

146

2.7 The principle, as you can see, is very straightforward. We have not included entries for labour costs or direct expenses to keep things simple, but these are treated in the same way. Instead of amounts being debited initially to the materials account, they would be debited to the labour costs or direct expenses accounts (with cash being credited). They would then be transferred to work in progress and the other entries would be as for materials. Overheads are slightly more (but not much more) problematic.

Accounting for labour costs

2.8 We will use an example to briefly review the principal bookkeeping entries for wages.

2.9 EXAMPLE: THE WAGES CONTROL ACCOUNT

The following details were extracted from a weekly payroll for 750 employees at a factory in Trinidad.

Analysis of gross pay

	Direct workers £	Indirect workers £	Total £
Ordinary time	36,000	22,000	58,000
Overtime: basic wage	8,700	5,430	14,130
premium	4,350	2,715	7,065
Shift allowance	3,465	1,830	5,295
Sick pay	950	500	1,450
Idle time	3,200	-	3,200
	56,665	32,475	89,140
Net wages paid to employees	£45,605	£24,220	£69,825

Task

Prepare the wages control account for the week.

2.10 SOLUTION

(a) **The wages control account** acts as a sort of **collecting place** for net wages paid and deductions made from gross pay. The gross pay is then analysed between **direct** and **indirect wages**.

(b) The first step is to determine which wage costs are **direct** and which are **indirect**. The direct wages will be debited to the **work in progress account** and the indirect wages will be debited to the **production overhead account**.

(c) There are in fact only two items of direct wages cost in this example, the ordinary time (£36,000) and the basic overtime wage (£8,700) paid to direct workers. All other payments (including the overtime premium) are indirect wages.

(d) The net wages paid are debited to the control account, and the balance then represents the deductions which have been made for income tax, national insurance, and so on.

WAGES CONTROL ACCOUNT

	£		£
Bank: net wages paid	69,825	Work in progress - direct labour	44,700
Deductions control accounts*		Production overhead control:	
(£89,140 – £69,825)	19,315	Indirect labour	27,430
		Overtime premium	7,065
		Shift allowance	5,295
		Sick pay	1,450
		Idle time	3,200
	89,140		89,140

* In practice there would be a separate deductions control account for each type of deduction made (for example, PAYE and National Insurance).

Activity 7.1

What items are included in a wages control account?

3   CONTROL ACCOUNTS

Control accounts

KEY TERM

A **control account** is an account which records total cost. In contrast, individual ledger accounts record individual debits and credits.

3.1   Obviously the previous section is highly simplified. This is to avoid obscuring the basic principles. For example, we have until now assumed that if £200 of materials are purchased the only entries made will be Dr Materials, Cr Cash. In practice, of course, this £200 might be made up of 20 different types of material, each costing £10, and if so each type of material is likely to have its own sub-account. These sub-accounts would be exactly like individual personal accounts in the creditors' ledger or the debtors' ledger. You have probably guessed that we need to use **control accounts** to summarise the detailed transactions (such as how the £200 of materials is made up) and to maintain the double entry in the nominal ledger.

KEY TERMS

- A **materials control account** (or **stores control account**) records the total cost of invoices received for each type of material (purchases) and the total cost of each type of material issued to various departments (the sum of the value of all materials requisition notes).

- A **wages control account** records the total cost of the payroll (plus employer's national insurance contributions) and the total cost of direct and indirect labour as recorded in the wages analysis sheets and charged to each production unit, job, or batch.

- A **production overhead control account** is a total record of actual expenditure incurred and the amount absorbed into individual units, jobs or batches. Subsidiary records for actual overhead expenditure items and cost records which show the overheads attributed to individual units or jobs must agree with or reconcile to the totals in the control account.

- A **work in progress control account** records the total costs of direct materials, direct wages and production overheads charged to units, jobs or batches, and the cost of finished goods which are completed and transferred to the distribution department. Subsidiary records of individual job costs and so on will exist for jobs still in production and for jobs completed.

3.2 The precise level of detail depends entirely upon the individual organisation. For example an organisation that makes different products might want a hierarchy of materials accounts as follows.

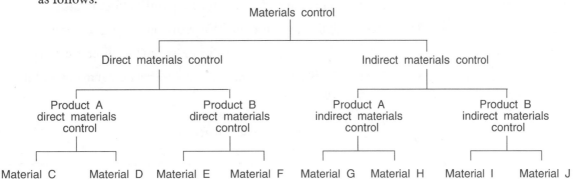

Coding

3.3 Each account in use needs to be classified by the use of coding. A suggested computer-based four-digit numerical coding account system is set out as follows.

Basic structure	Code number	Allocation
(a) First division	1000 – 4999	This range provides for cost accounts and is divided into four main departmental sections with ten cost centre subsections in each department, allowing for a maximum of 99 accounts in each cost centre
Second division	1000 – 1999 2000 – 2999 3000 – 3999 4000 – 4999	Departments 1 to 4
Third division	000 – 099 100 – 199 200 – 299 and so on	Facility for ten cost centres in each department
Fourth division	 01 – 39 40 – 79 80 – 99	Breakdown of costs in each cost centre direct costs indirect costs spare capacity
(b)	5000 – 5999	This range provides for the following. (i) Revenue accounts (ii) Work in progress accounts (iii) Finished goods accounts (iv) Cost of sales accounts (v) General expenses accounts (vi) Profit and loss account
(c)	6000 – 6999	This range provides for individual stores items
(d)	7000 – 7999	This range provides for individual debtor accounts
(e)	8000 – 8999	This range provides for individual creditor accounts
(f)	9000 – 9999	This range is used for balance sheet accounts including the following. (i) Stores control account (ii) Debtors' control account (iii) Creditors' control account

3.4 An illustration of the coding of direct labour (grade T) might be as follows.

Department 2

Cost centre	1	2	3	4
Direct labour (grade T)	2009	2109	2209	2309

3.5 The four digit code is explained as follows.

(a) The first digit, 2, refers to department 2.

(b) The second digit 0, 1, 2 or 3 refers to the cost centre which incurred the cost.

(c) The last two digits, 09, refer to 'direct labour costs, grade T'.

3.6 Obviously systems that you come across in practice will exhibit different features. The above describes only broad characteristics that are likely to be typical of all such systems.

Activity 7.2

The following data relate to the stores ledger control account of Fresh Ltd, an air freshener manufacturer, for the month of April 20X0.

	£
Opening stock	18,500
Closing stock	16,100
Deliveries from suppliers	142,000
Returns to suppliers	2,300
Cost of indirect materials issued	25,200

Tasks

(a) Calculate the value of the issue of direct materials during April 20X0.
(b) State the double entry to record the issue of direct materials in the cost accounts.

4 COST BOOKKEEPING SYSTEMS

4.1 There are two types of cost bookkeeping system, the **interlocking** and the **integrated**. Interlocking systems require separate ledgers to be kept for the cost accounting function and the financial accounting function, which means that the cost accounting profit and financial accounting profit have to be reconciled. Integrated systems, on the other hand, combine the two functions in one set of ledger accounts.

4.2 Modern cost accounting systems (computerised) integrate cost accounting information and financial accounting information and are known as **integrated systems.** You are much more likely to deal with integrated systems, and this is the system we shall be looking at in detail.

> **KEY TERM**
>
> An **integrated system** is a system where the cost accounting function and the financial accounting function are combined in one system of ledger accounts.

4.3 A system of **integrated accounts combines** the financial and cost accounts in one set of self-balancing ledger accounts.

4.4 In addition to the classifications used in the cost ledger, the following ledger accounts would be required.

- Debtors' and creditors' control accounts
- Bank account
- Fixed asset account
- Other assets and liabilities accounts
- Share capital account, retained profit account and other reserve accounts

4.5 The following diagram shows a cost accounting system which uses absorption costing. The entries in the individual accounts have been simplified. Study the diagram carefully, and work through the double entries represented in the diagram. Make sure that you understand the logic behind the flow of costs and then study the following example.

Cost accounting using absorption costing

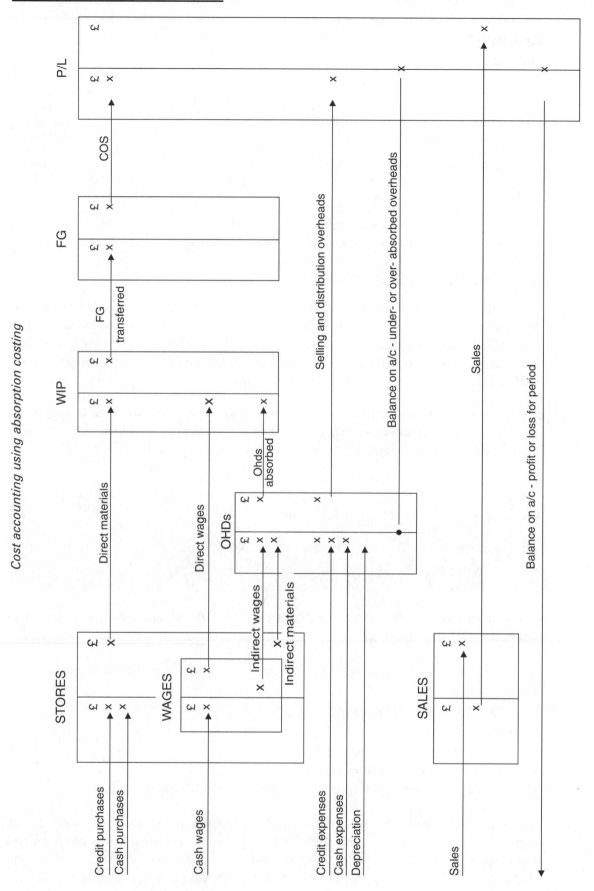

Dealing with overheads

4.6 We have already mentioned that the bookkeeping entries for overheads are not as straight forward as those for materials, labour and expenses. We shall now consider the way in which overheads are dealt with in a cost accounting system.

4.7 When an absorption costing system is in use, we now know that the amount of overhead included in the cost of an item is absorbed at a predetermined rate. The entries made in the cash book and the nominal ledger, however, are the actual amounts.

4.8 As we saw in an earlier chapter, it is highly unlikely that the actual amount and the predetermined amount will be the same. The difference is called **under- or over-absorbed overhead**. To deal with this in the cost accounting books, therefore, we need to have an account to collect under- or over-absorbed amounts for each type of overhead.

4.9 EXAMPLE: THE UNDER-/OVER-ABSORBED OVERHEAD ACCOUNT

Gnocci Ltd absorbs production overheads at the rate of £0.50 per operating hour and administration overheads at 20% of the production cost of sales. Actual data for one month was as follows.

Administration overheads	£32,000
Production overheads	£46,500
Operating hours	90,000
Production cost of sales	£180,000

What entries need to be made for overheads in the ledgers?

4.10 SOLUTION

PRODUCTION OVERHEADS ACCOUNT

	£		£
Cash	46,500	Absorbed into WIP (90,000 × £0.50)	45,000
		Under-absorbed overhead	1,500
	46,500		46,500

ADMINISTRATION OVERHEADS ACCOUNT

	£		£
Cash	32,000	To cost of sales (180,000 × 0.2)	36,000
Over-absorbed overhead	4,000		
	36,000		36,000

UNDER-/OVER-ABSORBED OVERHEAD ACCOUNT

	£		£
Production overhead	1,500	Administration overhead	4,000
Balance to profit and loss a/c	2,500		
	4,000		4,000

Less production overhead has been absorbed than has been spent so there is under-absorbed overhead of £1,500. More administration overhead has been absorbed (into cost of sales, note, not into WIP) and so there is over-absorbed overhead of £4,000. The net over-absorbed overhead of £2,500 is a credit in the profit and loss account.

4.11 EXAMPLE: INTEGRATED ACCOUNTS

Shown below are the opening balances for the month of September 20X0 for Vermicelli Ltd, with a summary bank account and information obtained from the stores department, the payroll department and the production department. The provisions for depreciation are also given below. During the month £196,000 worth of goods were sold (all on credit) for £278,000.

OPENING BALANCES - SEPTEMBER 20X0

	Dr £'000	Cr £'000
Raw materials stores account	30	
Work in progress account	20	
Finished goods account	60	
Debtors account	74	
Creditors account		85
Creditors for National Insurance & PAYE		19
Factory buildings account	250	
Provision for depreciation: factory and buildings		20
Equipment account	320	
Provision for depreciation: equipment		170
Share capital account		100
Share premium account		20
Profit and loss reserves		290
Cash and bank account		50
	754	754

STORES REPORT - SEPTEMBER 20X0

	£'000
Materials received from suppliers and invoiced	40
Materials issued to production	32
Materials issued to production service departments	8
Materials issued to administrative departments	2

PAYROLL REPORT - SEPTEMBER 20X0

	Gross wages £'000	PAYE & employees' NI £'000	Net £'000	Employer's NI £'000
Direct wages (£5.50 per hour)	33	8	25	2
Production indirect wages	7	1	6	-
Administrative staff wages and salaries	10	3	7	1
Selling staff wages and salaries	10	3	7	1
	60	15	45	4

PRODUCTION REPORT - SEPTEMBER 20X0

Production overhead absorption rate	£12.50 per direct labour hour
Value of work completed in the month	£150,000

CASH AND BANK ACCOUNT

	£'000		£'000
Debtors	290	Balance b/f	50
		Wages and salaries	45
		Production overhead	15
		Administration overhead	8
		Selling overhead	20
		Creditor for national insurance and PAYE	19
		Creditors	45
		Balance c/f (surplus)	88
	290		290
Balance b/f	88		

PROVISIONS FOR DEPRECIATION - SEPTEMBER 20X0

	£'000
Factory and buildings	2
Factory equipment	35
Office equipment	5
	42

Tasks

(a) Post the information given in the example to the integrated accounts of Vermicelli Ltd.

(b) Prepare a trial balance for Vermicelli Ltd, as at 30 September 20X0.

(c) Prepare a trading and profit loss account for Vermicelli Ltd for September 20X0.

4.12 SOLUTION

(a)   RAW MATERIALS STORES ACCOUNT

	£'000		£'000
Balance b/f	30	Work in progress account	32
Creditors	40	Production overhead account	8
		Administration overhead account	2
		Balance c/f	28
	70		70
Balance b/f	28		

WAGES AND SALARIES ACCOUNT

	£'000		£'000
Bank	45	Work in progress	33
Creditor for national insurance and PAYE	15	Production overhead	7
		Administration overhead	10
		Selling overhead	10
	60		60

PRODUCTION OVERHEAD ACCOUNT

	£'000		£'000
Raw materials stores	8	Work in progress	75
Wages and salaries	7		
Bank (expenses)	15		
Depreciation: buildings	2		
Depreciation: equipment	35		
Over-absorbed overhead (bal fig)	8		
	75		75

WORK IN PROGRESS ACCOUNT

	£'000		£'000
Balance b/f	20	Finished goods	150
Raw materials stores	32		
Wages and salaries	33		
Creditor for national insurance	2		
Production overhead	75	Balance c/f	12
	162		162
Balance b/f	12		

FINISHED GOODS ACCOUNT

	£'000		£'000
Balance b/f	60	Cost of sales	196
Work in progress	150	Balance c/f	14
	210		210
Balance b/f	14		

COST OF SALES ACCOUNT

	£'000		£'000
Finished goods	196	Profit and loss account	196

ADMINISTRATION OVERHEAD ACCOUNT

	£'000		£'000
Raw materials stores	2	Profit and loss account	26
Wages and salaries	10		
Bank (expenses)	8		
Creditor for national insurance	1		
Depreciation	5		
	26		26

SELLING OVERHEAD ACCOUNT

	£'000		£'000
Wages and salaries	10	Profit and loss account	31
Bank (expenses)	20		
Creditor for national insurance	1		
	31		31

UNDER-/OVER-ABSORBED OVERHEAD ACCOUNT

	£'000		£'000
Profit and loss account	8	Production overhead account	8

SALES ACCOUNT

	£'000		£'000
Profit and loss account	278	Debtors	278

TRADING AND PROFIT AND LOSS ACCOUNT

	£'000		£'000
Cost of sales	196	Sales	278
Gross profit c/d	82		
	278		278
Administration overhead	26	Gross profit b/d	82
Selling overhead	31	Over-absorbed overhead	8
Profit and loss reserves	33		
	90		90

DEBTORS ACCOUNT

	£'000		£'000
Balance b/f	74	Bank	290
Sales	278	Balance c/f	62
	352		352
Balance b/f	62		

CREDITORS ACCOUNT

	£'000		£'000
Bank	45	Balance b/f	85
Balance c/f	80	Raw materials stores	40
	125		125
		Balance b/f	80

CREDITOR FOR NATIONAL INSURANCE & PAYE

	£'000		£'000
Bank	19	Balance b/f	19
		Wages and salaries	15
Balance c/f	19	Employer's contributions:	
		Work in progress	2
		Administration overhead	1
		Selling overhead	1
	38		38
		Balance b/f	19

FACTORY BUILDINGS ACCOUNT

	£'000		£'000
Balance b/f	250	Balance c/f	250

PROVISION FOR DEPRECIATION: FACTORY AND BUILDINGS

	£'000		£'000
Balance c/f	22	Balance b/f	20
		Charge for September 19X8	2
	22		22
		Balance b/f	22

EQUIPMENT ACCOUNT

	£'000		£'000
Balance b/f	320	Balance c/f	320

PROVISION FOR DEPRECIATION: EQUIPMENT

	£'000		£'000
Balance c/f	210	Balance b/f	170
		Factory equipment charge	35
		Office equipment charge	5
	210		210
		Balance b/f	210

SHARE CAPITAL ACCOUNT

	£'000		£'000
Balance c/f	100	Balance b/f	100

SHARE PREMIUM ACCOUNT

	£'000		£'000
Balance c/f	20	Balance b/f	20

PROFIT AND LOSS RESERVES

	£'000		£'000
Balance c/f	323	Balance b/f	290
		Profit and loss account	33
	323		323
		Balance b/f	323

(b) The trial balance as at 30 September 20X0 is as follows.

	DR		CR
	£'000		£'000
Raw materials stores	28	Creditors	80
Work in progress	12	Creditor for national insurance	
Finished goods	14	and PAYE	19
Cash and bank	88	Provision for depreciation:	
Debtors	62	Factory and buildings	22
Factory and buildings	250	Equipment	210
Equipment	320	Share capital	100
		Share premium	20
		Profit and loss reserves	323
	774		774

The amount of production overhead transferred to WIP is calculated by multiplying the rate given (£12.50 per direct labour hour) by the number of direct labour hours, which was £33,000/£5.50 = 6,000.

$$£12.50 \times 6,000 = £75,000$$

We are not told that administration and selling overheads are absorbed into units produced, so we must assume that the actual costs are charged in full in the period in which they are incurred. A 'vertical' profit and loss account may make this clearer.

(c)   VERMICELLI LTD PROFIT & LOSS ACCOUNT
      30 SEPTEMBER 20X0

	£'000	£'000
Sales		278
Opening stocks (30 + 20 + 60)	110	
Direct materials purchased (40 – 8 – 2)	30	
Wages and salaries (33 + 2)	35	
Production overhead	75	
	250	
Closing stocks (28 + 12 + 14)	(54)	
Cost of sales		196
Gross profit		82
Administration overhead	26	
Selling overhead	31	
Over-absorbed overhead	(8)	
		(49)
Net profit		33

ASSESSMENT ALERT

In an assessment, be prepared to complete partially completed cost accounts, and always make sure that your debits equal your credits!

Activity 7.3

What would be the double entry to describe the following events in an integrated accounts system.

(a)   Materials costing £10,000 are purchased on credit and put into stock.   *DR RAW MATS   CR CREDITORS*
(b)   Finished units costed at £50,000 are made available for sale.   *DR FG   CR WIP.*
(c)   Materials valued at £5,000 are issued to the administration department.   *DR ADMIN O/HEADS   CR RAW MATS*
(d)   Indirect production wages of £20,000 are charged to the production department.   *DR: PRODUCTION O/HEAD   CR WAGES CONTROL*

Activity 7.4

In the absence of the accountant you have been asked to prepare a month's cost accounts for Liverpool Ltd, a company which operates a costing system which is fully **integrated** with the financial accounts. The cost clerk has provided you with the following information.

(a)   Balances at beginning of month

	£
Stores ledger control account	24,175
Work in progress control account	19,210
Finished goods control account	34,164
Creditors control account	15,187
Prepayments of production overheads brought forward from previous month	2,100

(b)   Information relating to events during the month

		£
Materials purchased		76,150
Materials issued from stores		29,630
Gross wages paid:	direct workers	15,236
	indirect workers	4,232
Recorded non-productive time of direct workers		5,230
Payments to creditors		58,320
Selling and distribution overheads incurred		5,240
Other production overheads incurred but not yet paid for		14,200
Sales		75,400
Cost of finished goods sold		59,830
Cost of goods completed and transferred into finished goods store during the month		62,130

(c)   Balances at end of month

	£
Physical stock value of work in progress at month end	24,800

(d)   The production overhead absorption rate is 150% of direct wages. $= £22\,854$

Task

Prepare the following accounts for the month.

Stores ledger control account
Work in progress control account
Finished goods control account
Production overhead control account
Creditors control account
Profit and loss account

Advantages and limitations of integrated cost accounting systems

4.13   The main **advantage** of integrated systems is the saving in administration time and costs. This is because only one set of accounts needs to be maintained instead of two. There is also no need to reconcile the profits of the separate cost and financial accounts.

4.14   The main **disadvantage** of integrated accounts is that one set of accounts is expected to fulfil two different purposes, the cost accounts provide internal management information and the financial accounts are used for external reporting. At times external reporting and internal management information may conflict. For example, for external reporting, stocks will be valued in accordance with SSAP 9. Cost accountants may however prefer to value stocks at marginal cost. It is clear therefore that in some circumstances it is more advantageous to have two separate systems.

Interlocking accounts

4.15   Before we move onto the next section of this chapter, we shall have a brief look at **interlocking accounts.**

4.16   An interlocking system features the following ledgers.

- The **financial ledger**
- The **cost ledger** which contains cost information

4.17 In addition to the usual accounts that are held in the financial and cost ledger, there are also the following control accounts.

- Cost ledger control account
- Financial ledger control account

4.18 The **cost ledger control account** includes certain items of cost, revenue or profit which are financial accounting items.

4.19 The **financial ledger control account** is a sort of 'dustbin' account which is used to keep the double entry system working.

4.20 We can summarise the principal accounts in a system of interlocking accounts as follows.

(a) The resources accounts

- Materials control account or stores control account
- Wages (and salaries) control account
- Production overhead control account
- Administration overhead control account
- Selling and distribution overhead control account

(b) Accounts which record the cost of production items from the start of production work through to cost of sales

- Work in progress control account
- Finished goods control account
- Cost of sales control account

(c) Sales account

(d) The costing profit and loss account

(e) The under-/over-absorbed overhead account

(f) Cost ledger control account (in the cost ledger)

(g) Financial ledger control account (in the financial ledger)

5 JOURNAL ENTRIES

5.1 Let us demonstrate the preparation of journal entries in an integrated system by means of an example.

5.2 EXAMPLE: JOURNAL ENTRIES

The following information relates to Cake Ltd.

	Gross wages £'000	PAYE and employees' NI £'000	Net £'000	Employer's NI £'000
Direct wages (£5.50 per hour)	33	8	25	2
Production indirect wages	7	1	6	-
Administrative staff wages and salaries	10	3	7	1
Selling staff wages and salaries	10	3	7	1
	60	15	45	4

Task

Prepare journal entries so as to record the above information in a set of integrated accounts.

5.3 SOLUTION

		£'000	£'000
DR	Wages and salaries control account	45	
CR	Cash/bank account		45
DR	Wages and salaries control account	15	
CR	Creditor for PAYE and NI		15
DR	WIP control account	33	
CR	Wages and salaries control account		33
DR	Production overhead control account	7	
CR	Wages and salaries control account		7
DR	Administration overhead control account	10	
CR	Wages and salaries control account		10
DR	Selling overhead control account	10	
CR	Wages and salaries control account		10
DR	WIP control account	2	
CR	Creditor for PAYE and NI		2
DR	Administration overhead control account	1	
CR	Creditor for PAYE and NI		1
DR	Selling overhead control account	1	
CR	Creditor for PAYE and NI		1

Activity 7.5

Crediton Debbit Ltd manufactures a range of products which are sold through a network of wholesalers and dealers. A set of integrated accounts is kept, and for the year 20X0 the following information is relevant.

(a) Production overhead is absorbed into the cost of products on the basis of a budgeted rate of 80% of direct labour cost.

(b) Finished stocks are valued at factory cost.

(c) The selling price to wholesalers and dealers includes a profit margin of 25% on actual production cost.

(d)

	31 March 19X8 £	30 April 19X8 £
Raw materials stock	17,200	15,160
Work in progress	5,600	4,750
Finished goods stock	10,500	12,090
Debtors for goods sold	9,200	11,140
Creditors for raw materials	7,600	9,420
Fixed assets at net book value	6,000	5,800

(e) Bank transactions for the month of April 20X0 were as follows.

	£
Bank balance at 31 March	1,500
Receipts from debtors	27,560
Payments made	
Direct labour	6,400
Creditors for raw materials	8,960
Production overhead	5,200
Administration overhead	700
Selling and distribution overhead	2,300

(f) Production overhead includes a monthly charge of £200 for depreciation and the opening balance on the production overhead control account each month is nil. Administration, selling and distribution overheads consist entirely of cash items.

162

Task

Use the information above to write up the following control accounts.

(a)   Raw materials stock
(b)   Work in progress
(c)   Finished goods stock
(d)   Production overhead

Key learning points

- A **control account** is an account which records total cost, unlike an individual ledger account which records individual debits and credits.

- There are two main types of cost bookkeeping system, **interlocking systems** and **integrated systems.**

- An **integrated system** is one in which the cost accounting function and the financial accounting function are combined in one system of ledger accounts.

- Integrated systems have the **advantage** of saving administrative time and effort because they only maintain one set of accounts.

- Integrated systems have the **disadvantage** of having to fulfil two different purposes which may, at some time or another conflict.

- The **wages control account** acts as a collecting place for wages before they are analysed into work in progress and production overhead control accounts.

Quick quiz

1   What is a control account?

2   What are the two types of cost bookkeeping system?

3   What are the two additional control accounts found in interlocking accounting systems known as?

4   Where are direct expenses and overheads collected?

Answers to quick quiz

1   An account which records total cost, as opposed to individual costs (which are recorded in individual ledger accounts).

2   Integrated and interlocking.

3   Financial ledger control account and cost ledger control account.

4   In the work in progress control account.

Answers to activities

Answer 7.1

Entries in a wages control account would include total cost of payroll plus employer's national insurance contributions. Entries would also include transfers to work-in-progress accounts in respect of direct labour, and transfers to overhead accounts in respect of indirect labour.

Answer 7.2

(a)   Since we are given no information on the issue of direct materials we need to construct a stores ledger control account.

STORES LEDGER CONTROL ACCOUNT

	£		£
Balance b/f	18,500	Creditors/cash (returns)	2,300
Creditors/cash	142,000	Overhead accounts	25,200
		WIP (balancing figure)	116,900
		Balance c/f	16,100
	160,500		160,500

The value of the issue of direct materials during April 20X0 was £116,900.

(b)   The issue of direct materials would therefore be recorded as follows.

DR	WIP control account	£116,900
CR	Stores ledger control account	£116,900

Answer 7.3

			£	£
(a)	DEBIT	Materials	10,000	
	CREDIT	Creditors		10,000
(b)	DEBIT	Finished goods	50,000	
	CREDIT	Work in progress		50,000
(c)	DEBIT	Administration overhead	5,000	
	CREDIT	Materials		5,000
(d)	DEBIT	Production overhead	20,000	
	CREDIT	Wages		20,000

Answer 7.4

STORES LEDGER CONTROL ACCOUNT

	£		£
Opening balance b/f	24,175	Work in progress control	
Creditors control		(materials issued)	29,630
(materials purchased)	76,150	Closing stock c/f	70,695
	100,325		100,325

WORK IN PROGRESS CONTROL ACCOUNT

	£		£
Opening balance b/f	19,210	Finished goods control	
Stores ledger account		(cost of goods transferred)	62,130
(materials issued)	29,630	Closing stock c/f	24,800
Wages control			
(direct wages)	15,236		
Production overhead control			
(overhead absorbed			
15,236 × 150%)	22,854		
	86,930		86,930

FINISHED GOODS CONTROL ACCOUNT

	£		£
Opening balance b/f	34,164	Profit and loss account	
Work in progress control		(cost of sales)	59,830
(cost of goods completed)	62,130	Closing stock c/f	36,464
	96,294		96,294

PRODUCTION OVERHEAD CONTROL ACCOUNT

	£		£
Prepayments b/f	2,100	Work in progress control	
Wages control (idle time		(overheads absorbed)	22,854
of direct workers)	5,230	Profit and loss account (under-	
Wages control (indirect		absorbed overhead) (bal.)	2,908
workers wages)	4,232		
Creditors control (other			
overheads incurred)	14,200		
	25,762		25,762

CREDITORS CONTROL ACCOUNT

	£		£
Cash account (payments)	58,320	Opening balance b/f	15,187
Creditors c/f	47,217	Stores ledger control	
		(materials purchased)	76,150
		Production overhead control	
		(other overheads)	14,200
	105,537		105,537

PROFIT AND LOSS ACCOUNT

	£		£
Finished goods control		Sales	75,400
(cost of goods sold)	59,830		
Gross profit c/f	15,570		
	75,400		75,400
Selling and distribution		Gross profit b/f	15,570
overheads	5,240		
Production overhead control			
(under-absorbed overhead)	2,908		
Net profit c/f	7,422		
	15,570		15,570

Tutorial notes

1 The value of materials transferred between batches will be recorded on the batch records and will not affect the cost accounts.

2 The balance on the direct wages control account may be regarded as a wages accrual and we have charged a higher amount for direct wages than was actually paid.

3 Direct wages incurred on the production of the capital equipment and the production overheads absorbed will be debited to the capital equipment under construction account and ultimately to the appropriate fixed asset account.

Answer 7.5

(a)   RAW MATERIALS STOCK

	£		£
Opening balance	17,200	Work in progress (bal figure)	12,820
Creditors (W1)	10,780	Balance c/d	15,160
	27,980		27,980
Balance b/d	15,160		

(b)   WORK IN PROGRESS

	£		£
Opening balance	5,600	Finished goods (bal figure)	25,190
Raw materials stock	12,820	Balance c/d	4,750
Direct wages	6,400		
Production overhead (W2)	5,120		
	29,940		29,940
Balance b/d	4,750		

(c)   FINISHED GOODS STOCK

	£		£
Opening balance	10,500	P&L account(Cost of sales)	23,600
Work in progress	25,190	Balance c/d	12,090
	35,690		35,690
Balance b/d	12,090		

Check	£
Production cost of sales	23,600
Profit margin (add 25%)	5,900
Sales	29,500

(d)   PRODUCTION OVERHEAD

	£		£
Cash	5,200	Work in progress	5,120
Depreciation	200	P&L account (under-absorbed)	280
	5,400		5,400

Workings

1   CREDITORS FOR RAW MATERIALS

	£		£
Cash	8,960	Opening balance	7,600
Balance c/f	9,420	Raw materials purchases(bal fig)	10,780
	18,380		18,380

2	Direct labour	£6,400
	Production overhead absorbed (80%)	£5,120

Chapter 8   Costing methods

Chapter topic list

Learning objectives

On completion of this chapter you will be able to:

	Performance criteria	Range statement
• understand job and batch costing systems	6.1.2, 6.2.3	6.1.1, 6.2.1
• deal with queries relating to job and batch costing systems		

BPP
PUBLISHING

1 WHAT IS A COSTING METHOD

> **KEY TERM**
>
> A **costing method** is a method of collecting costs which is designed to suit the way goods are processed or manufactured or the way that services are provided.

1.1 Each organisation's costing method will therefore have unique features but costing systems of firms in the same line of business will more than likely have common aspects. On the other hand, organisations involved in completely different activities, such as hospitals and car part manufacturers, will use very different costing methods.

2 JOB COSTING

2.1 The aim of **job costing** is simply to collect the cost information shown below.

	£
Materials	X
Labour	X
Expenses	X
Direct cost	X
Production overhead	X
Total production cost	X
Administration overhead	X
Selling overhead	X
Cost of sales	X

To the final figure is added a '**mark-up**' and the total is the selling price of the job.

2.2 In other words, all we are doing is looking at one way of putting together the pieces of information that we have studied separately so far.

What is a job

> **KEY TERM**
>
> A **job** is cost unit which consists of a single order or contract.

2.3 With other methods of costing it is usual to produce for stock, and management therefore decide in advance how many units of each type, site, colour, quality and so on will be produced during the coming year.

2.4 These decisions will all be taken without taking into account the identity of the customers who will eventually buy the products.

2.5 In job costing on the other hand, production is usually carried out in accordance with the **special requirements** of each customer. It is therefore usual for each job to **differ in one or more respects from every other job**, which means that a separate record must be maintained to show the details of a particular job.

2.6 The work relating to a job is usually carried out within a factory or workshop and moves through processes and operations as a **continuously identifiable unit**. The term job may also be applied to work such as property repairs, and the job costing method may be used in the costing of internal capital expenditure jobs.

Procedure for the performance of jobs

2.7 The normal procedure which is adopted in jobbing concerns involves the following.

(a) The prospective customer approaches the supplier and indicates the **requirements** of the job.

(b) A responsible official sees the prospective customer and agrees with him the **precise details of the items** to be supplied, for example the quantity, quality, size and colour of the goods, the date of delivery and any special requirements.

(c) The estimating department of the organisation then prepares an **estimate** for the job. This will include the cost of the materials to be used, the wages expected to be paid, the appropriate amount for factory, administration, selling and distribution overhead, the cost where appropriate of additional equipment needed specially for the job, and finally the supplier's profit margin. The total of these items will represent the **quoted selling price**.

(d) At the appropriate time, the job will be 'loaded' on to the factory floor. This means that as soon as all materials, labour and equipment are available and subject to the scheduling of other orders, the job will be started. In an efficient organisation, the start of the job will be timed to ensure that while it will be ready for the customer by the promised date of delivery it will not be loaded too early, otherwise storage space will have to be found for the product until the date it is required by (and was promised to) the customer.

Collection of job costs

2.8 A separate record must be maintained to show the details of individual jobs. The process of collecting job costs may be outlined as follows.

(a) **Materials requisitions are sent to stores.**

(b) **The material requisition note will be used to cost the materials issued to the job** concerned, and this cost may then be recorded on a **job cost sheet**. The cost may include items already in stock, at an appropriate valuation, and/or items specially purchased.

(c) **The job ticket is passed to the worker who is to perform the first operation.** The times of his starting and finishing the operation are recorded on the ticket, which is then passed to the person who is to carry out the second operation, where a similar record of the times of starting and finishing is made.

(d) When the job is completed, the **job ticket is sent to the cost office**, where the time spent will be costed and recorded on the job cost sheet.

(e) The **relevant costs** of materials issued, direct labour performed and direct expenses incurred as recorded on the job cost sheet **are charged to the job account** in the work in progress ledger. This may include meeting the special requirements of the customer.

(f) **The job account is debited with the job's share of the factory overhead**, based on the absorption rate(s) in operation. If the job is incomplete at the end of an accounting period, it is valued at factory cost in the closing balance sheet (where a system of absorption costing is in operation).

(g) **On completion of the job**, the job account is charged with the appropriate administration, selling and distribution overhead, after which **the total cost of the job can be ascertained.**

(h) The difference between the agreed selling price and the total actual cost will be the supplier's profit (or loss).

2.9 Here is a proforma job account, which will be one of the accounts in the work in progress control account.

JOB ACCOUNT

	£		£
Materials issued	X	Finished jobs	X
Direct labour	X		
Direct expenses	X		
Factory overhead at predetermined rate	X		
Other overheads	X		X
	X		X

Activity 8.1

What does the word 'job' mean when we talk about job costing? Give three examples.

Job cost sheet (or card)

2.10 An example of a job cost sheet is shown on the next page.

Job cost sheets show:

- detail of relatively small jobs;
- a summary of direct materials, direct labour and so on for larger jobs.

2.11 When jobs are completed, **job cost sheets** are transferred from the **work in progress** category to **finished goods**. When delivery is made to the customer, the costs become a **cost of sale**. If the completed job was carried out in order to build up finished goods stocks (rather than to meet a specific order) the quantity of items produced and their value are recorded on **finished goods stores ledger cards**.

Rectification costs

KEY TERM

Rectification cost is the cost incurred in rectifying sub-standard output.

2.12 If the finished output is found to be sub-standard, it may be possible to rectify the fault. The sub-standard output will then be returned to the department or cost centre where the fault arose.

JOB COST CARD													Job No.	B641	

Customer Mr J White
Customer's Order No.
Vehicle make Peugot 205 GTE

Job Description Repair damage to offside front door

Estimate Ref. 2599
Invoice No.
Vehicle reg. no. G 614 SOX

Quoted price £338.68
Invoice price £355.05
Date to collect 14.6.X0

Material						Labour								Overheads			
				Cost								Cost				Cost	
Date	Req. No.	Qty.	Price	£	p	Date	Emp-loyee	Cost Ctre	Hrs.	Rate	Bonus	£	p	Hrs	OAR	£	p
12.6	36815	1	75.49	75	49	12.6	018	B	1.98	6.50	-	12	87	7.9	2.50	19	75
12.6	36816	1	33.19	33	19	13.6	018	B	5.92	6.50	-	38	48				
12.6	36842	5	6.01	30	05						13.65	13	65				
13.6	36881	5	3.99	19	95												
Total C/F				158	68	Total C/F						65	00	Total C/F		19	75

Expenses						Job Cost Summary	Actual		Estimate	

			Cost				£	p	£	p
Date	Ref.	Description	£	p		Direct Materials B/F	158	68	158	68
						Direct Expenses B/F	50	00		
						Direct Labour B/F	65	00	180	00
12.6	-	N. Jolley Panel-beating	50	-		Direct Cost	273	68		
						Overheads B/F	19	75		
							293	43		
						Admin overhead (add 10%)	29	34		
						= Total Cost	322	77	338	68
						Invoice Price	355	05		
Total C/F			50	-		Job Profit/Loss	32	28		

Comments

Job Cost Card Completed by _____

2.13 **Rectification costs** can be treated in two ways.

(a) If rectification work is not a frequent occurrence, but arises on occasions with specific jobs to which it can be traced directly, then the rectification costs should be **charged as a direct cost to the jobs concerned.**

(b) If rectification is regarded as a normal part of the work carried out generally in the department, then the rectification costs should be **treated as production overheads**. This means that they would be included in the total of production overheads for the department and absorbed into the cost of all jobs for the period, using the overhead absorption rate.

Job costing and computerisation

2.14 **Job costing cards** exist in **manual** systems, but it is increasingly likely that in large organisations the job costing system will be **computerised**, using accounting software specifically designed to deal with job costing requirements. A computerised job accounting system is likely to contain the following features.

(a) Every job will be given a job code number, which will determine how the data relating to the job is stored.

(b) A separate set of codes will be given for the type of costs that any job is likely to incur. Thus, 'direct wages', say, will have the same code whichever job they are allocated to.

(c) In a sophisticated system, costs can be analysed both by job (for example all costs related to Job 456), but also by type (for example direct wages incurred on all jobs). It is thus easy to compare actual and expected costs and to make comparisons between jobs.

(d) A job costing system might have facilities built into it which incorporate other factors relating to the performance of the job. In complex jobs, sophisticated planning techniques might be employed to ensure that the job is performed in the minimum time possible. **Time management features** therefore may be incorporated into job costing software.

Cost plus pricing

2.15 In this chapter we have described the usual method of fixing selling prices within a jobbing concern. It is known as **cost plus pricing** because a desired profit margin is added to total costs to arrive at the selling price.

2.16 The **disadvantages** of cost plus pricing are as follows.

(a) There are no incentives to **control costs** as a profit is guaranteed.

(b) There is no motive to tackle **inefficiencies** or **waste**.

(c) It doesn't take into account any significant differences in actual and estimated volumes of activity. Since the overhead absorption rate is based upon estimated volumes, there may be **under-/over-absorbed overheads** not taken into account.

(d) Because overheads are apportioned in an arbitrary way, this may lead to **under and over pricing.**

2.17 Consider the following formula.

	%
Cost of sales	100
Plus profit	25
Equals sales	125

Profit may be expressed either as a percentage of cost of sales (such as 25% (25/100) **mark-up** using the formula above) as in cost plus pricing or as a percentage of sales (such as 20% (25/125) **margin**).

2.18 The **cost plus system** is often adopted where **one-off jobs** are carried out to **customers' specifications**.

Activity 8.2

Three of the following documents were used to establish the direct costs of job C1027. Identify the documents in question.

Stock card 8754/1262
Payroll (week-ending 26 September 20X0)
Factory electricity bill for the quarter to 29 September 20X0
GRN No 45725
M Bobb's clock card (w/e 26 September 20X0)
Materials requisition note no 20019
Industrial Refuse Ltd - weekly invoices for skip hire
M Bobb's time sheet (w/e 26 September 20X0)
Fred Davis - invoice for sub-contracting work 'per quotation'

3 JOB COSTING FOR INTERNAL SERVICES

3.1 **Job costing systems** may be used to control the costs of **internal service departments**, eg the maintenance department. A job costing system enables the cost of a specific job to be charged to a user department. Therefore instead of apportioning the total costs of service departments, each job done is charged to the individual user department.

3.2 An **internal job costing system** for service departments will have the following advantages.

(a) **Realistic apportionment.** The identification of expenses with jobs and the subsequent charging of these to the department(s) responsible means that costs are borne by those who incurred them.

(b) **Increased responsibility and awareness.** User departments will be aware that they are charged for the specific services used and may be more careful to use the facility more efficiently. They will also appreciate the true cost of the facilities that they are using and can take decisions accordingly.

(c) **Control of service department costs.** The service department may be restricted to charging a standard cost to user departments for specific jobs carried out or time spent. It will then be possible to measure the efficiency or inefficiency of the service department by recording the difference between the standard charges and the actual expenditure.

(d) **Budget information.** This information will ease the budgeting process, as the purpose and cost of service department expenditure can be separately identified.

Activity 8.3

East and West Ltd is a company that carries out jobbing work. One of the jobs carried out in May was job 2409, to which the following information relates.

Direct material Y:	400 kilos were issued from stores at a cost of £5 per kilo.
Direct material Z:	800 kilos were issued from stores at a cost of £6 per kilo. 60 kilos were returned.
Department P:	300 labour hours were worked, of which 100 hours were done in overtime.
Department Q:	200 labour hours were worked, of which 100 hours were done in overtime.

Overtime work is not normal in Department P, where basic pay is £4 per hour plus an overtime premium of £1 per hour. Overtime work was done in Department Q in May because of a request by the customer of another job to complete his job quickly. Basic pay in Department Q is £5 per hour and overtime premium is £1.50 per hour. Overhead is absorbed at the rate of £3 per direct labour hour in both departments.

Tasks

(a) Calculate the direct materials cost of job 2409
(b) Calculate the direct labour cost of job 2409
(c) Calculate the full production cost of job 2409 using absorption costing

4 THE PRINCIPLES OF JOB COSTING

4.1 An example may help to illustrate the principles of job costing, and the way in which the costing of individual jobs fits in with the recording of total costs in control accounts. Study the following example very carefully and make sure that you understand the solution.

4.2 EXAMPLE: JOB COSTING PRINCIPLES

Stripey Zebra Ltd is a jobbing company. On 1 October 20X0, there was one uncompleted job in the factory. The job card for this work is summarised as follows.

Job Card, Job No H1

Costs to date	£
Direct materials	630
Direct labour (120 hours)	350
Factory overhead (£2 per direct labour hour)	240
Factory cost to date	1,220

During October, three new jobs were started in the factory, and costs of production were as follows.

Direct materials	£
Issued to: job H1	2,390
job H2	1,680
job H3	3,950
job H4	4,420
Damaged stock written off from stores	2,300

Material transfers	£
Job H3 to job H2	250
Job H1 to H3	620

Materials returned to store	£
From job H1	870
From job H4	170

Direct labour hours recorded	
Job H1	430 hrs
Job H2	650 hrs
Job H3	280 hrs
Job H4	410 hrs

The cost of labour hours during October 20X0 was £3 per hour, and production overhead is absorbed at the rate of £2 per direct labour hour. Production overheads incurred during the month amounted to £3,800. Completed jobs were delivered to customers as soon as they were completed, and the invoiced amounts were as follows.

Job H1	£5,500
Job H3	£8,000
Job H4	£7,500

Administration and marketing overheads are added to the cost of sales at the rate of 20% of factory cost. Actual costs incurred during October 20X0 amounted to £3,200.

Tasks

(a) Prepare the job accounts for each individual job during October 20X0 (the accounts should only show the cost of production, and not the full cost of sale).

(b) Prepare the summarised job cost cards for each job, and calculate the profit on each completed job.

(c) Show how the costs would be shown in the company's cost control accounts.

4.3 SOLUTION

(a) *Job accounts*

JOB H1

	£		£
Balance b/f	1,220	Job H3 a/c	620
Materials (stores a/c)	2,390	(materials transfer)	
Labour (wages a/c)	1,290	Stores a/c (materials returned)	870
Production overhead (o'hd a/c)	860	Cost of sales a/c (balance)	4,270
	5,760		5,760
-			

JOB H2

	£		£
Materials (stores a/c)	1,680	Balance c/f	5,180
Labour (wages a/c)	1,950		
Production overhead (o'hd a/c)	1,300		
Job H3 a/c (materials transfer)	250		
	5,180		5,180

JOB H3

	£		£
Materials (stores a/c)	3,950	Job H2 a/c (materials transfer)	250
Labour (wages a/c)	840		
Production overhead (o'hd a/c)	560	Cost of sales a/c (balance)	5,720
Job H1 a/c (materials transfer)	620		
	5,970		5,970

JOB H4

	£		£
Materials (stores a/c)	4,420	Stores a/c (materials returned)	170
Labour (wages a/c)	1,230		
Production overhead (o'hd a/c)	820	Cost of sales a/c (balance)	6,300
	6,470		6,470

(b) *Job cards, summarised*

	Job H1	*Job H2*	*Job H3*	*Job H4*
	£	£	£	
Materials	1,530*	1,930	4,320 **	4,250
Labour	1,640	1,950	840	1,230
Production overhead	1,100	1,300	560	820
Factory cost	4,270	5,180	(c/f) 5,720	6,300
Admin & marketing o'hd (20%)	854		1,144	1,260
Cost of sale	5,124		6,864	7,560
Invoice value	5,500		8,000	7,500
Profit/(loss) on job	376		1,136	(60)

* £(630 + 2,390 − 620 − 870)   ** £(3,950 + 620 − 250)

(c) *Control accounts*

STORES CONTROL (incomplete)

	£		£
WIP a/c (returns)	1,040	WIP a/c	
		(2,390 + 1,680 + 3,950 + 4,420)	12,440
		Profit and loss a/c:	
		stock written off	2,300

WORK IN PROGRESS CONTROL

	£		£
Balance b/f	1,220	Stores control a/c (returns)	1,040
Stores control a/c	12,440	Cost of sales a/c	
Wages control a/c	5,310	*(4,270 + 5,720 + 6,300)	16,290
Production o'hd control a/c	3,540	Balance c/f (Job No H2)	5,180
	22,510		22,510

* 1,770 hours at £3 per hour

COST OF SALES CONTROL

	£		£
WIP control a/c	16,290	Profit and loss	19,548
Admin & marketing o'hd a/c			
(854 + 1,144 + 1,260)	3,258		
	19,548		19,548

SALES

	£		£
Profit and loss	21,000	CLC	21,000
		(5,500 + 8,000 + 7,500)	
	21,000		21,000

PRODUCTION OVERHEAD CONTROL

	£		£
CLC	3,800	WIP a/c	3,540
(overhead incurred)		Under-absorbed o'hd a/c	260
	3,800		3,800

UNDER-/OVER-ABSORBED OVERHEADS

	£		£
Production o'hd control a/c	260	Admin & marketing o'hd a/c	58
		Profit and loss a/c	202
	260		260

ADMIN & MARKETING OVERHEAD CONTROL

	£		£
CLC (overhead incurred)	3,200	Cost of sales a/c	3,258
Over-absorbed o'hd a/c	58		
	3,258		3,258

PROFIT AND LOSS

	£		£
Cost of sales a/c	19,548	Sales a/c	21,000
Stores a/c (stock written off)	2,300		
Under-absorbed overhead a/c	202	Loss (CLC) - balance	1,050
	22,050		22,050

FINANCIAL LEDGER CONTROL (CLC) (incomplete)

	£		£
Sales a/c	21,000	Production overhead a/c	3,800
P & L a/c (loss)	1,050	Admin and marketing o'hd a/c	3,200

The loss of £1,050 is the sum of the profits/losses on each completed job £(376 + 1,136 - 60) = £1,452, minus the total of under-absorbed overhead (£202) and the stock write-off (£2,300).

ASSESSMENT ALERT

In an assessment, you may be asked to determine the amount of profit to be added to a job price. Remember that profit may be expressed either as a percentage of job cost (such as 25% (25/100) mark up) or as a percentage of price (such as 20% (25/125) margin).

Activity 8.4

A curtain-making business manufactures quality curtains to customers' orders. It has three production departments (X, Y and Z) which have overhead absorption rates (per direct labour hour) of £12.86, £12.40 and £14.03 respectively.

Two pairs of curtains are to be manufactured for customers. Direct costs are as follows.

	Job TN8	*Job KT2*
Direct material	£154	£108
Direct labour	20 hours dept X	16 hours dept X
	12 hours dept Y	10 hours dept Y
	10 hours dept Z	14 hours dept Z

Labour rates are as follows: £3.80(X); £3.50 (Y); £3.40 (Z)

The firm quotes prices to customers that reflect a required profit of 25% on selling price.

Task

Calculate the total cost and selling price of each job.

5 BATCH COSTING

KEY TERM

A **batch** is a cost unit which consists of a separate, readily identifiable group of product units which maintain their separate identity throughout the production process.

5.1 The procedures for **costing batches** are very similar to those for costing jobs.

BPP PUBLISHING

(a)   The batch is treated as a **job** during production and the costs are collected in the manner already described in this chapter.

(b)   Once the batch has been completed, the **cost per unit** can be calculated as the total batch cost divided by the number of units in the batch.

5.2   EXAMPLE: BATCH COSTING

A company manufactures model cars to order and has the following budgeted overheads for the year, based on normal activity levels.

Department	Budgeted overheads £	Budgeted activity
Welding	6,000	1,500 labour hours
Assembly	10,000	1,000 labour hours

Selling and administrative overheads are 20% of factory cost. An order for 250 model cars type XJS1, made as Batch 8638, incurred the following costs.

Materials	£12,000
Labour	100 hours welding shop at £2.50/hour
	200 hours assembly shop at £1/hour

£500 was paid for the hire of special X-ray equipment for testing the welds.

Task

Calculate the cost per unit for Batch 8638.

5.3   SOLUTION

The first step is to calculate the overhead absorption rate for the production departments.

$$\text{Welding} \quad = \quad \frac{£6,000}{1,500} \quad = \quad £4 \text{ per labour hour}$$

$$\text{Assembly} \quad = \quad \frac{£10,000}{1,000} \quad = \quad £10 \text{ per labour hour}$$

Total cost - Batch no 8638

		£	£
Direct material			12,000
Direct expense			500
Direct labour	$100 \times 2.50 =$	250	
	$200 \times 1.00 =$	200	
			450
Prime cost			12,950
Overheads	$100 \times 4 =$	400	
	$200 \times 10 =$	2,000	
			2,400
Factory cost			15,350
Selling and administrative cost (20% of factory cost)			3,070
Total cost			18,420

$$\text{Cost per unit} = \frac{£18,420}{250} = £73.68$$

Activity 8.5

Lyfsa Kitchen Units Ltd crafts two different sizes of standard unit and a DIY all-purpose unit for filling up awkward spaces. The units are built to order in batches of around 250 (although the number varies according to the quality of wood purchased), and each batch is sold to NGJ Furniture Warehouses Ltd.

The costs incurred in May 19X3 were as follows.

	Big unit	Little unit	All-purpose
Direct materials purchased	£5,240	£6,710	£3,820
Direct labour			
Skilled (hours)	1,580	1,700	160
Semi-skilled (hours)	3,160	1,900	300
Direct expenses	£1,180	£1,700	£250
Selling price of batch	£33,180	£27,500	£19,500
Completed at 31 May 20X0	100%	80%	25%

The following information is available.

All direct materials for the completion of the batches have been recorded. Skilled labour is paid £5 per hour, semi-skilled £4 per hour. Administration expenses total £4,400 per month and are to be allocated to the batches on the basis of direct labour hours. Direct labour costs, direct expenses and administration expenses will increase in proportion to the total labour hours required to complete the little units and the all-purpose units. On completion of the work the practice of the manufacturer is to divide the calculated profit on each batch 20% to staff as a bonus, 80% to the company. Losses are absorbed 100% by the company.

Tasks

(a) Calculate the profit or loss made by the company on big units.
(b) Project the profit or loss likely to be made by the company on little units and all-purpose units.
(c) Comment on any matters you think relevant to management as a result of your calculations.

Key learning points

- **Job costing** is the costing method used where each cost unit is separately identifiable.

- Each job is given a **number** to distinguish it from other jobs.

- Costs for each job are collected on a **job cost sheet** or **job card.**

- Material costs for each job are determined from **material requisition notes**.

- Labour times on each job are recorded on a **job ticket**, which is then costed and recorded on the job cost sheet. Some labour costs, such as overtime premium or the cost of rectifying sub-standard output, might be charged either directly to a job or else as an overhead cost, depending on the circumstances in which the costs have arisen.

- **Overhead** is absorbed into the cost of jobs using the predetermined overhead absorption rates.

- The usual method of fixing prices within a jobbing concern is **cost plus pricing**.

- An **internal job costing system** can be used for costing the work of service departments.

- **Batch costing** is similar to job costing in that each batch of similar articles is separately identifiable. The **cost per unit** manufactured in a batch is the total batch cost divided by the number of units in the batch.

Quick quiz

1   What is a job?

2   What is cost plus pricing?

3   In which situations may job costing systems be used?

4   How would you calculate the cost per unit of a completed batch?

Answers to quick quiz

1 A cost unit which consists of a single order or contract.

2 A pricing method whereby a desired profit margin is added to total costs to arrive at the selling price.

3 To control costs of internal service departments, where the costs of specific jobs are charged directly to user departments.

4 $$\frac{\text{Total batch cost}}{\text{Number of units in the batch}}$$

Answers to activities

Answer 8.1

A job is a cost unit which consists of a single order (or contract) usually carried out in accordance with the special requirements of each customer. This means that each job will be at least slightly different from every other job and so separate records must be maintained to show the details of a particular job.

Examples are numerous.
(a) A haircut
(b) Writing a book
(c) The Channel Tunnel
(d) A tailor-made suit
(e) A highly-specialised machine
(f) An audit
(g) Jobs done by domestic plumbers, builders and so on

You may have compiled a totally different list.

Answer 8.2

The documents most likely to be needed to establish *direct* costs are the materials requisition note, M Bobb's time sheet and the sub-contractor's invoice.

Details of materials used could probably, but not necessarily, have been obtained from the stock card too. The payroll would not be analysed in sufficient detail. The cost of electricity is not (so far as we are told) *directly* traceable to the job in question. The GRN and the clock card are of no relevance. The skip hire invoice appears to be an ongoing cost, not directly traceable to this job.

Answer 8.3

(a)

	£
Direct material Y (400 kilos × £5)	2,000
Direct material Z (800 – 60 kilos × £6)	4,440
Total direct material cost	6,440

(b)

	£
Department P (300 hours × £4)	1,200
Department Q (200 hours × £5)	1,000
Total direct labour cost	2,200

Overtime premium will be charged to overhead in the case of Department P, and to the job of the customer who asked for overtime to be worked in the case of Department Q.

(c)

	£
Direct material cost	6,440
Direct labour cost	2,200
Production overhead (500 hours × £3)	1,500
	10,140

Answer 8.4

			Job TN8		Job KT2
			£		£
Direct material			154.00		108.00
Direct labour:	dept X	(20 × 3.80)	76.00	(16 × 3.80)	60.80
	dept Y	(12 × 3.50)	42.00	(10 × 3.50)	35.00
	dept Z	(10 × 3.40)	34.00	(14 × 3.40)	47.60
Total direct cost			306.00		251.40
Overhead:	dept X	(20 × 12.86)	257.20	(16 × 12.86)	205.76
	dept Y	(12 × 12.40)	148.80	(10 × 12.40)	124.00
	dept Z	(10 × 14.03)	140.30	(14 × 14.03)	196.42
Total cost			852.30		777.58
Profit (note)			284.10		259.19
Quoted selling price			1,136.40		1,036.77

(*Note.* If profit is 25% on selling price, this is the same as $33^1/3\%$ (25/75) on cost.)

Answer 8.5

(a)   *Big units*

		£	£
Direct materials			5,240
Direct labour			
Skilled 1,580 hours at £5		7,900	
Semi-skilled 3,160 hours at £4		12,640	
			20,540
Direct expenses			1,180
Administrative expenses			
4,740 hours at £0.50 (see below)			2,370
			29,330
Selling price			33,180
Calculated profit			3,850
Divided:	staff bonus 20%		770
	profit for company 80%		3,080

$$\text{Administration expenses absorption rate} = \frac{£4,400}{8,800} \text{ per labour hour}$$

$$= £0.50 \text{ per labour hour}$$

(h)

		Little units		All-purpose	
		£	£	£	£
Direct materials			6,710		3,820
Direct labour					
Skilled	1,700 hrs at £5	8,500		160 hrs at £5	800
Semi-skilled	1,900 hrs at £4	7,600		300 hrs at £4	1,200
Direct expenses		1,700			250
Administration					
expenses:	3,600 hrs at £0.50	1,800		460 hrs at £0.50	230
		19,600			2,480
Costs to					
completion	20/80 × 19,600	4,900		75/25 × 2,480	7,440
			24,500		9,920
Total costs			31,210		13,740
Selling price			27,500		19,500
Calculated profit/(loss)			(3,710)		5,760
Divided:	Staff bonus 20%		-		1,152
	(Loss)/profit for company		(3,710)		4,608

Note that whilst direct labour costs, direct expenses and administration expenses increase in proportion to the total labour hours required to complete the little units and the all-purpose units, there will be no further material costs to complete the batches.

(c)   Little units are projected to incur a loss. There are two possible reasons for the loss.

   (i)   The estimation process may be inadequate. For example, it may have been incorrect to assume that the make-up of the costs to completion is the same as the make-up of the costs already incurred. It is possible that all of the skilled work has already been carried out and only unskilled labour is required to complete the batch. If the loss is the result of inadequate estimating, the estimation procedure should be reviewed to prevent recurrence.

   (ii) It is the result of a lack of cost control. If this is the case, appropriate action should be taken to exercise control in future.

Part D

Standard costing and variance analysis

Chapter 9   Standard costing

Chapter topic list

1   Standard costs and standard costing

2   How standards are set

3   Performance standards

Learning objectives

On completion of this chapter you will be able to:

	Performance criteria	Range statement
• identify standard costs in accordance with organisational costing procedures	6.1.1, 6.2.2	6.1.1, 6.2.1
• ensure that information relating to standard costs is clearly and correctly coded, analysed and recorded	6.1.2, 6.2.3	6.1.1, 6.2.1
• calculate standard costs in accordance with organisational policies and procedures	6.1.3	6.1.1

BPP PUBLISHING

1 STANDARD COSTS AND STANDARD COSTING

What is a standard?

> **KEY TERM**
>
> A **standard** represents what we think should happen. It is our best 'guesstimate' of how long something will take to produce, what quantity of materials it will require, how much it will cost and so on.

1.1 The **materials standard** for a product is our best estimate of how much material is needed to make the product in kilograms, litres, metres or whatever (standard materials usage) multiplied by our best estimate of the price we will have to pay for each kilogram, litre, metre or whatever (standard materials price). For example, we might think that two square metres of material should be needed to make a curtain and that the material should cost £10 per square metre. The standard material cost of the curtain is therefore 2 × £10 = £20.

1.2 Likewise the **labour standard** for a product is an estimate of how many hours are needed to make the product multiplied by the amount the labour force needed to make the product is paid per hour.

1.3 The whole idea of a best guesstimate might sound a bit of a hit and miss affair to you. It may seem as if standard setting has no technical basis and that we can make it up as we go along. You would be wrong. As we shall now explain, there is a proper approach to setting standards.

What is standard costing?

> **KEY TERM**
>
> **Standard costing** is the preparation of standard costs for use in the following situations.
>
> - In costing as a means of valuing stocks and the cost of production. It is an alternative method of valuation to methods like FIFO, LIFO or replacement costing.
>
> - In variance analysis, which is a means of controlling the business.

The standard cost card

1.4 A **standard cost card** (or standard cost sheet) can be prepared for each product. The card will normally show the **quantity** and **price** of each **direct material** to be consumed, the **time** and **rate** of each **grade of direct labour** required, the **overhead recovery** and the **full cost**. The **standard selling price** and the **standard profit** per unit may also be shown.

1.5 A distinction should be made in the standard between the following overhead costs.

(a) **Fixed and variable production overheads,** unless variable overheads are insignificant in value, in which case all production overheads are regarded as fixed costs.

(b) **Production overhead and other overheads** (administration and marketing). In many costing systems, administration and marketing overheads are excluded from the standard unit cost, so that the standard cost is simply a standard production cost.

1.6 A simple standard cost card might therefore look like the one shown as follows.

STANDARD COST CARD				
PRODUCT 1234				
DESCRIPTION	QUANTITY	COST PER KG/HOUR/ETC	EXTENSION	TOTAL
Materials			£	£
Flour	*3 kg*	*4.00*	*12.00*	
Water	*9 litres*	*2.00*	*18.00*	
SUB-TOTAL				*30.00*
Labour				
Duckers	*6 hrs*	*1.50*	*9.00*	
Divers	*8 hrs*	*2.00*	*16.00*	
SUB-TOTAL				*25.00*
Direct cost				*55.00*
Variable production o/h	*14 hrs*	*0.50*		*7.00*
Standard variable cost				*62.00*
Fixed production o/h	*14 hrs*	*4.50*		*63.00*
Standard full production cost				*125.00*
Administration o/h				*15.00*
STANDARD COST OF SALE				*140.00*
Standard profit				*20.00*
STANDARD SELLING PRICE				*160.00*

1.7 In a computer system cost cards could be assembled on a spreadsheet, or by means of a tailor-made programme drawing its information from a database.

Issue of raw material stock at standard cost

1.8 In Chapter 2, we considered the different methods of valuing materials issues and stocks. We briefly mentioned that issues and stock could be valued at a **pre-determined cost,** or what is known as a **standard cost.**

1.9 This method is therefore quite simple, since all issues and all closing stock will be valued at the same pre-determined cost.

For example, material A has a standard cost of £8 per unit, it therefore follows that:

(a) if 200 units of material A are issued, the issues will be valued at 200 × £8 = £1,600;

(b) if 700 units of material A are held in stock at the year end, the stock valuation of material A will be 700 × £8 = £5,600.

Activity 9.1

(a) In what senses is a standard cost a 'standard'?

(b) Why is standard costing used?

2   HOW STANDARDS ARE SET

Establishing standard material costs

2.1   We have already seen that the standard materials cost for a unit of output is calculated as follows.

KEY TERM

Standard materials cost = standard materials usage × standard materials price

To set a standard materials cost we therefore need to establish the **standard materials usage** and the **standard materials price**.

Standard usage of materials

2.2   To ascertain how much material should be used to make a product, technical specifications have to be prepared for the product. This will be done by experts in the production department. On the basis of these technical and engineering specifications and in the light of experience, a **bill of materials** will be drawn up which lists the **quantity of materials** required to make a unit of the product. These quantities can include allowances for wastage of materials if that is normal and unavoidable.

Standard prices of materials

2.3   The proper approach to setting a standard cost for a particular material is to study the market for that material and become aware of any likely future trends. If your company makes apple pies, news of a disastrous apple crop failure clearly has implications for raw materials prices and the amounts at which standards should be set.

2.4   In practice it is not always possible or practicable to acquire full information. In such circumstances it is likely that **standard prices** would be set on the basis of **current prices** and any notification from suppliers of changes (for example a new catalogue or price list).

2.5   Sometimes businesses are able to enter into a contract stating that such and such a price will be charged for such and such a period. Obviously this adds a good deal of certainty to the standard setting process.

2.6   Standards should also take into account any **discount** that may be available for bulk purchase, so long as it is economical to buy in sufficiently large quantities to earn the discounts, after considering the costs of holding the stock.

Establishing standard labour costs

2.7   In principle it is easy to set **standards for labour**.

(a) Find out how long it should take to do a job.

(b) Multiply this time by the rate that the person who does the job is paid.

The result is the **standard labour cost** for that job.

> **KEY TERM**
>
> **Standard labour cost** = time it should take to do a job × standard labour rate

2.8 In practice, of course, it is not this straightforward. For example, an experienced worker may be able to do the job in less time than a novice, and two equally experienced workers may take a different length of time to do the same job. Some time must be spent recording actual performance before a realistic standard can be established.

2.9 EXAMPLE: LABOUR STANDARDS

Fix-a-car Ltd employs two female mechanics, Georgina, who is an apprentice, and Clarissa, who has given loyal service for ten years. The accountant is looking through last week's figures and decides to note down the time each mechanic took to perform each of ten MOTs.

Georgina	*Clarissa*
Minutes	Minutes
63	30
55	28
50	35
57	25
49	32
52	33
58	29
57	31
70	30
69	27

Georgina is presently paid £4.50 per hour and Clarissa £8 per hour. Calculate the standard time for performing an MOT, the standard labour cost for performing an MOT and the cost of a standard hour.

2.10 SOLUTION

The total time taken for 20 MOTs is 880 minutes, an average of 44 minutes per MOT. Georgina takes a total of 580 minutes and Clarissa 300 minutes. Multiplied by their respective hourly rates the total cost is £83.50 or an average of £4.18 per MOT.

Thus, an hour of MOT work costs, on average,

$$\frac{60}{44} \times £4.18 = £5.70$$

We have therefore calculated the following for MOTs.

Standard time	44 minutes
Standard labour cost per MOT	£4.18
Cost of one standard hour	£5.70

2.11 These figures have considerable shortcomings however. They take no account of the time of day when the work was performed, or the type or age of vehicle concerned. We cannot tell to what extent the difference in performance of the two mechanics is due to their relative experience and to what extent it is due to other factors: possibly Georgina does the more difficult jobs to gain experience, while Clarissa works on cars that she regularly maintains for established customers who ask for her.

On the other hand it is quite likely that a better controlled set of measurements would give very similar results to those obtained using historical figures. In a case like this there is probably very little point in trying to be more scientific and 'accurate'. Even if the garage performed 20 MOTs a day, the first set of figures would have to be quite significantly wrong for a more accurate estimation to make any material difference to the accuracy of the costing.

(If, however, we were dealing with a high volume business where, say, 10,000 units were produced an hour, then small differences in times and costs per unit (or batch or whatever) would have a considerable impact on the accuracy of the costing. In such cases, the taking of more precise measurements in controlled conditions and the use of sophisticated statistical techniques would be worthwhile.)

2.12 How would these figures affect Georgina and Clarissa if they were used as standards? So far as Georgina is concerned a standard time of 44 minutes is a good target to aim at as she is expected to improve her performance, but she is not expected to be as fast as the more experienced mechanic Clarissa. For Clarissa the standard could be demotivating as she may not work so hard if she knows she has half as long again as she needs to do an MOT. A 'time saved bonus' for MOTs taking less than 44 minutes is a good idea in this case: Clarissa will not slack off if she is financially rewarded for her hard work, and Georgina has a further incentive to speed up her own work.

Work study and standard costs

2.13 The point about accuracy might be developed here. In the example no special effort was made to record the times taken to perform the MOTs. The standard was calculated using **historical data**.

2.14 This approach is widely used in practice. It has two **advantages**. There is no extra expense in obtaining the information, and it is not distorted by employees who, knowing they are being measured, work more slowly than usual to ensure that easy standards are set.

2.15 The information is, however, distorted by past inefficiencies and 'engineered standards' are therefore considered to be preferable. These are based upon a detailed study of the operations involved in a task. You may have heard of 'time and motion studies', and this is essentially what is involved although the phrase is rather dated. The most commonly used techniques are the following.

(a) **Analytical estimating**. This involves breaking down a job into fairly 'large' units and estimating a time for each unit.

(b) **Predetermined motion time study (PMTS)**. This approach uses times established for basic human motions and so the physical motions required to perform the task would first need to be ascertained by observation.

(c) **Synthetic timing**. This technique is used if it is not possible to actually measure how long a job takes, perhaps because the job is still at the drawing board stage.

2.16 The standard times established by such methods are adjusted to allow for any delays that are unavoidable, and also include an allowance for rest, relaxation, calls of nature, fluctuating performance ('off days') and other contingencies such as machine breakdowns.

2.17 You may be wondering why anybody should bother to go to such extreme lengths. Suppose rivets are made in a repetitive operation which is thought to take five seconds per unit produced and operatives are paid a standard £5 per hour. If there are 100 operatives working a seven hour day it is feasible to produce 504,000 (100 × 60/5 × 60 × 7) rivets at a cost of £3,500 (100 × 7 × £5) per day.

If the operation actually takes 6 seconds, not 5, then to produce 504,000 rivets it will really take 840 hours and cost £4,200 or 20% more than expected. Where large volumes and large sums of money are involved it is clearly worth being as accurate as possible.

Some terminology

2.18 Students are sometimes confused by the concept of a **standard hour**. Contrary to what you might expect, a standard hour is not a unit of time. In the previous example a standard hour would be 720 rivets, this being the number of rivets that could be produced by one operative in one hour if the operative was working in the **standard way** at the **standard rate**. In the Georgina/Clarissa example a standard hour is 1.36 MOTs. In other words a standard hour is a **quantity of work**, not a period of time. You may also come across the term **standard minute**: again this is a quantity of work (12 rivets in our example).

2.19 The person working in the standard way at the standard rate is said to be working at **standard performance**.

2.20 Other terms, like **ideal standard** and **attainable standard** are also of particular relevance to labour costs but we shall come back to these later in the chapter.

Activity 9.2

After extensive work study Carter Ltd has established that all of its production processes are carried out by means of combinations from a set of 10 basic labour operations. A standard time for each operation has been calculated by taking the mean of all observations.

COST / OPERATION

Operation			Time (hours)	
1	X	4 – 80	1 ½	7 – 20
2	Y	5 – 50	1	5 – 50
3	X	4 – 80	¼	~~6 – 00~~ 1 – 20
4	Z	6 – 50	2	13 – 00
5	X	4 – 80	½	2 – 40
6	Y	5 – 50	2	11 – 00
7	Z	6 – 50	3	19 – 50
8	X	4 – 80	1	4 – 80
9	X	4 – 80	¼	1 – 20
10	Y	5 – 50	½	2 – 75

Operations 2, 6 and 10 can only be done by trade Y workers and operations 4 and 7 only by grade Z workers.

Grade	Basic wage (per hour)
X	£4.80
Y	£5.50
Z	£6.50

The company now wishes to establish standard direct labour costs for each of its seven major products and its two enhanced packages. The operations involved for each product are as follows.

Product	Operations per unit
A	2, 4, 5
B	2, 5, 6, 10
C	3, 6, 8, 9
Sharp C	1, 3, 4, 6
D	1, 2, 6, 7, 10
E	3, 4, 5, 10
F	1, 4, 9
F (augmented)	3, 6, 7, 8
G	1, 5, 9, 10

Task

Calculate the standard direct labour cost of one unit of each of the nine products.

Establishing standard costs for expenses

2.21 Cost accounting textbooks are usually silent on the way to set standard costs for expenses, and certainly there is little to add to what you already know about standard setting for materials and labour.

(a) If a contract has been entered into (for cleaning, say) then the standard cost can be set at the amount specified in the contract.

(b) Certain expenses are like materials in that there is a (fluctuating) market rate for a specific quantity and the amount likely to be consumed can be determined by 'engineering' methods (studying the relationship between what is put in and what comes out). Examples are gas and electricity.

2.22 An advantage (for standard setting purposes) with many expenses is that they are fixed over the period for which the standard is being set. The annual buildings insurance premium, for example, will be known for certain on 1 January: it will not turn out to have been different when the year's actual results are determined.

2.23 In other cases expenses can be made to conform to a standard. Discretionary costs, for example, need only be incurred up to a certain level. Suppose you had £10,000 to spend on staff training. Once £10,000 had been spent this would be the end of staff training for the year.

2.24 EXAMPLE: STANDARD COSTS FOR EXPENSES

Edmund Ltd uses a number of gas-fired furnaces to make its products. All are connected to a single meter, but all have their own gauges which show how many therms have been consumed. A gas heater in the factory office is also connected to the meter. The gas central heating in the main administrative office is separately metered.

During the past year one of Edmund Ltd's furnaces produced 2,000 units and used 943 therms. Information from the gas bills for the whole of the period is as follows.

	Administrative office	Factory
	£	£
27.1.X1	2,989.48	8,259.37
24.4.X1	2,527.14	6,482.09
29.7.X1	1,398.26	9,961.24
28.10.X1	2,493.82	8,662.55
26.1.X2	3,477.77	8,729.48

Standing charges are £25 per quarter for the administrative office and £50 per quarter for the factory. The price per therm throughout 20X1 was £0.442, but it rose by 10% in January 20X2.

Calculate the total expected cost of gas for the administrative office for 20X0 and the expected cost of gas per unit of production for the individual furnace referred to.

Note. Assume that activity will continue at the same level in 20X2 as in 20X1.

2.25 SOLUTION

(a) For the administrative office it is reasonable to suppose that gas usage on a daily basis does not vary much although obviously it varies according to the season. We can therefore calculate an annual amount by using the accruals principle.

	£
1.1.X1 to 27.1.X1 (27/91 × (2,989.48 – 25.00))	879.57
28.1.X1 to 24.4.X1 (2,527.14 – 25.00)	2,502.14
25.4.X1 to 29.7.X1 (1,398.26 – 25.00)	1,373.26
30.7.X1 to 28.10.X1 (2,493.82 – 25.00)	2,468.82
29.10.X1 to 31.12.X1 (64/91 × (3,477.77 – 25.00))	2,428.32
	9,652.11
Add 10%	965.21
	10,617.32
Add standing charge (4 × £25)	100.00
Total expected cost	10,717.32

(b) The furnace referred to used 0.4715 therms for each unit of production in 20X1 (943 ÷ 2,000). In 20X2, therefore, the cost per unit of production will be as follows.

$$0.4715 \text{ therms} \times (0.442 \times 1.1) = £0.229 \text{ per unit}$$

Note that we could now estimate the cost of gas if planned activity was to double the production from this furnace: 4,000 units would cost £916 in direct fuel expenses.

Standards and inflation

2.26 One point to bear in mind is that inflation should be considered when standards are being set. For example, when establishing standard material costs, it is unlikely that the **standard materials usage** of a unit of product will change from one year to the next. It is however, likely that the **standard materials price** will increase in line with **inflation**.

2.27 Similarly, when establishing standard labour costs, in general, the time it should take to do a job is unlikely to change from year to year. The **standard labour rate** is, however, likely to increase in line with **inflation**.

2.28 When revising standards therefore, it is important that you take into account how inflation might have an effect on materials prices, labour rates and expenses.

3 PERFORMANCE STANDARDS

3.1 Do not forget that **standards are averages**. Even under ideal working conditions, it would be unrealistic to expect every unit of activity or production to take exactly the same time, using exactly the same amount of materials, and at exactly the same cost. Some variations are inevitable, but for a reasonably large volume of activity, it would be fair to expect that on average, standard results should be achieved.

3.2   Standard costs are thus 'standard' not only in the sense 'this product has been produced in a standard way, using the standard amount of materials and so on' but also in the sense 'this product has been produced to a certain standard'. There are four different types of performance standard that an organisation could aim for.

KEY TERMS

- **Ideal standards** are based on the most favourable operating conditions, with no wastage, no inefficiencies, no idle time and no breakdowns. Variances from ideal standards are useful for pinpointing areas where a close examination may result in large savings, but they are likely to have an unfavourable motivational impact. Employees will often feel that the goals are unattainable and not work so hard.

- **Attainable standards** are based on efficient (but not perfect) operating conditions. Some allowance is made for wastage, inefficiencies, machine breakdowns and fatigue. If well-set they provide a useful psychological incentive, and for this reason they should be introduced whenever possible. The consent and co-operation of employees involved in improving the standard are required.

- **Current standards** are standards based on current working conditions (current wastage, current inefficiencies). The disadvantage of current standards is that they do not attempt to improve on current levels of efficiency, which may be poor and capable of significant improvement.

- **Basic standards** are standards which are kept unaltered over a long period of time, and may be out-of-date. They are used to show changes in efficiency or performance over an extended time period. Basic standards are perhaps the least useful and least common type of standard in use.

Activity 9.3

Kingston Ltd makes one product, the tudor. Two types of labour are involved in the preparation of a tudor, skilled and semi-skilled. Skilled labour is paid £10 per hour and semi-skilled £5 per hour. Twice as many skilled labour hours as semi-skilled labour hours are needed to produce a tudor, four semi-skilled labour hours being needed.

A tudor is made up of three different direct materials. Seven kilograms of direct material A, four litres of direct material B and three metres of direct material C are needed. Direct material A costs £1 per kilogram, direct material B £2 per litre and direct material C £3 per metre.

Variable production overheads are incurred at Kingston Ltd at the rate of £2.50 per direct labour (skilled) hour.

A system of absorption costing is in operation at Kingston Ltd. The basis of absorption is direct labour (skilled) hours. For the forthcoming accounting period, budgeted fixed production overheads are £250,000 and budgeted production of the tudor is 5,000 units.

Task

Using the above information to draw up a standard cost card for the tudor.

ASSESSMENT ALERT

Make sure that you can draw up a standard cost card such as the one in activity 9.3 above - this is first the sort of task that you may be asked to complete in an assessment.

Activity 9.4

LW Ltd makes and sells a single product, G, with the following standard specification for materials.

	Quantity Kilograms	Price per kilogram £
Direct material L	10	30
Direct material W	6	45

It takes 30 direct labour hours to produce one unit of G with a standard direct labour cost of £5.50 per hour.

The annual sales/production budget is 1,200 units evenly spread throughout the year.

The budgeted production overhead, all fixed, is £252,000 and expenditure is expected to occur evenly over the year, which the company divides into twelve calendar months. Absorption is based on units produced.

The budgeted sales quantity in one particular month was actually sold for a total of £120,000 at the standard selling price.

Task

Calculate the standard product cost and the gross profit of each unit sold.

Activity 9.5

The following times were recorded for the performance of a task in the last month.

Worker	Time	Time
Lynn	1 hour 45 minutes	2 hours
Alison	2 hours 5 minutes	1 hour 55 minutes
Jed	1 hour 15 minutes	1 hour 15 minutes
Kate	2 hours 10 minutes	1 hour 30 minutes
Nick	1 hour 45 minutes	1 hour 37 minutes
Edmund	1 hour 39 minutes	1 hour 57 minutes
Bob	2 hours	1 hour 30 minutes
Roger	2 hours 15 minutes	1 hour 43 minutes
Tina	1 hour 20 minutes	1 hour 35 minutes
Tim	2 hours 20 minutes	2 hours 2 minutes
Clive	1 hour 35 minutes	1 hours 52 minutes
Graham	1 hour 59 minutes	2 hours 5 minutes
Barry	1 hour 40 minutes	2 hours
Glen	1 hour 57 minutes	1 hour 53 minutes

The standard time for the performance of the job is 2 hours and 30 minutes, but this was set several years ago when most staff were unfamiliar with the equipment in use. It is estimated that at least 15 minutes of idle time may be unavoidable.

Task

Determine four performance standards for the job in question.

Activity 9.6

The following information has been collected about the materials used by Sutton Ltd, an organisation which uses standard costing.

Material	Supplier	Information source	Unit cost £	20X2 standard £	20X3 standard £
AB30	4073	20X3 catalogue	1.74	1.68	1-74
AB35	4524	20X2 catalogue	5.93	5.93	6-27
		Invoice (10/X2)	6.05		
		Telephone enquiry to 4524	6.00		
BB29	4333	X2/X3 catalogue	15.72	15.00	16-30
BB42	4929	Invoice (5/X2)	2.36	2.40	2-01
	-	New supplier quotation (11/X2)	1.94		
CA19	4124	Contract to 12/X3	20.07	20.07	20-07
		Invoice (12/X2)	21.50		
CD26	4828	-	2.50		2-50 2-59

Sutton Ltd uses the materials in a variety of combinations to make four different products. Technical specifications for usage (in units of material per batch) have been determined as follows.

Material	Guildford	Dorking	Reigate	Coulsdon
AB30	20	20	10	5
AB35	-	10	-	-
BB29	-	-	4	-
BB42	8	5	-	12
CA19	20	9	-	5
CD26	6	-	3	-

Tasks

(a)   What are the 20X2 standard materials costs for each product?

(b)   As a last resort standard costs are set by adding the current annual rate of inflation to the most recent available price, but more certain information is used if it is available (for example, catalogue prices are usually guaranteed for 12 months). Your task is to calculate the new standard costs for 20X3. Very large quantities are used so it is important to calculate to the penny. The RPI is 3.7%.

RETAIL PRICE INDEX (INFLATION)

Key learning points

- A **standard** represents what we think should happen.

- A **standard cost** is a predetermined unit of cost.

- **Standard costing** is a means of valuing stocks and the issue of materials to production and a way of exerting control over a business.

- A **standard cost card/sheet** shows full details of the components making up the standard cost of a product.

- Setting **materials standards** involves determining how much material is needed to produce a product and how much that material should cost.

- Setting **labour standards** is generally a matter of estimating how long it will take to do a piece of work. This can be done on a rough and ready basis or by detailed work study.

- **Standard costs** can be set for expenses just as they can for any other cost.

- Standards are basically set by developing an awareness of market conditions and by understanding technical requirements. They can also be set so as to encourage improvements in performance.

- **Inflation** should always be considered when setting standards.

Quick quiz

1   What details would you expect to see on a standard cost card?

2   What is the formula for standard materials cost?

3   What is the formula for standard labour cost?

4   What are the advantages of using historical data to calculate labour standards?

5   How would you explain the term standard performance?

6   List four types of performance standard.

7   How often are standard cost revisions usually made?

Answers to quick quiz

1   The quantity and price of direct material. The time and rate of each grade of direct labour. Overhead recovery, full cost, standard selling price and standard profit.

2   Standard materials usage × standard materials price.

3   Time that it should take to do a job × standard labour rate.

4   No extra costs are involved in getting the information, and the information is not distorted by employees working more quickly or slowly than usual.

5   A person who is working in a standard way at a standard rate is said to be working at standard performance.

6   Ideal, attainable, current and basic.

7   Once a year.

Answers to activities

Answer 9.1

(a)   A standard cost is standard in two senses.

(i)   It is a uniform cost that is applied to all like items, irrespective of their actual cost.
(ii)   It is a measure of expected performance, that is, a standard to be achieved.

(b)   Standard costing is used for two main reasons.

(i)   As a means of valuing stocks and the cost of production.
(ii)   In variance analysis, which is a means of controlling the business.

Answer 9.2

This activity is a test of your ability to analyse information in a way that avoids laborious computations as much as a test of your understanding of standard setting.

Operation	Grade	Rate £	Time Hours	Cost £
1			1.50	7.20
2	Y	5.50	1.00	5.50
3			0.25	1.20
4	Z	6.50	2.00	13.00
5			0.50	2.40
6	Y	5.50	2.00	11.00
7	Z	6.50	3.00	19.50
8			1.00	4.80
9			0.25	1.20
10	Y	5.50	0.50	2.75

(*Tutorial note.* The operation is done by grade X labour at £4.80 per hour unless otherwise indicated.

	A	B	C	Sharp C	D	E	F	Augmented F	G
1				7.20	7.20		7.20		7.20
2	5.50	5.50			5.50				
3			1.20	1.20		1.20		1.20	
4	13.00			13.00		13.00	13.00		
5	2.40	2.40				2.40			2.40
6		11.00	11.00	11.00	11.00			11.00	
7					19.50			19.50	
8		4.80						4.80	
9		1.20					1.20		1.20
10		2.75			2.75	2.75			2.75
Standard cost	20.90	21.65	18.20	32.40	45.95	19.35	21.40	36.50	13.55

Answer 9.3

STANDARD COST CARD - PRODUCT TUDOR

Direct materials	Cost	Requirement	£	£
A	£1 per kg	7 kgs	7	
B	£2 per litre	4 litres	8	
C	£3 per m	3 m	9	
				24
Direct labour				
Skilled	£10 per hour	8 hours	80	
Semi-skilled	£5 per hour	4 hours	20	
				100
Standard direct cost				124
Variable production overhead	£2.50 per hour	8 hours		20
Standard variable cost of production				144
Fixed production overhead	£6.25 (W) per hour	8 hours		50
Standard full production cost				194

Working

$$\text{Overhead absorption rate} = \frac{£250,000}{5,000 \times 8} = £6.25 \text{ per skilled labour hour}$$

Answer 9.4

Standard product cost and gross profit

	£
Direct material L	300
Direct material W	270
Direct labour	165
Direct cost	735
Production overhead (£252,000/1,200)	210
Total product cost	945
Selling price (120,000/(1,200/12))	1,200
Gross profit	255

Answer 9.5

(a) The *ideal standard*, based on the most favourable operating conditions, seems to be one hour. This is the time achieved by Jed less the 15 minutes idle time (since we are not sure it is *completely* unavoidable). However, in view of the other performances it seems unlikely that anybody could achieve this. Further investigation should be made to determine whether Jed's two attempts include idle time or not: it may be that they were rare occasions when idle time was avoided.

(b) The *current standard* can be taken as the average (the arithmetic mean) of all the times recorded.

Worker	Time Minutes	Time Minutes
Lynn	105	120
Alison	125	115
Jed	75	75
Kate	130	90
Nick	105	97
Edmund	99	117
Bob	120	90
Roger	135	103
Tina	80	95
Tim	140	122
Clive	95	112
Graham	119	125
Barry	100	120
Glen	117	113
	1,545	1,494

$$\text{Arithmetic mean} = \frac{(1,545 + 1,494)}{2 \times 14} = 108.5 \text{ minutes} = 1 \text{ hour } 48 \text{ minutes}$$

(c) An *attainable standard* is one that makes some allowance for wastage and inefficiencies. Simply by looking at the times that most come roughly in the range 1 hour 40 minutes to 2 hours. (1 hour 35 minutes to 2 hours if you do know how to calculate quartiles). A reasonably attainable standard would therefore be 1 hour 40 minutes or slightly less, giving most staff something to aim for.

(d) The *basic standard* is given in the question as 2 hours and 30 minutes. This is clearly very outdated and of little value.

Answer 9.6

(a)

Material	Standard cost £	Guildford £	Dorking £	Reigate £	Coulsdon £
AB30	1.68	33.60	33.60	16.80	8.40
AB35	5.93	-	59.30	-	-
BB29	15.00	-	-	60.00	-
BB42	2.40	19.20	12.00	-	28.80
CA19	20.07	401.40	180.63	-	100.35
CD26	2.50	15.00	-	7.50	-
Total standard materials cost		469.20	285.53	84.30	137.55

(b)

Material	Supplier	Information source	Unit cost £	20X2 standard £	20X3 standard £	Note
AB30	4073	20X3 catalogue	1.74	1.68	1.74	(i)
AB35	4524	20X2 catalogue	5.93	5.93		
		Invoice (10/X2)	6.05		6.27	(ii)
		Telephone enquiry to 4524	6.00			
BB29	4333	X2/X3 catalogue	15.72	15.00	16.30	(iii)
BB42	4929	Invoice (5/X2)	2.36	2.40		
	-	New supplier quotation (11/X2)	1.94		2.01	(iv)
CA19	4124	Contract to 12/X3	20.07	20.07	20.07	(v)
		Invoice (12/X2)	21.50			
CD26	4828	-		2.50	2.59	(vi)

Notes

(i) AB30 is costed on the basis of the 20X3 catalogue price which is assumed to be guaranteed for 12 months.

(ii) AB35's new standard cost is on the basis of the most recent invoiced cost plus 3.7%. (The telephone enquiry figure is suspiciously 'round'.)

(iii)   BB29's current standard cost looks like an underestimate. Do not allow this to influence your calculation for 20X3.

(iv)   BB42 should be bought from the new supplier, on the evidence available. The standard cost is £1.94 plus 3.7%.

(v)   For CA19 the contractually agreed price should be used as the standard cost. Enquiries should be made as to why this was not the cost invoiced in December 20X2.

(vi)   In the absence of other information 3.7% is added to the 20X2 standard cost for CD26.

Chapter 10   Calculation of variances

Chapter topic list

1   Introduction to variances

2   Materials variances

3   Labour variances

4   Fixed overhead variances

5   Control ratios

Learning objectives

On completion of this chapter you will be able to:

	Performance criteria	Range statement
• calculate and analyse materials (usage and price) and labour (rate and efficiency) variances	6.1.4	6.1.2
• systematically check information against the overall usage and stock control practices	6.1.5	6.1.1-2
• calculate and analyse the following overhead variances	6.2.6	6.2.3

    ○   expenditure
    ○   efficiency
    ○   volume
    ○   capacity

BPP PUBLISHING

1 INTRODUCTION TO VARIANCES

1.1 Having set **standards** (as described in the previous chapter), what are we going to do with them? We mentioned that we could use materials standards to value materials issues and materials stock. But what about labour standards? And standards for expenses? **The principal reason most organisations use standard costs is for control.**

1.2 At the beginning of this Interactive Text we introduced you to the term 'variance'. When costs are incurred in an organisation they are compared with the estimated standard cost, and if there is a difference it is known as a **variance**. Generally, somebody will be responsible for a variance and will be asked to explain why it occurred.

1.3 The analysis of variances is a very important aspect of costing. Variance analysis simply aims to find the difference between what costs *were* and what they *should have been*.

1.4 **Standards represent what should happen.** Suppose for example that 10,000 units of product X should require 10,000 kg of material A costing £10,000. This is therefore the standard for product X. Let us now consider the actual results for product X - 11,000 kg of material A costing £12,000 were required to make 10,000 units of product X. We can therefore deduce the following.

(a) We had to spend £2,000 more on materials than we should have to make 10,000 units of product X.

(b) We used 1,000 kg more of material A than we should have to make 10,000 units of product X.

1.5 These differences that we have identified are the **variances** that we were explaining above.

> **KEY TERMS**
>
> - A **variance** is the difference between an actual result and an expected standard cost or revenue.
>
> - **Variance analysis** is the process by which the *total* difference between standard and actual results is analysed.

1.6 Variances may be either **favourable** or **adverse**.

(a) A **favourable** variance means that actual results were better than expected results (ie standards).

(b) An **adverse** variance means that actual results were worse than expected results (ie standards).

1.7 This chapter looks at the main types of variance for materials, labour and fixed overheads, and the processes involved in calculating them.

2 MATERIALS VARIANCES

Why materials variances arise

2.1 Standards are estimates: they are predictions of what will happen. However, how accurate these estimates turn out to be will depend upon what happens after they have been set.

202

2.2   For example, suppose you are expecting a good coffee bean harvest, and therefore set a **standard material price** of £10 per kg of coffee. If your prediction is correct, and a good harvest results, then your standard of £10 will be correct. However, if your prediction is not correct, and prices are in fact £15 per kg of coffee beans, then **your standard will be inaccurate.**

2.3   If your standard is inaccurate, then the actual costs incurred will be different to the standard costs estimated - and this is where our **differences** or **variances** arise.

2.4   Think back to how the **materials standard cost** is calculated.

$$\text{materials standard cost} = \text{standard usage} \times \text{standard price}$$

2.5   Now think about how a variance could arise. Consider the following.

- If actual usage were different to standard usage
- If actual price were different to standard price
- If actual usage *and* actual price were different to standard usage and standard price

Calculating materials variances

2.6   EXAMPLE: MATERIALS TOTAL VARIANCES

The following standards have been set for product LW.

	Standard cost	*Standard usage*
Material A	£2.20 per kg	2kg per unit

Actual production in January was 10,000 units and actual cost of material A was £46,000. Usage in January was exactly as expected.

Task

Calculate the materials total variance for January.

2.7   SOLUTION

	£
10,000 units should have cost (× £2.20 × 2kg)	44,000
but did cost	46,000
Materials total variance	2,000 (A)

2.8   EXAMPLE: MATERIALS PRICE AND USAGE VARIANCES

In February, the standards stayed the same but the actual production figures were as follows.

Actual production	10,000 units
Material A	21,000 kg costing £47,250

Calculate the materials price and the materials usage variance for February.

2.9 SOLUTION

	£
21,000 kg should have cost (× £2.20)	46,200
but did cost	47,250
Materials price variance	1,050
10,000 units should have taken (× 2 kg)	20,000 kg
but did take	21,000 kg
Materials usage variance in kg	1,000 kg
× standard cost per kg	× £2.20
Materials usage variance	£2,200

Three variances may therefore be calculated for materials.

> **KEY TERMS**
>
> - The **materials total variance** is the difference between what the output actually cost and what it should have cost, in terms of material. It can be divided into the following two sub-variances.
>
> - The **materials price variance** is the difference between the standard cost and the actual cost of the *actual* quantity of material used or purchased. In other words, it is the difference between what the material did cost and what it should have cost.
>
> - The **materials usage variance** is the difference between the standard quantity of materials that *should* have been used for the number of units *actually* produced, and the actual quantity of materials used, valued at the standard cost per unit of material. In other words, it is the difference between how much material should have been used and how much material was used, valued at standard cost.

Adverse and favourable variances

2.10 All of the examples we have seen so far have been cases where **more money was paid out** or **more materials were used than expected**. These are called **adverse variances** because they have adverse consequences. They mean that **less profit** is made than we hoped.

2.11 Sometimes, of course, things will be cheaper than usual or we will use them more efficiently. When less money is paid than expected or fewer materials are used than expected the variances are said to be **favourable variances**. They mean that **more profit** is made than we hoped.

2.12 EXAMPLE: ADVERSE AND FAVOURABLE VARIANCES

It is now April and actual data is as follows.

Production	9,500 units
Material A	20,000 kg costing £42,000

Have a go at calculating the variances yourself before looking at the solution.

2.13 SOLUTION

(a) Let's begin by calculating the **materials total variance**.

	£
9,500 units should have cost (9,500 × 2kg × £2.20)	41,800
but did cost	42,000
	200 (A)

The (A) indicates that overall the variance is **adverse**.

(b) We can now go on to calculate the individual components of the total variance (ie the price and usage variances).

	£
20,000 kg should have cost (× £2.20)	44,000
but did cost	42,000
Materials price variance	2,000 (F)

The (F) indicates that this is a **favourable** variance because less money was spent than expected.

9,500 units should take (× 2 kg)	19,000 kg
but did take	20,000 kg
Materials usage variance in kg	1,000 kg (A)
× standard cost per kg	× £2.20
Materials usage variance in £	£2,200 (A)

The (A) indicates that this is an **adverse** variance, because more materials were used than standard for 9,500 units.

(c) Let's check that the total variance is the sum of the two individual variances.

	£
Price variance	2,000 (F)
Usage variance	(2,200) (A)
Total variance	(200) (A)

Remember that adverse variances are **negative** (*less* profit) and favourable variances are **positive** (*more* profit).

Material variances and opening and closing stock

2.14 Suppose that a company uses raw material P in production, and that this raw material has a standard price of £3 per metre. During one month 6,000 metres are bought for £18,600, and 5,000 metres are used in production. At the end of the month, stock will have been increased by 1,000 metres. In variance analysis, the problem is to determine the materials price variance. Should it be calculated on the basis of materials purchased (6,000 metres) or on the basis of materials used (5,000 metres)?

2.15 The answer to this problem depends on how **closing stocks** of the raw materials will be valued.

(a) If they are **valued at standard cost**, (1,000 units at £3 per unit) the **price variance is calculated on material purchases** in the period.

(b) If they are **valued at actual cost** (FIFO) (1,000 units at £3.10 per unit) the **price variance is calculated on materials used in production** in the period.

Reasons for materials variances

2.16 As well as calculating the variances, it is important to understand why they might arise.

2.17 Possible reasons for a **materials price variance** may include the following.

(a) Purchase of a **cheaper** (favourable) or **more expensive** (adverse) substitute, than anticipated when the standard cost was set

(b) Bulk buying leading to unforeseen **discount** (favourable)

(c) **More care** taken in purchasing materials (favourable) or **less care** (adverse)

(d) Material price **increase** (adverse) or **decrease** (favourable)

2.18 Possible reasons for a **materials usage variance** may include the following.

(a) **Defective material** (adverse) or material used of a **higher quality** than standard (favourable)

(b) Material used more **efficiently** (favourable) or **excessive waste** (adverse)

(c) **Theft** (adverse)

(d) **Stricter quality control** (adverse)

Interdependence between variances

2.19 An important additional consideration is that variances should not be seen in isolation. In the example in Paragraph 2.8 above, the production manager was asked to explain why he had used 1,000 units more than he should have done. He said that the latest batch of material A had been rather **poor quality** and it had had to be thrown away. On further investigation it transpired that the buying department had indeed bought a lower grade of material, retailing at £2.10 per kg rather than the standard £2.20. This shows how important it is to understand the real reason for variances. **The actions of one part of a business affect the outcome of other parts.**

Activity 10.1

(a) A company had a favourable materials usage variance of £4,000 in February 20X3. What does this mean? *difference in usage × standard cost*

(b) If there was a materials usage variance does this mean that there must also have been a materials price variance? *No.*

(c) Explain the following in words.

	£
Standard cost (1,200 kg)	6,288
Actual cost (1,200 kg)	6,564
	276

(d) Calculate the materials total variance and its sub-variances given the following information.

Product A has a standard direct materials cost of £10 (5 kg of material M). During April 20X3 100 units of product A were manufactured using 520 kg of material M at a cost of £1,025.

3 LABOUR VARIANCES

3.1 **Labour variances** are very similar to materials variances but they have different names, presumably because it is thought rather undignified to talk about 'usage' of people and the 'price' of people.

3.2 There are two types of sub-variance that you need to understand and calculate for labour. The money variance is called the **rate variance** and the quantity variance is called the **efficiency variance**.

3.3 Apart from the different names there is no difference between a labour variance and a materials variance.

> **KEY TERMS**
>
> - The **labour total variance** is the difference between what the output should have cost and what it did cost, in terms of labour. It can be divided into the following two sub-variances.
>
> - The **labour rate variance** is the difference between the standard cost and the actual cost for the actual number of hours paid for. In other words, it is the difference between what the labour did cost and what it should have cost.
>
> - The **labour efficiency variance** is the difference between the hours that *should* have been worked for the number of units *actually* produced, and the actual number of hours worked, valued at the standard rate per hour. In other words, it is the difference between how many hours should have been worked and how many hours were worked, valued at the standard rate per hour.

3.4 EXAMPLE: LABOUR VARIANCES

Suppose that the labour standard for the production of a unit of product B is as follows.

> 4 hours of grade S labour at £3 per hour

During May 200 units of product B were made and the direct labour cost of grade S labour was £2,440 for 785 hours work.

Task

Calculate the following variances.

(a) The direct labour total variance
(b) The direct labour efficiency variance
(c) The direct labour rate variance

3.5 SOLUTION

(a) Let us begin by calculating the **direct labour total variance**.

	£
200 units of product B should have cost (× £12)	2,400
but did cost	2,440
Direct labour total variance	40 (A)

(b) Having learned that direct labour costs were £40 more than they should have been, we can now look at why this happened.

(c) **Labour rate variance.** This variance is calculated by taking the number of labour hours 'purchased' ie paid for, and comparing what they did cost with what they should have cost.

	£
785 hours of grade S labour should cost (× £3)	2,355
but did cost	2,440
Labour rate variance	85 (A)

The variance is **adverse** because **actual rates of pay were higher than expected**.

(d) **Labour efficiency variance.** This variance is calculated by taking the amount of output produced (200 units of product B) and comparing how long it should have taken to make them with how long it did take. The difference is the **efficiency variance**, expressed in hours of work. It should be converted into £ by applying the **standard rate per labour hour**.

200 units of product B should take (× 4 hours)	800 hrs
but did take	785 hrs
Labour efficiency variance in hrs	15 hrs (F)
× standard rate per hour	× £3
Labour efficiency variance in £	£45 (F)

The variance is **favourable** because the **labour force has been more efficient** than expected.

(e) **Summary**

	£
Labour rate variance	85 (A)
Labour efficiency variance	45 (F)
Direct labour total variance	40 (A)

Activity 10.2

When are materials price variances recorded?

Activity 10.3

(a) Why might an adverse labour rate variance arise?

(b) Give two possible reasons for an adverse materials price variance.

(c) What variances might arise if temporary student labour is used on a job?

Activity 10.4

Pogle Ltd manufactures one product, the clanger. The following direct standard costs apply to the clanger.

	£
Direct material 10 kgs at £5 per kg	50
Direct labour 5 hours at £6 per hour	30

In July production was 10,000 units and actual data for the month was:

(a) Actual materials consumed 106,000 kgs costing £530,500
(b) Actual labour hours worked 50,200 hours, costing £307,200

Task

Calculate the materials price and usage variances, and the labour rate and efficiency variances.

Reasons for labour variances

3.6 Reasons for labour rate variances may include the following.

(a) Wage rate increases (adverse)

(b) Excessive overtime with over premiums charged to (direct) labour costs (adverse)

(c) Using more skilled (and hence more expensive) labour (adverse) or less skilled (and hence less expensive) labour (favourable) than allowed for when the standard was set

3.7 **Favourable labour efficiency variances** will be reflected in output being produced more quickly than expected. Reasons may include the following.

(a)   Highly motivated or skilled staff

(b)   Better quality equipment or materials than anticipated when the standard was set

3.8   By contrast adverse labour efficiency variances will be reflected in output being lower than the standard set. Reasons may include the following.

- Deliberate go-slows
- Untrained or unskilled workforce
- Substandard material being used
- Errors in allocating time to jobs

Interdependence between variances

3.9   Do not forget that variances **should not be looked at in isolation**. There may be a favourable labour rate variance if apprentices are used instead of the expected skilled labour but this could lead to an adverse efficiency variance if the apprentices do not work as efficiently.

3.10 On the other hand, more highly skilled workers may be more efficient but their rate per hour will be more. Moreover, if the purchasing department purchases cheaper materials than standard there will be a favourable material price variance but there may be an adverse labour efficiency variance: cheaper material is often of a poorer quality and hence the labour force may take longer to produce a certain quantity of 'good' units.

4   FIXED OVERHEAD VARIANCES

4.1   You may have noticed that the method of calculating cost variances for variable cost items is essentially the same for labour and materials. Fixed overhead variances are very different. In an absorption costing system, they are **an attempt to explain the under- or over-absorption of fixed production overheads in production costs**. You should of course, know all about under/over absorption of fixed overheads. We looked at this topic in detail in Chapter 5. If you need reminding, however, skim through Section 6 of that chapter again.

4.2   You will find it easier to calculate and understand **fixed overhead variances**, if you keep in mind the whole time that you are trying to 'explain' (put a name and value to) any under- or over-absorbed overhead.

Remember that the **absorption rate** is calculated as follows.

$$\textbf{Overhead absorption rate } = \frac{\text{Budgeted fixed overhead}}{\text{Budgeted activity level}}$$

4.3   If either of the following are incorrect, then we will have an under- or over-absorption of overhead.

- The numerator (number on top) = Budgeted fixed overhead
- The denominator (number on bottom) = Budgeted activity level

4.4   The **fixed overhead total variance** may be broken down into two parts as follows.

- An **expenditure variance**
- A **volume variance**. This in turn may be split into two parts.

  -   A **volume efficiency variance**
  -   **volume capacity variance**

The fixed overhead expenditure variance

4.5 The fixed overhead expenditure variance occurs if the numerator is incorrect. It measures the under- or over-absorbed overhead caused by the **actual total overhead** being different from the budgeted total overhead.

4.6 Therefore, fixed overhead expenditure variance = **Budgeted expenditure – Actual Expenditure.**

The fixed overhead volume variance

4.7 As we have already stated, the fixed overhead volume variance is made up of the following sub-variances.

- Fixed overhead efficiency variance
- Fixed overhead capacity variance

These variances arise if the denominator (ie the budgeted activity level) is incorrect.

4.8 The fixed overhead efficiency and capacity variances measure the under- or over-absorbed overhead caused by the **actual activity level** being different from the budgeted activity level used in calculating the absorption rate.

4.9 There are two reasons why the **actual activity** level may be different from the **budgeted activity level** used in calculating the absorption rate.

(a) The workforce may have worked more or less efficiently than the standard set. This deviation is measured by the **fixed overhead efficiency variance.**

(b) The hours worked by the workforce could have been different to the budgeted hours (regardless of the level of efficiency of the workforce) because of overtime and strikes etc. This deviation from the standard is measured by the **fixed overhead capacity variance.**

How to calculate the variances

4.10 In order to clarify the overhead variances which we have encountered in this section, consider the following definitions which are expressed in terms of how each overhead variance should be calculated.

KEY TERMS

- **Fixed overhead total variance** is the difference between fixed overhead incurred and fixed overhead absorbed. In other words, it is the under- or over-absorbed fixed overhead.

- **Fixed overhead expenditure variance** is the difference between the budgeted fixed overhead expenditure and actual fixed overhead expenditure.

- **Fixed overhead volume variance** is the difference between actual and budgeted volume multiplied by the standard absorption rate per *unit*.

- **Fixed overhead volume efficiency variance** is the difference between the number of hours that actual production should have taken, and the number of hours actually taken (that is, worked) multiplied by the standard absorption rate per *hour*.

- **Fixed overhead volume capacity variance** is the difference between budgeted hours of work and the actual hours worked, multiplied by the standard absorption rate per *hour*.

4.11 You should now be ready to work through an example to demonstrate all of the fixed overhead variances.

4.12 EXAMPLE: FIXED OVERHEAD VARIANCES

Suppose that a company budgets to produce 1,000 units of product E during August 20X3. The expected time to produce a unit of E is five hours, and the budgeted fixed overhead is £20,000. The standard fixed overhead cost per unit of product E will therefore be as follows.

5 hours at £4 per hour = £20 per unit

Actual fixed overhead expenditure in August 20X3 turns out to be £20,450. The labour force manages to produce 1,100 units of product E in 5,400 hours of work.

Task

Calculate the following variances.

(a) The fixed overhead total variance
(b) The fixed overhead expenditure variance
(c) The fixed overhead volume variance $b + c = a$
(d) The fixed overhead volume efficiency variance $d + e = c$
(e) The fixed overhead volume capacity variance

4.13 SOLUTION

All of the variances help to assess the under- or over-absorption of fixed overheads, some in greater detail than others.

(a) **Fixed overhead total variance**

	£
Fixed overhead incurred	20,450
Fixed overhead absorbed (1,100 units × £20 per unit)	22,000
Fixed overhead total variance	1,550 (F)
(= under-/over-absorbed overhead)	

The variance is favourable because more overheads were absorbed than budgeted.

(b) **Fixed overhead expenditure variance**

	£
Budgeted fixed overhead expenditure	20,000
Actual fixed overhead expenditure	20,450
Fixed overhead expenditure variance	450 (A)

The variance is adverse because actual expenditure was greater than budgeted expenditure.

(c) **Fixed overhead volume variance**

The production volume achieved was greater than expected. The fixed overhead volume variance measures the difference at the standard rate.

	£
Actual production at standard rate (1,100 × £20 per unit)	22,000
Budgeted production at standard rate (1,000 × £20 per unit)	20,000
Fixed overhead volume variance	2,000 (F)

The variance is **favourable** because output was greater than expected.

(i) The labour force may have worked efficiently, and produced output at a faster rate than expected. Since overheads are absorbed at the rate of £20 per unit, more will be absorbed if units are produced more quickly. This **efficiency variance** is exactly the same in hours as the direct labour efficiency variance, but is valued in £ at the standard absorption rate for fixed overhead.

(ii) The labour force may have worked longer hours than budgeted, and therefore produced more output, so there may be a **capacity variance**.

(d) **Fixed overhead volume efficiency variance**

The volume efficiency variance is calculated in the same way as the labour efficiency variance.

1,100 units of product E should take (× 5 hrs)	5,500 hrs
but did take	5,400 hrs
Fixed overhead volume efficiency variance in hours	100 hrs (F)
× standard fixed overhead absorption rate per hour	× £4
Fixed overhead volume efficiency variance in £	£400 (F)

The labour force has produced 5,500 standard hours of work in 5,400 actual hours and so output is 100 standard hours (or 20 units of product E) higher than budgeted for this reason and the variance is **favourable**.

(e) **Fixed overhead volume capacity variance**

The volume capacity variance is the difference between the budgeted hours of work and the actual active hours of work (excluding any idle time).

Budgeted hours of work	5,000 hrs
Actual hours of work	5,400 hrs
Fixed overhead volume capacity variance	400 hrs (F)
× standard fixed overhead absorption rate per hour	× £4
Fixed overhead volume capacity variance in £	£1,600 (F)

Since the labour force worked 400 hours longer than budgeted, we should expect output to be 400 standard hours (or 80 units of product E) higher than budgeted and hence the variance is **favourable**.

The variances may be summarised as follows.

Expenditure variance	450 hrs (A)
Efficiency variance	400 hrs (F)
Capacity variance	1,600 hrs (F)
Over-absorbed overhead (total variance)	£1,550 (F)

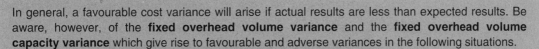

Graphical approach

4.14 BD Ltd budgets to produce 100 units of product A. Each unit of product A requires five machine hours and the budgeted fixed overhead is £10,000.

Two possible overhead absorption rates can be calculated from this information. BD Ltd could use an overhead absorption rate of £10,000/100 = £100 **per unit** or a machine hour rate of £10,000/(100 × 5) = £20 **per machine hour**.

4.15 If 100 units are produced or 500 machine hours worked, £10,000 of fixed overheads is absorbed. If 60 units are produced or 300 machine hours worked, £6,000 of fixed overheads is absorbed. Plotting this information on a graph produces a **line, the slope of which represents the fixed overhead absorption rates** of £100 per unit or £20 per machine hour. Whichever absorption rate is used, as the activity level increases, the fixed overhead absorbed into production increases.

Graph of BD Ltd's fixed overhead absorption rate

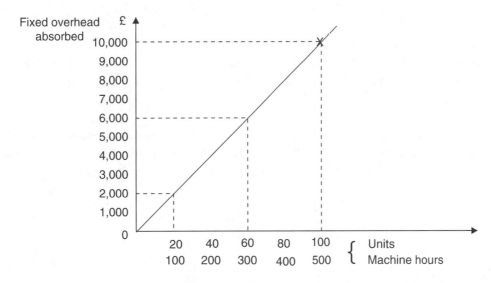

4.16 Now suppose that BD Ltd actually takes 700 machine hours to produce 120 units of product A and incurs £9,000 of fixed overheads. Let's reflect this information on a graph.

4.17 Obviously, **fixed overheads cost £1,000 less than anticipated**. Fixed overheads are a fixed cost, they do not vary with the level of activity in the way in which variable costs such as direct labour and direct materials do. And so the only reason for the difference must be that BD Ltd paid £1,000 less than anticipated. This difference of £1,000 is called the **fixed overhead expenditure variance** and, because the expenditure was less than expected, the variance is **favourable.**

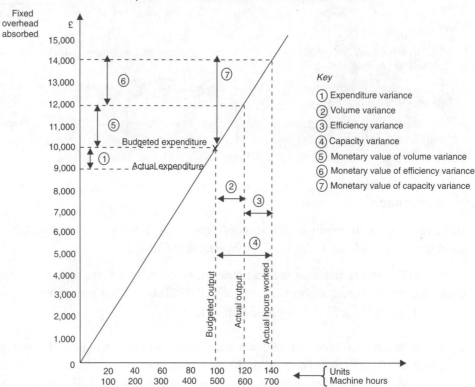

Graph of BD Ltd's fixed overhead variances

You can see on the vertical axis of the graph (①) that the variance is the **difference between the budgeted expenditure and the actual expenditure.**

4.18 A production level of 120 units (or 600 machine hours of production) means that **production was 20 units or 100 machine hours greater than planned**. An additional £2,000 (20 units × £100 or 100 hours × £20) of overheads was therefore absorbed into production costs, resulting in a favourable adjustment to the profit and loss account. This £2,000 is called the **fixed overhead volume variance** and, because it has had a positive impact on profits, it is a **favourable** variance. You can see on the graph (②) that the variance is the **difference between the budgeted production level** (of 100 units or 500 machines hours) and **the actual production level** (of 120 units or 600 standard hours of production).

4.19 Look at how the financial implication of this volume variance is shown on the graph (⑤). Can you see that if the slope of the line representing the overhead absorption rate changes, the variance in monetary terms would change. The graph below might make this clearer for you.

Graph of volume variances at various overhead absorption rates

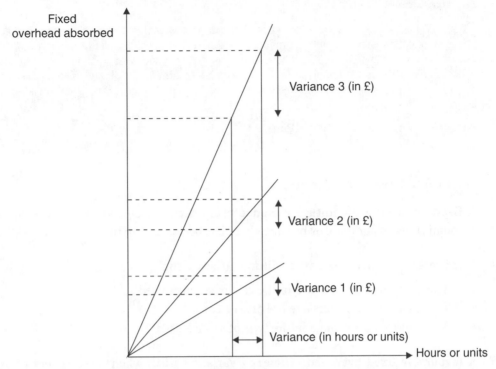

As the absorption rate increases (in other words, as the slope of the line increases), so does the variance in monetary terms, while the variance in hours or units remains the same.

4.20 **700 machine hours were worked but only 600 machine hours of work were produced,** which does not appear to be particularly efficient. In the hours worked (at the budgeted efficiency level), 100 extra hours of production should have been produced than actually were produced. This means that an additional $100 \times £20 = £2,000$ of absorbed fixed overhead should have been charged to the profit and loss account. The 100 hours is a measure of the inefficiency with which the machines were working and so £2,000 must be charged to the profit and loss account because of the inefficiency. This is the **(adverse) fixed overhead efficiency variance,** a subdivision of the volume variance. You can see the variance on the graph of the variances (③) as the **difference between the number of hours production that should have been achieved (600) and the number of hours that were worked (700).**

4.21 Although the **budgeted capacity was $100 \times 5 = 500$ hours, the machines worked for 700 hours**. Since we would expect output to be greater than budgeted if more hours are worked than budgeted, the financial implications of this difference of 200 hours ($200 \times £20 = £4,000$) must be credited to the profit and loss account. This is known as the **fixed overhead capacity variance** (a subdivision of the volume variance) and, because we would expect output to be higher than budgeted, the variance is **favourable.** This is shown on the graph (④) he **difference between the budgeted number of machine hours and the actual number of machine hours.**

4.22 Our graph is drawn to scale and so you can see the monetary value of the variances on the vertical axis (⑤), (⑥) and (⑦), but you **do not need to draw yours to scale.** It can be drawn freehand - you just need to ensure that you have not made any mistakes when calculating the fixed overhead absorption rate and that you have correctly marked on your graph the information provided.

ASSESSMENT ALERT

Watch out for overhead variance questions providing additional information in the form of graphs. For example, a question is likely to present overhead variance information in the form of bar charts **as well as** in written form. The assessor for unit 6 is concerned that in the past too many candidates have focused upon the recall of formulae to arrive at required variances and failed to show competence - additional graphical information should enable competence to be achieved by more than one method.

You should use whichever method you feel most comfortable with.

Reasons for fixed overhead variances

4.23 A **fixed overhead expenditure variance** could occur because of services being used more economically (favourable), or because there has been a saving in costs incurred.

4.24 An **adverse fixed overhead expenditure variance** might occur in the following situations.

- There has been an increase in the cost of services used
- There has been an excessive use of services
- There has been a change in the type of service used

4.25 A **favourable fixed overhead efficiency variance** arises when the recovery of overhead is higher than standard because potential output is higher than expected due to labour efficiency. An **adverse fixed overhead efficiency variance** arises when the recovery of overhead is lower than standard because potential output is lower than expected output due to labour inefficiency.

4.26 An **adverse fixed overhead capacity variance** occurs because actual activity level is less than budgeted activity level. This may be due to poor production scheduling, leading to bottlenecks and low output, unexpected machine breakdowns, strikes or shortage of labour or materials, acts of God (such as floods) and so on.

4.27 Favourable fixed overhead capacity variances arise when actual time worked is greater than budgeted time, for example when the labour force work overtime.

4.28 Do not worry if you find fixed overhead variances more difficult to grasp than the other variances we have covered. Most students do. Read over this section again and then try the following activities.

Activity 10.5

Lynn Ltd produces and sells one product only, the Koob, the standard cost for one unit being as follows.

	£
Direct material A - 10 kilograms at £20 per kg	200
Direct material B - 5 litres at £6 per litre	30
Direct wages - 5 hours at £6 per hour	30
Fixed overhead	50
Total standard cost	310

The fixed overhead included in the standard cost is based on an expected monthly output of 900 units. Fixed overhead is absorbed on the basis of direct labour hours.

During April 20X3 the actual results were as follows.

Production	800 units
Material A	7,800 kg used, costing £159,900
Material B	4,300 litres used, costing £23,650

Direct wages   4,200 hours worked for £24,150
Fixed overhead   £47,000

Tasks

(a)   Calculate price and usage variances for each material.

(b)   Calculate labour rate and efficiency variances.

(c)   Using the graphical approach, calculate fixed overhead expenditure, volume, efficiency and capacity variances.

Activity 10.6

Constance & Co Ltd expected to produce 14,000 units of its product during September 20X3. The standard time for a unit of the product is 2 hours and the budgeted fixed overhead was £70,000. Production overheads are absorbed on the basis of hours worked.

In the event the actual fixed overhead expenditure was £67,500. The number of hours worked was 28,400 and 12,000 units were produced.

Task

Calculate all of the fixed overhead variances for September 20X3.

---

5   CONTROL RATIOS

Efficiency, capacity and production volume ratios

5.1   You may also meet labour activity being measured by ratios, for example, as follows.
(a)   Efficiency ratio (or productivity ratio)
(b)   Capacity ratio
(c)   Production volume ratio, or activity ratio (the product of efficiency and capacity ratios).

Efficiency ratio	Capacity ratio	Production volume ratio
$$\dfrac{\text{Standard hours to make actual output}}{\text{Actual hours worked}}$$	$\times \ \dfrac{\text{Actual hours worked}}{\text{Hours budgeted}}$	$= \ \dfrac{\substack{\text{Output measured in expected} \\ \text{or standard hours}}}{\text{Hours budgeted}}$

These ratios are usually expressed as percentages.

5.2   EXAMPLE: RATIOS

Rush and Fluster Ltd budgets to make 25,000 standard units of output (in four hours each) during a budget period of 100,000 hours.

Actual output during the period was 27,000 units which took 120,000 hours to make.

Task

Calculate the efficiency, capacity and production volume ratios.

5.3   SOLUTION

(a)   Efficiency ratio $\dfrac{(27,000 \times 4) \text{ hours}}{120,000 \text{ hours}}$ $\times \ 100\% \ = $ 90%

(b)   Capacity ratio $\dfrac{120,000 \text{ hours}}{100,000 \text{ hours}}$ $\times \ 100\% \ = $ 120%

(c)   Production volume ratio $\dfrac{(27{,}000 \times 4)\text{ hours}}{100{,}000\text{ hours}}$ $\times\ 100\%\ =$ 108%

(d)   The production volume ratio of 108% (more output than budgeted) is explained by the 120% capacity working, offset to a certain extent by the poor efficiency (90% × 120% = 108%).

Key learning points

- A **variance** is the difference between actual results and expected results. **Variance analysis** is the process by which the total difference between actual results and expected results is analysed.

- In general, a **favourable** variance arises when actual results are better than expected results, an **adverse** variance means that actual results were worse than expected.

- **Total**, **price** and **usage** variances may be calculated for materials.

- **Total**, **rate** and **efficiency** variances may be calculated for labour.

- **Fixed overhead variances** include the following.

  o   **Expenditure** variance
  o   **Volume** variance (which may be split into **efficiency** and **capacity**)

- When considering the reasons why variances have occurred, it is important to remember that they should not be looked at in isolation, since there may be **interdependence between variances**.

- Variances can be calculated using diagrams.

Quick quiz

1   What is a materials usage variance?

2   What do favourable variances mean in terms of profit?

3   Are adverse variances positive or negative?

4   List three possible reasons why an adverse materials usage variance might occur.

5   The fixed overhead volume variance is broken down into which two parts?

6   What is the fixed overhead total variance and what is it equivalent to?

7   Which of the following formulae is correct?

(a)   Efficiency ratio × capacity ratio = production volume ratio
(b)   Efficiency ratio × production volume ratio = capacity ratio
(c)   Capacity ratio × production volume ratio = efficiency ratio

Answers to quick quiz

1   The difference between the standard quantity of materials that should have been used for the number of units actually produced, and the actual quantity of materials used, valued at the standard cost per unit of material.

2   They mean the actual profits are higher than expected profits.

3   Negative

4   - Material is defective
    - There is an excessive waste of material
    - Theft
    - Stricter quality control

5   The volume efficiency variance and the volume capacity variance.

6   It is the difference between fixed overhead incurred and fixed overhead absorbed. It is equivalent to the under- or over-absorbed overhead.

7 (a) Efficiency ratio × capacity ratio = production volume ratio

Answers to activities

Answer 10.1

(a) A favourable materials usage variance arises when less of a material is used than the standard quantity for the number of units produced. This quantity is valued at the standard materials cost.

(b) No.

(c) The calculation shows that 1,200 kg of a material were purchased for £5.47 per kg. The standard cost is £5.24 per kg, so an adverse price variance of 23p per kg arose (1,200 × £0.23 = £276).

		£
(d)	100 units should cost (× £10)	1,000
	but did cost	1,025
	Materials total variance	25 (A)

	£
520 kg should cost	1,040
but did cost	1,025
Materials price variance	15 (F)

100 units should take (× 5kg)	500 kgs
but did take	520 kgs
Materials usage variance (in kgs)	20 kgs (A)
× standard cost (per kg)	× £2
Materials usage variance (in £)	£40 (A)

Answer 10.2

A full standard costing system, which values stocks of raw materials at standard cost, is usually in operation if standard costing is used at all. If this is the case, materials price variances will be extracted at the time of purchase.

If raw materials are valued at actual cost (FIFO) the price variance has to be calculated on materials *used* in the period, but this is very inconvenient administratively.

Answer 10.3

(a) The main reason for an adverse labour rate variance is an increase in the wage rate above the standard rate.

(*Tutorial note.* If you mentioned overtime, this is not (usually) correct. Overtime hours are usually recorded at basic (standard) rate when calculating labour costs (and thus labour rate variances). The premium is an overhead, and an allowance may already be made in the overhead absorption rate for a certain amount of overtime. The overtime hours probably will give rise to a labour efficiency variance.)

(b) Two possible reasons are a price increase and careless purchasing (failing to take a discount, using the wrong supplier and so on). A third is that a higher quality of material was purchased deliberately.

(c) The temporary labour is likely to be paid a lower rate than standard, leading to a favourable labour rate variance. However, the temporary staff are likely to be less efficient than experienced staff, resulting in an adverse labour efficiency variance and perhaps adverse materials usage variance also.

Answer 10.4

	£
106,000 kgs should cost (× £5)	530,000
but did cost	530,500
Materials price variance	500 (A)

10,000 units should have used (× 10 kgs)	100,000 kgs
but did use	106,000 kgs
Materials usage variance (in kilos)	6,000 kgs (A)
× standard cost per kilo	× £5
Materials usage variance (in £)	£30,000 (A)

	£
50,200 hours should have cost (× £6)	301,200
but did cost	307,200
Labour rate variance	6,000 (A)
10,000 units should take (× 5 hours)	50,000 hrs
but did take	50,200 hrs
Labour efficiency (in hours)	200 hrs (A)
× standard rate per hour	× £6
Labour efficiency variance (in £)	£1,200 (A)

Answer 10.5

(a) *Price variance - A*

	£
7,800 kgs should have cost (× £20)	156,000
but did cost	159,900
Price variance	3,900 (A)

Usage variance - A

800 units should have used (× 10 kgs)	8,000 kgs
but did use	7,800 kgs
Usage variance in kgs	200 kgs (F)
× standard cost per kilogram	× £20
Usage variance in £	£4,000 (F)

Price variance - B

	£
4,300 units should have cost (× £6)	25,800
but did cost	23,650
Price variance	2,150 (F)

Usage variance - B

800 units should have used (× 5 l)	4,000 l
but did use	4,300 l
Usage variance in litres	300 (A)
× standard cost per litre	× £6
Usage variance in £	£1,800 (A)

(b) *Labour rate variance*

	£
4,200 hours should have cost (× £6)	25,200
but did cost	24,150
Rate variance	1,050 (F)

Labour efficiency variance

800 units should have taken (× 5 hrs)	4,000 hrs
but did take	4,200 hrs
Efficiency variance in hours	200 hrs (A)
× standard rate per hour	× £6
Efficiency variance in £	£1,200 (A)

(c) Overhead absorption rate per labour hour = £50/5 = £10
Budgeted expenditure = £50 × 900 = £4,500
Actual output in hours = 800 × 5 = 4,000

To plot a line which has a gradient the same as the overhead absorption rate per hour we need to know two points that it passes through.

If 5,000 labour hours are worked, overhead absorbed = £10 × 5,000 = £50,000
If 4,000 labour hours are worked, overhead absorbed = £10 × 4,000 = £40,000

The line therefore passes through (4,000 , 40,000) and (5,000 , 50,000).

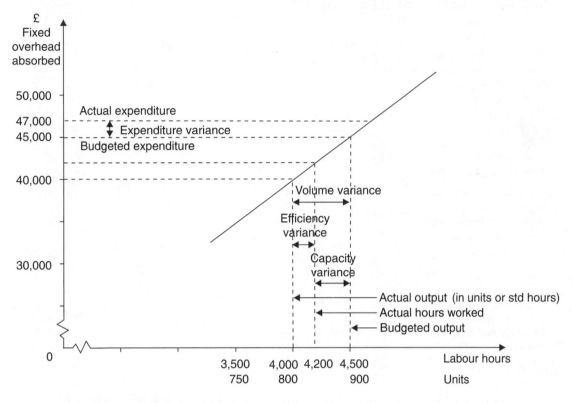

Expenditure variance = £45,000 – £47,000 = £2,000 (A). The variance is **adverse** because the actual expenditure is greater than the budgeted expenditure.

Volume variance is the difference between actual output and budgeted output. In monetary terms this is (4,000 – 4,500) hrs × £10 per hour = £5,000. The variance is **adverse** because the actual output is less than the budgeted output and so less overhead will be absorbed than expected.

Efficiency variance is the difference between actual output in standard hours and actual hours. In monetary terms this is (4,000 – 4,200) hrs × £10 per hour = £2,000. The variance is **adverse** because 4,200 hours of work should have been produced but only 4,000 were produced and so less overheads were absorbed than should have been.

Capacity variance is the difference between budgeted output and actual hours worked = (4,500 – 4,200) hrs × £10 per hour = £3,000. The variance is **adverse** because we would expect production levels to be less than budgeted if fewer hours are worked.

Answer 10.6

The overhead absorption rate is $\dfrac{£70,000}{14,000 \times 2}$ = £2.50 per hour or £5 per unit

	£
Total fixed overhead incurred	67,500
Total fixed overhead absorbed (12,000 units × £5)	60,000
Under-absorbed overhead = total variance	7,500 (A)

	£
Budgeted fixed overhead expenditure	70,000
Actual fixed overhead expenditure	67,500
Expenditure variance	2,500 (F)

12,000 units should have taken (× 2 hrs)	24,000 hrs
but did take	28,400 hrs
Efficiency variance (in hrs)	4,400 hrs (A)
× standard absorption rate per hour	× £2.50
Efficiency variance (in £)	£11,000 (A)

Budgeted activity level	28,000 hrs
Actual activity level	28,400 hrs
Capacity variance (in hrs)	400 hrs (F)
× standard rate per hour	× £2.50
Capacity variance (in £)	£1,000 (F)

Summary

	£
Expenditure variance	2,500 (F)
Efficiency variance	11,000 (A)
Capacity variance	1,000 (F)
Total variance	7,500 (A)

Chapter 11 Variance analysis

Chapter topic list

1 Statement of variances

2 Diagrammatic presentation of variances

3 Deriving actual data from standard cost details and variances

4 Presenting variance analysis information to management

Learning objectives

On completion of this chapter you will be able to:

	Performance criteria	Range statement
• compare standard costs against actual costs and analyse any variances	6.1.4	6.1.1-2
• systematically check information against the overall usage and stock control practices	6.1.5	6.1.1-2
• prepare variances reports with variances clearly identified and presented in an intelligible form	6.3.1	6.3.1-2
• identify any unusual or unexpected results and report them to management	6.3.2	6.3.1-2
• identify any reasons for significant variances and present explanations to management	6.3.3	6.3.1-2
• produce the results of variance analysis and the explanations of specific variances for management	6.3.4	6.3.1-2
• deal with any variance analysis queries	6.3.5	6.3.1-2

BPP PUBLISHING

1 STATEMENT OF VARIANCES

1.1 So far, we have considered how different types of variance are calculated without considering how they may be presented in a statement, or in a report to management.

1.2 An example will now be introduced to revise the variance calculations already encountered in Chapter 10.

1.3 EXAMPLE: STATEMENT OF VARIANCES

Dollar Princess Ltd manufactures one product, the opalette. The company operates a standard costing system and analysis of variances is made every month. The standard cost card for the product is as follows.

STANDARD COST CARD - OPALETTE

		£
Direct materials	0.5 kilos at £4 per kilo	2.00
Direct wages	2 hours at £2.00 per hour	4.00
Fixed overhead	2 hours at £3.70 per hour	7.40
Standard cost		13.40

Budgeted output for the month of June 20X0 was 5,100 units. Actual results for June 20X0 were as follows.

Production was 4,850 units
Materials consumed in production amounted to 2,300 kilos at a total cost of £9,800
8,500 labour hours were worked at a cost of £16,800
Fixed overheads amounted to £42,300

Task

Calculate all cost variances for the month ended 30 June 20X0.

1.4 SOLUTION

		£
(a)	2,300 kg of material should cost (× £4)	9,200
	but did cost	9,800
	Materials price variance	600 (A)

(b)	4,850 opalettes should use (× 0.5 kgs)	2,425 kg
	but did use	2,300 kg
	Materials usage variance in kgs	125 kg (F)
	× standard cost per kg	× £4
	Materials usage variance in £	£ 500 (F)

		£
(c)	8,500 hours of labour should cost (× £2)	17,000
	but did cost	16,800
	Labour rate variance	200 (F)

(d)	4,850 opalettes should take (× 2 hrs)	9,700 hrs
	but did take	8,500 hrs
	Labour efficiency variance in hours	1,200 hrs (F)
	× standard cost per hour	× £2
	Labour efficiency variance in £	£2,400 (F)

		£
(e)	Budgeted fixed overhead (5,100 units × 2 hrs × £3.70)	37,740
	Actual fixed overhead	42,300
	Fixed overhead expenditure variance	4,560 (A)

		£
(f)	Actual production at standard rate (4,850 units × £7.40)	35,890
	Budgeted production at standard rate (5,100 units × £7.40)	37,740
	Fixed overhead volume variance	1,850 (A)

Variance reports

1.5 Once all of the cost variances have been calculated, as in Paragraph 1.4, they should ideally be summarised in a **variance report**. The following for example, is not uncommon.

VARIANCE REPORT

Month June 20X0
Budgeted output 5,100 units
Actual output 4,850 units

	Actual costs	*Output*	*Standard costs* *Unit cost*	*Total cost*	*Total* *Variance*
	£	Units	£	£	£
Materials	9,800	4,850	2.00	9,700	100 (A)
Labour	16,800	4,850	4.00	19,400	2,600 (F)
Fixed overhead	42,300	4,850	7.40	35,890	6,410 (A)
	68,900		13.40	64,900	3,910 (A)

1.6 This report effectively **compares actual costs with 'flexed' budget figures**. This means that the budgeted figures have been recalculated to show what would have been expected if the actual production volume had been known in advance.

Significance of variances

1.7 Once you have completed your variance report, it should be clear which variances, if any, are **significant**. Variances are usually considered to be significant if they are more than a certain proportion of actual costs. For example, in Paragraph 1.5, we can calculate the following percentages in order to determine how significant each variance is.

(a) $\dfrac{\text{Materials total variance}}{\text{Actual materials cost}}$ $=$ $\dfrac{100}{9,800}$ $=$ 1%

(b) $\dfrac{\text{Labour total variance}}{\text{Actual labour cost}}$ $=$ $\dfrac{2,600}{16,800}$ $=$ 16%

(c) $\dfrac{\text{Fixed overhead total variance}}{\text{Actual fixed overhead cost}}$ $=$ $\dfrac{6,410}{42,300}$ $=$ 15%

As a **general guideline,** if the variance as a percentage of actual costs is greater than 5%, then it might be considered to be significant. (However, your organisation may have its own levels of significance which may be greater or less than 5%.)

1.8 The calculations in Paragraph 1.7 show that the labour and overhead total variances are significant. Significant variances should be investigated to find out why they have arisen.

Activity 11.1

Bradford Ltd manufactures one product, and the entire product is sold as soon as it is produced. There are no opening or closing stocks and work in progress is negligible. The company operates a standard costing system and analysis of variances is made every month. The standard cost card for the product, an alista, is as follows.

STANDARD COST CARD - ALISTA

		£
Direct materials	1 kilos at £2 per kilo	2.00
Direct wages	4 hours at £1.00 per hour	4.00
Fixed overhead	3 hours at £3.50 per hour	10.50
Standard cost		16.50

Budgeted output for the month of April 20X0 was 8,000 units. Actual results for April 20X0 were as follows.

Production was 9,000 units

Materials consumed in production amounted to 10,000 kilos at a total cost of £22,000

30,000 labour hours were worked at a cost of £32,000

Fixed overheads amounted to £82,000

Tasks

(a) Calculate all cost variances for the month ended 30 April 20X0.

(b) Prepare a variance report.

Activity 11.2

What are the following variances and why might they occur?

(a) Materials price variance
(b) Materials usage variance
(c) Labour rate variance
(d) Labour efficiency variance
(e) Fixed overhead expenditure variance

2 DIAGRAMMATIC PRESENTATION OF VARIANCES

2.1 It is possible to present variance analysis information **diagrammatically**. We begin by drawing horizontal and vertical axes.

- The horizontal axis represents quantity (of hours, kilograms and so on)
- The vertical axis represents price (per kg, per hour and so on).

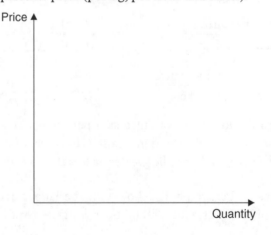

2.2 We will show you how to present material variances but the same approach can be used for the other variable cost variances (labour and variable overhead).

2.3 Suppose that the standard material cost of product A is £12 (3 kgs × £4 per kg) and that, in April 20X0, 100 units of product A are made using 280 kgs of material which cost £1,148.

To produce 100 units, the **standard material usage** is 100×3 kgs = 300 kgs at a **standard price** of £4 per kg, resulting in a **standard cost** of 300 kgs $\times$ £4 = £1,200. We can show the standards (300 kgs and £4 per kg) on the axes as follows.

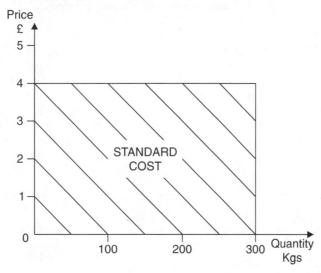

The area of the rectangle ($300 \times 4 = 1,200$) represents the standard cost of £1,200.

2.4 However, 280 kgs were actually used instead of the standard 300 kgs. This **usage variance** can be shown on the axes as follows.

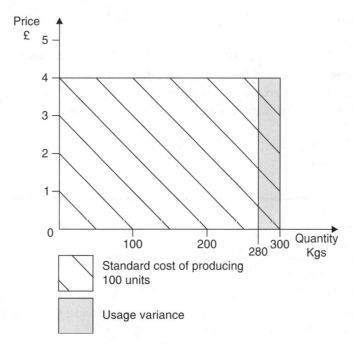

The rectangle representing the **usage variance** has an area of $20 \times 4 = 80$. Let's calculate the usage variance in the usual way just so you can see where the 80 comes from.

100 units should have used ($\times$ 3kgs)	300	kgs
but did use	280	kgs
Usage variance in kgs	20	kgs (F)
$\times$ standard price per kg	$\times$ £4	
Usage variance in £	£80	(F)

2.5 The actual price paid for each of the 280 kgs was £1,148 ÷ 280 = £4.10. We can therefore represent the **price variance** as follows.

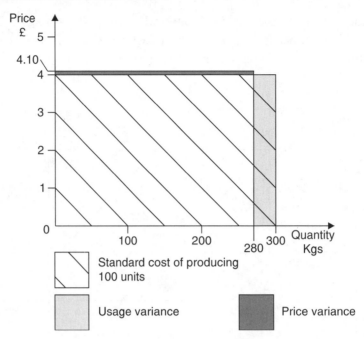

The area of the rectangle representing the price variance is $0.10 \times 280 = 28$. Again we'll just compare this with the variance calculated in the normal way.

	£
280 kgs should have cost ($\times$ £4)	1,120
but did cost	1,148
Price variance	28 (A)

2.6 The rectangle representing the price variance adds to or increases the area of the rectangle representing the standard material cost and hence the price variance must be **adverse**. On the other hand, the rectangle representing the usage variance falls within the rectangle representing standard material cost and so the usage variance is therefore **favourable**.

2.7 Try the following activity to make sure that you understand this particular presentation process.

Activity 11.3

Standard labour cost of product X - 10 hrs at £5 per hour
Actual production in week 52 - 25 units of product X
Actual hours worked in week 52 - 200
Actual wages paid in week 52 - £900

Draw a diagram representing the rate and efficiencies variances which occurred in week 52. State whether the variances are adverse or favourable.

2.8 You may find a diagram easier to understand than a statement such as 'There was a favourable rate variance of £100 and a favourable efficiency variance of £250'. The sizes of the rectangles representing the variances and their position with relation to the standard cost rectangle give some idea of the relative sizes of the variances and the direction (adverse or favourable).

3 DERIVING ACTUAL DATA FROM STANDARD COST DETAILS AND VARIANCES

3.1 In an assessment, you are most likely to be provided with data about actual results and you will have to calculate the variances. One way in which your understanding of the topic can be assessed, however, is if you are provided with information about variances from which you have to '**work backwards**' to determine the actual results. Let's have a look at an example.

3.2 EXAMPLE: WORKING BACKWARDS

The standard direct material cost of Product X is £96 (16 kgs × £6 per kg) and the standard direct labour cost is £72 (6 hours × £12 per hour).

The following variances were among those reported in control period 10 in relation to Product X.

Direct materials price: £18,840 favourable
Direct materials usage: £480 adverse
Direct labour rate: £10,598 adverse
Direct labour efficiency: £8,478 favourable

Actual direct wages cost £171,320 and £5.50 was paid for each kg of direct material. There was no opening or closing stocks of the material.

Task

Calculate the following.

(a)   Actual output
(b)   Actual hours worked
(c)   Average actual wage rate per hour
(d)   Actual number of kilograms purchased and used

3.3 SOLUTION

(a)

	£
Total direct wages cost	171,320
Adjust for variances:	
labour rate	(10,598)
labour efficiency	8,478
Standard direct wages cost	169,200

∴ Actual output   = Total standard cost ÷ unit standard cost
                    = £169,200 ÷ £72
                    = 2,350 units

(b)

	£
Total direct wages cost	171,320.0
Less rate variance	(10,598.0)
Standard rate for actual hours	160,722.0
÷ standard rate per hour	÷ £12.0
Actual hours worked	13,393.5 hrs

(c)   Average actual wage rate per hour = actual wages/actual hours = £171,320/13,393.5 = £12.79 per hour.

(d)   Number of kgs purchased and used = x

	£
x kgs should have cost (× £6)	6.0x
but did cost (× £5.50)	5.5x
Direct material price variance	0.5x

∴   £0.5x = £18,840
∴   x = 37,680 kgs

Activity 11.4

XYZ Ltd uses standard costing. The following data relate to labour grade II.

Actual hours worked	10,400 hours
Standard allowance for actual production	9,800 hours
Standard rate per hour	£5
Rate variance (adverse)	£416

What was the actual rate of pay per hour?

Activity 11.5

The standard material content of one unit of product A is 10kgs of material X which should cost £10 per kilogram. In June 20X0, 5,750 units of product A were produced and there was an adverse materials usage variance of £1,500.

Task

Calculate the quantity of material X used in June 20X0.

4   PRESENTING VARIANCE ANALYSIS INFORMATION TO MANAGEMENT

Report design

4.1   There is little point preparing variance analysis information if it goes no further than the accounting technician who prepares it. Information requires **dissemination**.

4.2   Although information can be disseminated **orally**, **informally**, the majority of variance analysis information is passed around an organisation in some sort of written report.

4.3   In general, reports should have the following characteristics.

(a)   They should be **clear**.

(b)   They should anticipate a reader's reactions and questions and answer them in the report itself.

(c)   They should not contain language which may be unfamiliar to the reader.

(d)   Formats should not change without good reason and definitions of terms should be consistent over time.

(e)   Account should be taken of different readers with different levels of understanding.

(f)   In general, they should be as simple as possible and should not assume too much expertise on the part of the reader.

(g)   Some management reports can simply be a few words whereas in more complex cases numbers can be useful. Pictures can help to show trends over time. Colours can also be used. Remember that different people find it easier to understand different kinds of communication and so variety is important.

Tables

4.4   Reports are usually produced as a **table of numbers** using a standard format, often comparing two sets of numbers. Actual results against standard can be reported in this way. It is common, however, for internal reports to use excessive detail and to report numbers with far too many digits. In general, numbers should be presented to two or three significant digits. A third digit should only be used to avoid crude rounding or because the report contains numbers of different magnitude. Using significant digits avoids spurious accuracy (the pretence that numbers are precisely accurate) and eases communication, since readers can take in approximate magnitude, key relationships and essential trends (and can perform mental arithmetic).

4.5 Think about the purpose your report is intended to fulfil before deciding what exactly to include.

Reporting to management

4.6 You should now have a clear idea of how to calculate the following variances.

- Materials price
- Materials usage
- Labour rate
- Labour efficiency
- Fixed overhead expenditure
- Fixed overhead volume
- Fixed overhead efficiency
- Fixed overhead capacity

If you are unsure about how to calculate any of these, look back at your notes and go through the activities and examples relating to this topic.

ASSESSMENT ALERT

Have you noticed how the labour efficiency variance (in hours) is equal to the fixed overhead efficiency variance (in hours)? When preparing cost variances in an assessment, you can carry out a quick check by making sure that these two variances are the same.

4.7 We have also considered the reasons why variances arise and the interdependence between them. So, what should we do with all of this information now? As we have already mentioned, there is little point preparing variance analysis information if it goes no further than the accounting technician, so we should present our results and analysis in the form of a **report for management** at the end of each period under consideration.

4.8 An extensive example of such a report will now be introduced, both to revise the variance calculations encountered in Chapter 10, and also to combine the variances into a report for management.

4.9 EXAMPLE: VARIANCE ANALYSIS REPORTS

McIntosh plc uses a standard costing system and for the single product that the firm produces the following standard costs apply.

	£
Direct material 5 kgs at £2 per kg	10
Direct wages 4 hours at £3 per hour	12
Fixed overhead 4 hours at £2 per hour	8
Total standard cost	30

In September 20X0 production is budgeted at 5,000 units and actual data for the month is as follows.

(a) Production 5,400 units
(b) Actual materials consumed 30,000 kgs, costing £57,000
(c) Actual labour hours worked 23,300, costing £72,500

(d)   Actual fixed overhead cost £38,000

Tasks

(a)   Prepare a variance report, detailing total materials, labour and overhead variances.

(b)   Calculate all the material, labour and fixed overhead sub-variances of the total variances in your variance report.

(c)   Prepare a report for management which includes a variance schedule and explanations of why the variances that you have calculated in (b) might have arisen.

4.10   SOLUTION

(a)   McINTOSH PLC VARIANCE REPORT

Month   *September*
Budgeted output   5,000 units
Actual output   5,400 units

	Actual costs	*Output*	*Standard costs* *Unit cost*	*Total cost*	*Total* *variance*
	£	Units	£	£	£
Materials	57,000	5,400	10	54,000	3,000 (A)
Labour	72,500	5,400	12	64,800	7,700 (A)
Fixed overhead	38,000	5,400	8	43,200	5,200 (F)
	167,500		30	162,000	5,500 (A)

(b)   (i)

	£
30,000 kgs should cost (× £2)	60,000
but did cost	57,000
Materials price variance	3,000 (F)

(ii)

5,400 units should have used (× 5 kgs)	27,000 kgs
but did use	30,000 kgs
Materials usage variance (in kgs)	3,000 kgs (A)
× standard cost per kg	× £2
Materials usage variance (in £)	£6,000 (A)

(iii)

	£
23,300 hours should have cost (× £3)	69,900
but did cost	72,500
Labour rate variance	2,600 (A)

(iv)

5,400 units should take (× 4 hrs)	21,600 hrs
but did take	23,300 hrs
Labour efficiency variance (in hrs)	1,700 hrs (A)
× standard rate per hour	× £3
Labour efficiency variance (in £)	£5,100 (A)

(v)

	£
Budgeted fixed overhead (4 × £2 × 5,000)	40,000
Actual fixed overhead	38,000
Fixed overhead expenditure variance	2,000 (F)

(vi)

5,400 units should have taken (× 4 hrs)	21,600 hrs
but did take	23,300 hrs
Fixed overhead efficiency variance (in hrs)	1,700 hrs (A)
× standard rate per hour	× £2
Fixed overhead efficiency variance (in £)	£3,400 (A)

(vii)		
	Budgeted activity level	20,000 hrs
	Actual activity level	23,300 hrs
	Fixed overhead capacity variance (in hrs)	3,300 hrs (F)
	× standard rate per hr	× £2
	Fixed overhead capacity variance (in £)	£6,600 (F)

(c) REPORT

To: McIntosh plc management
From: A Technician
Date: 15 October 20X0
Subject: Variance analysis report - September 20X0

This report contains a variance schedule which lists all of the cost variances for the period under consideration. Specific variances are explained where possible.

McINTOSH PLC
VARIANCE SCHEDULE

	(F)	(A)	
Cost variances	£	£	£
Materials price	3,000		
Materials usage		6,000	
Labour rate		2,600	
Labour efficiency		5,100	
Fixed overhead expenditure	2,000		
Fixed overhead efficiency		3,400	
Fixed overhead capacity	6,600		
	11,600	17,100	5,500 (A)

Explanation of variances

(a) **Favourable materials price variance.** This variance may have arisen because unforeseen discounts were received by purchasing staff.

(b) **Adverse materials usage variance.** This variance may have arisen because the material may have been defective, or there may have been excessive waste during production.

(c) **Adverse labour rate variance** This variance may have arisen because of wage rate increases, or excessive overtime being worked (and charged to direct labour costs).

(d) **Adverse labour efficiency variance.** This variance may arise if there are an increased number of machine breakdowns (thus resulting in increased idle time).

(e) **Favourable fixed overhead expenditure variance.** This variance may arise if there had been more economical use of services.

(f) **Adverse fixed overhead efficiency variance.** This variance might arise if output is lower than expected (because of labour inefficiency).

(g) **Favourable fixed overhead capacity variance.** This variance might arise because the workforce worked longer hours than expected, perhaps because of extra overtime hours.

(*Note.* There are many reasons for the above variances - we have only noted one or two specific reasons. Look back at the explanations given in Chapter 10 for a full range of possibilities.)

Activity 11.6

Ross Ltd uses a standard costing system and for the single product that the firm produces the following standard costs apply.

	£
Direct material 5 kgs at £3 per kg	15
Direct wages 4 hours at £4 per hour	16
Fixed overhead 4 hours at £1 per hour	4
Total standard cost	35

In April production is budgeted at 6,000 units and actual data for the month is as follows.

(a)   Production 6,200 units
(b)   Actual materials consumed 33,000 kgs, costing £97,000
(c)   Actual labour hours worked 25,800, costing £106,000
(d)   Actual fixed overhead cost £23,000

Tasks

(a)   Prepare a variance report, detailing total materials, labour and overhead variances.

(b)   Calculate all the material, labour and fixed overhead sub-variances of the total variances in your variance report.

(c)   Prepare a variance schedule for Ross Ltd for April 20X0.

ASSESSMENT ALERT

Variances are commonly assessed in Unit 6 Assessments. Make sure that you are able to calculate all of the variances covered in this Interactive Test and be able to comment on the possible causes of variances also.

Key learning points

- A **variance report** is a report which summarises cost variances.

- Variances should not be looked at in isolation, since one variance might be **interdependent** or **interrelated** with another.

- Variance information may also be presented **diagrammatically.**

- Sometimes you may have to **work backwards** in order to derive actual data from standard cost details and variances.

- Significant variances are investigated and it is usual to report the **reasons** for the occurrence of these variances.

Quick quiz

1   If 3,000 kg of material A should have cost £9,000, but did cost £10,400, what is the materials price variance?

2   When preparing a statement that reconciles standard cost of production to actual cost of production, should you *add* or *subtract* an adverse variance to the standard cost of production in order to calculate the actual cost of production?

3   Explain why a favourable materials price variance might be interrelated with an adverse materials usage variance.

4   The standard direct material cost of product ER is £50 (10kg × £5). In period 1, the materials price variance was found to be £2,100 favourable, whilst the materials usage variance was £1,500 adverse. £4.50 was paid for each kg of direct material.

Using the above information, calculate the actual number of kilograms purchased and used.

5   What are the main reasons for the occurrence of adverse fixed overhead capacity variances?

6   What type of variance will arise if actual hours worked are greater than budgeted hours worked?

7   What is the main method that is used to pass variance analysis information around an organisation?

Answers to quick quiz

1   £1,400 (Adverse)

2   Add (since the actual costs of production are higher than standard costs when the sum of the cost variances is adverse).

3   If cheaper materials are purchased, then this will give rise to a favourable price variance. However, the cheaper materials are likely to result in increased wastage and therefore an adverse materials usage variance will result.

4   Let number of kgs purchased and used = x

	£
x kgs should have cost	5.0x
but did cost (× £4.50)	4.5x
Direct materials price variance	0.5x

∴ £0.5x = £2,100
∴ x = 4,200 kg

5   • Excessive idle time
     • Shortage of plant capacity
     • Strikes

6   A favourable fixed overhead volume capacity variance.

7   By means of a written **report for management**.

Answers to activities

Answer 11.1

			£
(a)	(i)	10,000 kg of material should cost (× £2)	20,000
		but did cost	22,000
		Materials price variance	2,000 (A)
	(ii)	9,000 opalettes should use (× 1 kg)	9,000 kg
		but did use	10,000 kg
		Materials usage variance in kgs	1,000 kg (A)
		× standard cost per kg	× £2
		Materials usage variance in £	£2,000 (A)

			£
	(iii)	30,000 hours of labour should cost (× £1)	30,000
		but did cost	32,000
		Labour rate variance	2,000 (A)
	(iv)	9,000 opalettes should take (× 4 hrs)	36,000 hrs
		but did take	30,000 hrs
		Labour efficiency variance in hours	6,000 hrs (F)
		× standard cost per hour	× £1
		Labour efficiency variance in £	£6,000 (F)

			£
	(v)	Budgeted fixed overhead (8,000 units × 3 hrs × £3.50)	84,000
		Actual fixed overhead	82,000
		Fixed overhead expenditure variance	2,000 (F)

		£
(vi)	Actual production at standard rate (9,000 units × £10.50)	94,500
	Budgeted production at standard rate (8,000 units × £10.50)	84,000
	Fixed overhead volume variance	10,500 (F)

(b) BRADFORD LTD
VARIANCE REPORT

Month April 20X0
Budgeted output 8,000 units
Actual output 9,000 units

	Actual costs	*Output*	*Standard costs* *Unit cost*	*Total cost*	*Total* *Variance*
	£	*Units*	£	£	£
Materials	22,000	9,000	2.00	18,000	4,000 (A)
Labour	32,000	9,000	4.00	36,000	4,000 (F)
Fixed overhead	82,000	9,000	10.50	94,500	12,500 (F)
	136,000		16.50	148,500	12,500 (F)

Answer 11.2

(a) **Materials price variance**. This variance shows the difference between **actual price paid** for materials and their **standard price**. Such a variance may occur for the following reasons.

- Managers responsible for buying decisions have paid too much for the materials
- Inflation
- Seasonal variations in prices
- Rush orders - quick delivery may lead to higher prices
- Bulk purchase discounts (unforeseen)

(b) **Materials usage variance**. This variance indicates that the quantity of materials consumed was larger or smaller than standard. Such a variance may occur for the following reasons.

- Materials wastage was higher or lower than it should have been
- The quantity of rejects was above or below standard

(c) **Labour rate variance**. This variance is the difference between the actual labour cost paid to the workforce, and the standard labour cost. A rate variance might occur for the following reasons.

- Unexpected overtime working with overtime paid at a premium rate
- Productivity bonuses added on to basic rates

(d) **Labour efficiency variance**. This variance indicates that the actual production time needed to do the work was longer or less than expected for the period. Such a variance might occur for the following reasons.

- Weak supervision of the workforce
- A badly-motivated workforce might lead to poor labour productivity
- Machine breakdowns
- Bottlenecks in production leading to an idle workforce
- Shorter batch runs than expected so time is spent setting up between batch runs

(e) **Fixed overhead expenditure variance**. This variance indicates that the actual fixed overhead expenditure is greater or less than the budgeted fixed overhead expenditure. Such a variance might occur for the following reasons.

- Higher or lower than expected power costs
- Higher or lower than expected depreciation costs
- Higher or lower than expected accommodation costs
- Other items of fixed overhead expenditure being higher or lower than expected

Answer 11.3

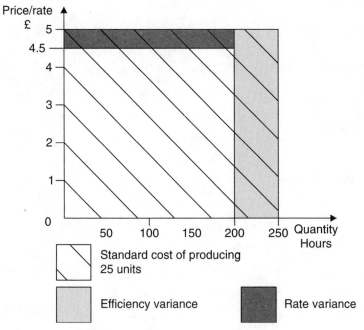

Price/rate £

Legend:

(hatched box) Standard cost of producing 25 units

(grey box) Efficiency variance

(dark box) Rate variance

Actual rate per hour = £900/200 = £4.50.

Both variances are favourable.

Answer 11.4

Rate variance per hour worked = $\dfrac{£416}{10,400}$ = £0.04 (A)

Actual rate per hour = £(5.00 + 0.04) = £5.04.

Answer 11.5

Let the quantity of material X used = Y

5750 units should have used (× 10kgs)	57,500 kgs
but did use	− Y kgs
Usage variance in kgs	(Y − 57,500) kgε
× standard price per kg	× £10
Usage variance in £	£1,500 (A)

∴ 10(Y − 57,500) = 1,500
   Y − 57,500 = 150
∴ Y = 57,650 kgs

Answer 11.6

(a) ROSS LTD VARIANCE REPORT

Month April

Budgeted output 6,000 units
Actual output 6,200 units

	Actual costs	*Output*	*Standard costs* *Unit cost*	*Total cost*	*Total variance*
	£	Units	£	£	£
Materials	97,000	6,200	15	93,000	4,000 (A)
Labour	106,000	6,200	16	99,200	6,800 (A)
Fixed overhead	23,000	6,200	4	24,800	1,800 (F)
	226,000		35	217,000	9,000 (A)

Part D: Standard costing and variance analysis

(b)　(i)

	£
33,000 kgs should cost (× £3)	99,000
but did cost	97,000
Materials price variance	2,000 (F)

(ii)

6,200 units should have used (× 5 kgs)	31,000 kgs
but did use	33,000 kgs
Materials usage variance (in kgs)	2,000 kgs (A)
× standard cost per kg	× £3
Materials usage variance (in £)	£6,000 (A)

(iii)

	£
25,800 hours should have cost (× £4)	103,200
but did cost	106,000
Labour rate variance	2,800 (A)

(iv)

6,200 units should take (× 4 hrs)	24,800 hrs
but did take	25,800 hrs
Labour efficiency variance (in hrs)	1,000 hrs (A)
× standard rate per hour	× £4
Labour efficiency variance (in £)	£4,000 (A)

(v)

	£
Budgeted fixed overhead (4 × £1 × 6,000)	24,000
Actual fixed overhead	23,000
Fixed overhead expenditure variance	1,000 (F)

(vi)

6,200 units should have taken (× 4 hrs)	24,800 hrs
but did take	25,800 hrs
Fixed overhead efficiency variance (in hrs)	1,000 hrs (A)
× standard rate per hour	× £1
Fixed overhead efficiency variance (in £)	£1,000 (A)

(vii)

Budgeted activity level	24,000 hrs
Actual activity level	25,800 hrs
Fixed overhead capacity variance (in hrs)	1,800 hrs (F)
× standard rate per hr	× £1
Fixed overhead capacity variance (in £)	£1,800 (F)

(c)　ROSS LTD
VARIANCE SCHEDULE

	(F) £	(A) £	£
Cost variances			
Materials price	2,000		
Materials usage		6,000	
Labour rate		2,800	
Labour efficiency		4,000	
Fixed overhead expenditure	1,000		
Fixed overhead efficiency		1,000	
Fixed overhead capacity	1,800		
	4,800	13,800	9,000 (A)

List of key terms
and index

BPP PUBLISHING

ORDER FORM

Any books from our AAT range can be ordered by telephoning 020-8740-2211. Alternatively, send this page to our address below, fax it to us on 020-8740-1184, or email us at **publishing@bpp.com.** Or look us up on our website: www.bpp.com

We aim to deliver to all UK addresses inside 5 working days; a signature will be required. Order to all EU addresses should be delivered within 6 working days. All other orders to overseas addresses should be delivered within 8 working days.

To: BPP Publishing Ltd, Aldine House, Aldine Place, London W12 8AW

Tel: 020-8740 2211   **Fax: 020-8740 1184**   **Email: publishing@bpp.com**

Mr / Ms (full name): _____

Daytime delivery address: _____

_____

Postcode: _____   Daytime Tel: _____

Please send me the following quantities of books.

	5/00 Interactive Text	8/00 DA Kit	8/00 CA Kit
FOUNDATION			
Unit 1 Recording Income and Receipts	☐	☐	
Unit 2 Making and Recording Payments	☐	☐	
Unit 3 Ledger Balances and Initial Trial Balance	☐		☐
Unit 4 Supplying information for Management Control	☐	☐	
Unit 20 Working with Information Technology (8/00 Text)	☐		
Unit 22/23 Achieving Personal Effectiveness	☐		
INTERMEDIATE			
Unit 5 Financial Records and Accounts	☐		☐
Unit 6 Cost Information	☐		
Unit 7 Reports and Returns	☐	☐	
Unit 21 Using Information Technology	☐		
Unit 22: see below			
TECHNICIAN			
Unit 8/9 Core Managing Costs and Allocating Resources	☐		☐
Unit 10 Core Managing Accounting Systems	☐	☐	☐
Unit 11 Option Financial Statements (Accounting Practice)	☐		
Unit 12 Option Financial Statements (Central Government)	☐		
Unit 15 Option Cash Management and Credit Control	☐	☐	
Unit 16 Option Evaluating Activities	☐		
Unit 17 Option Implementing Auditing Procedures	☐		
Unit 18 Option Business Tax FA00(8/00 Text)	☐		
Unit 19 Option Personal Tax FA00(8/00 Text)	☐		
TECHNICIAN 1999			
Unit 17 Option Business Tax Computations FA99 (8/99 Text & Kit)	☐	☐	
Unit 18 Option Personal Tax Computations FA99 (8/99 Text & Kit)	☐	☐	

TOTAL BOOKS   ☐   +   ☐   +   ☐   =   ☐

Postage and packaging:
                                                              @ £9.95 each = £ ☐
UK: £2.00 for each book to maximum of £10

Europe (inc ROI and Channel Islands): £4.00 for first book, £2.00 for each extra   —   P & P   £ ☐

Rest of the World: £20.00 for first book, £10 for each extra

▶ Unit 22 Maintaining a Healthy Workplace Interactive Text (postage free)   ☐   @ £3.95   £ ☐

                                                                    GRAND TOTAL £ ☐

I enclose a cheque for £ _____ (cheques to BPP Publishing Ltd) or charge to **Mastercard/Visa/Switch**

Card number ☐☐☐☐☐☐☐☐☐☐☐☐☐☐☐☐☐☐☐☐

Start date _____ **Expiry date** _____ **Issue no. (Switch only)** ___

Signature _____

REVIEW FORM & FREE PRIZE DRAW

All original review forms from the entire BPP range, completed with genuine comments, will be entered into one of two draws on 31 January 2001 and 31 July 2001. The names on the first four forms picked out on each occasion will be sent a cheque for £50.

Name: _____   **Address:** _____

_____

_____

How have you used this Interactive Text?
(Tick one box only)

☐ Home study (book only)

☐ On a course: college _____

☐ With 'correspondence' package

☐ Other _____

Why did you decide to purchase this Interactive Text? *(Tick one box only)*

☐ Have used BPP Texts in the past

☐ Recommendation by friend/colleague

☐ Recommendation by a lecturer at college

☐ Saw advertising

☐ Other _____

During the past six months do you recall seeing/receiving any of the following?
(Tick as many boxes as are relevant)

☐ Our advertisement in *Accounting Technician* magazine

☐ Our advertisement in *Pass*

☐ Our brochure with a letter through the post

Which (if any) aspects of our advertising do you find useful?
(Tick as many boxes as are relevant)

☐ Prices and publication dates of new editions

☐ Information on Interactive Text content

☐ Facility to order books off-the-page

☐ None of the above

Have you used the companion Assessment Kit for this subject?   ☐ Yes   ☐ No

Your ratings, comments and suggestions would be appreciated on the following areas

	Very useful	Useful	Not useful
Introductory section (How to use this Interactive Text etc)	☐	☐	☐
Chapter topic lists	☐	☐	☐
Chapter learning objectives	☐	☐	☐
Key terms	☐	☐	☐
Assessment alerts	☐	☐	☐
Examples	☐	☐	☐
Activities and answers	☐	☐	☐
Key learning points	☐	☐	☐
Quick quizzes and answers	☐	☐	☐
List of key terms and index	☐	☐	☐
Icons	☐	☐	☐

	Excellent	Good	Adequate	Poor
Overall opinion of this Text	☐	☐	☐	☐

Do you intend to continue using BPP Interactive Texts/Assessment Kits? ☐ Yes ☐ No

Please note any further comments and suggestions/errors on the reverse of this page.

Please return to: Nick Weller, BPP Publishing Ltd, FREEPOST, London, W12 8BR

REVIEW FORM & FREE PRIZE DRAW (continued)

Please note any further comments and suggestions/errors below

FREE PRIZE DRAW RULES

1   Closing date for 31 January 2001 draw is 31 December 2000. Closing date for 31 July 2001 draw is 30 June 2001.

2   Restricted to entries with UK and Eire addresses only. BPP employees, their families and business associates are excluded.

3   No purchase necessary. Entry forms are available upon request from BPP Publishing. No more than one entry per title, per person. Draw restricted to persons aged 16 and over.

4   Winners will be notified by post and receive their cheques not later than 6 weeks after the relevant draw date.

5   The decision of the promoter in all matters is final and binding. No correspondence will be entered into.